Refining Privacy in Tort Law

Patrick O'Callaghan

Refining Privacy in Tort Law

Springer

Patrick O'Callaghan
Newcastle Law School
Newcastle University
Newcastle Upon Tyne
United Kingdom

Dissertation, University of Bremen
1st Supervisor: Prof. Dr. Gert Brüggemeier
2nd Supervisor: Prof. Dr. Lesley Jane Smith
Date of Doctoral Colloquium: 27/3/2009

ISBN 978-3-642-31883-2 ISBN 978-3-642-31884-9 (eBook)
DOI 10.1007/978-3-642-31884-9
Springer Heidelberg New York Dordrecht London

Library of Congress Control Number: 2012948287

Printed on acid-free paper

Springer is part of Springer Science+Business Media (www.springer.com)

For my parents

Edel sei der Mensch
Hilfreich und gut!
Denn das allein
Unterscheidet ihn
Von allen Wesen,
Die wir kennen.

Der edle Mensch
Sei hilfreich und gut!
Unermüdet schaff er
Das Nützliche, Rechte,
Sei uns ein Vorbild
Jener geahneten Wesen.

Goethe, *Das Göttliche*

Preface

This is a book about privacy interests in English tort law. Despite the recent recognition of a misuse of private information tort, English law remains underdeveloped. The presence of gaps in the law can be explained, to some extent, by a failure on the part of courts and legal academics to reflect on the meaning of privacy. Through comparative, critical and historical analysis, this book seeks to refine our understanding of privacy by considering our shared experience of it. To this end, the book draws on the work of Norbert Elias and Karl Popper among others and compares the English law of privacy with the highly elaborate German law. In doing so, the book reaches the conclusion that an unfortunate consequence of the way English privacy law has developed is that it gives the impression that justice is only for the rich and famous. If English courts are to ensure equalitarian justice, the book argues that they must reflect on the value of privacy and explore the bounds of legal possibility.

Chapter 1 provides the methodology for this study and explains why privacy needs to be conceptualised. I argue that it is not possible to provide a precise definition of the concept. Drawing on Karl Popper's critical rationalism, I suggest that the scholar's task is to refine privacy and the methods of legal protection. We do this by reflecting on privacy's content: our shared experience of it. In Chap. 2, I propose three 'genuine conjectures' about our shared experience. First, I argue that privacy is an essential constituent of personhood—normative agency depends on it. Second, privacy has proprietary characteristics. My third conjecture is that personality (and therefore privacy) is ontologically dependent on the community. These conjectures are not analytically distinct; they overlap to a considerable extent. For this reason, I argue that if we neglect even one of these informing purposes in our privacy laws, we are failing in our task to probe the Rawlsian 'limits of the practicably possible'. Drawing on the work of Norbert Elias, in Chap. 3 I suggest that since antiquity there has been a 'privacy curve'. As the curve inclines, the individual gradually emerges from the collective and concern for personal privacy becomes more pronounced. I seek to establish gradients in this privacy curve by paying close attention to the history of laws and legal literature on personality rights. The chapter provides support for the proposition that my three conjectures shed light on our shared experience of privacy. In Chap. 4, I seek to 'test' the methods of legal protection in English tort law by considering how three hard cases might be decided by a German court. This provides us with instructive insights about English law and helps us to identify gaps in protection. Finally, in Chap. 5, I consider whether English law adheres to the regulative ideals of justice and the rule of law. I conclude that the narrow focus on protecting informational privacy means that privacy law is seen as being the preserve of the rich and famous. This would be bad enough on its own but this state of affairs is particularly troubling given the egalitarian justifications for the introduction of the Human Rights Act.

The book is based on my doctoral dissertation, defended at the University of Bremen on 27 March 2009. In the meantime, I have revised the structure and updated the text. I have already published portions of Chaps. 4 and 5 of this book in 'Privacy in Pursuit of a Purpose' (2009) 17 (2) *Tort Law Review* 100–113. I am grateful to Thomson Reuters (Australia) for the permission to reproduce this material here.

I owe a debt to my doctoral supervisor Gert Brüggemeier who has encouraged me to think hard about tort law within its historical, economic and social contexts. I have been inspired by his approach to scholarship and am deeply grateful for his guidance. I must also express my gratitude to Aurelia Colombi Ciacchi for making my stay in Bremen possible in the first place and for her continued support. I am particularly grateful to my mentor and friend, Richard Mullender, from whom I have learned a great deal. At various times over the past few years, I am fortunate to have benefitted from collaboration and conversations with a number of friends and colleagues. Sincere thanks are due to Lesley Jane Smith, Mel Kenny, Sjef van Erp, Giovanni Comandé, Peter Rott, Nuno Ferreira and Joanna Krzeminska-Vamvaka. I am also grateful to Prof John Blackie for participating in the Kolloquium in 2009.

I must thank the European Commission for the funding I received under the Fifth Framework Programme and Anke Seyfried at Springer for her patience and hard work.

I cannot thank Carol enough for her help and support and for reading earlier drafts with such a critical eye. Thanks also to my brother and sisters for their care and encouragement. But my deepest gratitude goes to my parents; they taught me more than any book ever could. This book is dedicated to them.

Newcastle-upon-Tyne Patrick O'Callaghan
May 2012

Author's Note

A comparativist faces many hurdles in his research, not least those of a linguistic variety. In places, I have drawn on the expertise of others, particularly the helpful translations of major German court decisions on the web site of the Institute for Transnational Law, University of Texas (www.utexas.edu/law/academics/centers/transnational). As a general rule, however, all translations are my own unless otherwise indicated.

In opting for particular terms of art, I have taken what I regard as pragmatic decisions. I refer to 'tort law' rather than civil liability but I am mindful that this is a common law construct and is not an entirely appropriate way to describe the delictual branch of the German law of obligations. The attentive reader may notice other curious terms. The way privacy laws are structured means I have to distinguish between 'public persons' (which includes public figures and celebrities) and the potentially oxymoronic 'non-public persons' (by which I simply mean individuals who are not subjected to media attention and/or do not actively seek it).

As for more technical details, I have used short title referencing in this book. Full references can be found in the bibliography at the end. Where possible, I have used the *Neue Juristische Wochenschrift* (NJW) citations for German cases.

Contents

Abbreviations

§/§§	paragraph/paragraphs
a	article
ABGB	Allgemeines Bürgerliches Gesetzbuch
AC	Law Reports, Appeal Cases
ad	adversus (objection)
AfP	Archiv für Presserecht
All ER	All England Law Reports
ALR	Allgemeines Landrecht
Amb	Ambler's Chancery Reports
Art/Arts	Article/Articles
Atk	Atkyns' Chancery Reports
BAG	Bundesarbeitsgericht
Bd	Band (Volume)
BGB	Bürgerliches Gesetzbuch
BGH	Bundesgerichtshof
BGHZ	Entscheidungen des Bundesgerichtshofs in Zivilsachen
Burrow	Burrow's King's Bench Reports
BVerfG	Bundesverfassungsgericht
BVerfGE	Entscheidungen des Bundesverfassungsgerichts
C civ	Code civil
CA	Court of Appeal
Cass Civ	Cour de Cassation
Ch/ Ch D	Law Reports, Chancery Division
ch/chs	chapter/chapters
Comm	Commentary
CPD	Law Reports, Common Pleas Division
Croke Jac	Croke's King's Bench Reports tempore James
De Gex & Smale	De Gex & Smale's Chancery Reports
De GF & J	De Gex, Fisher & Jones Chancery Reports
Dyer	Dyer's King's Bench Reports

ECHR	European Convention on Human Rights and Fundamental Freedoms
ECtHR	European Court of Human Rightsed/eds editor/editors
edn	edition
EGStPO	Einführungsgesetz zur Strafprozessordnung
EHRR	European Human Rights Reports
Eliz	Elizabeth (Queen)
EMLR	Entertainment & Media Law Reports
Eq	Equity Cases, Law Reports
ER	English Reports
EWCA Civ	England and Wales Court of Appeal, Civil Division
EWHC	England and Wales High Court
EWHC (Admin)	England and Wales High Court (Administrative Court)
f/ff	folio/folios
FLR	Family Law Reports
FSR	Fleet Street Reports
Gai	Gaius
GG	Grundgesetz
GRUR	Gewerblicher Rechtsschutz und Urheberrecht
Hare	Hare's Reports
Hen	Henry (King)
Hil	Hilary Term
HL	House of Lords
HL Deb	House of Lords Debates
HLC	Clark & Finnelly's House of Lords Reports New Series
HRA	Human Rights Act
JZ	Juristen-Zeitung
KB	Law Reports, King's Bench
Keilw	Keilwey's King's Bench Reports
KG JW	Kammergericht Juristische Wochenschrift
KUG	Kunsturhebergesetz
LG	Landgericht
lib	liber (book)
LJCh (NS)	Law Journal Reports, Chancery (New Series)
Lofft	Lofft's King's Bench Reports
LR	Law Reports
LT	Law Times Reports
LUG	Literaturhebergesetz
m	memorandum
Macnaghten & Gordon	Macnaghten & Gordon's Chancery Reports
Mer	Merivale's Chancery Reports
NJW	Neue Juristische Wochenschrift
NJW-RR	Neue Juristische Wochenschrift—Rechtsprechungsreport
no	number

NZLR	New Zealand Law Reports
OLG	Oberlandesgericht
para/paras	paragraph/paragraphs
pl	plea
pt	part
Q	Question
QB	Law Reports, Queen's Bench
Rep	Report
Res	Resolution
rev	revised
RG	Reichsgericht
RGBl	Reichsgesetzblatt
RGZ	Entscheidungen des Reichsgerichts in Zivilsachen
RPC	Reports of Patent, Design and Trade Mark Cases
StGB	Strafgesetzbuch
Swanston	Swanston's Chancery Reports
T	Title
Tab	Table
Taunton	Taunton's Common Pleas Reports
tit	titulus (title)
TLR	Times Law Report
Trin	Trinity Term
Ulp D	Ulpian Digesta
VC	Vice-chancellor
Vol/Vols	Volume/Volumes
WBl	William Blackstone's King's Bench Reports
Wils KB	Wilson's King's Bench and Common Pleas Reports
WLR	Weekly Law Reports
YB	Yearbooks
ZUM	Zeitschrift für Urheber- und Medienrecht?

Chapter 1
Refining Privacy

The gods did not reveal, from the beginning, all things to us; but in the course of time through seeking we may learn and know things better. But as for certain truth, no man has known it, nor shall he know it; and even if by chance he were to utter the final truth, he would himself not know it: for all is but a woven web of guesses

- Xenophanes

1.1 Introduction

In his seminal essay on privacy, Bloustein notes that 'the words we use to identify and describe basic human values are necessarily vague and ill-defined.'[1] What does he mean by this? A sceptical interpretation is that 'abstract concepts' lack any 'natural content' and so can mean whatever we want them to mean.[2] But I prefer a second interpretation. On this account, words such as *dignity* and *liberty* have sufficient force so that we are in some measure cognisant of their content. But the words are sufficiently vague at the same time so that some degree of reasonable disagreement about what they represent can be accommodated. In this way, these words project *universality* but allow for *reasonable pluralism*.[3] When human rights lawyers talk about dignity, for instance, they do so in a way that suggests they are certain that there is either some objective definition of it, or, at the very least, that others intuitively know what they mean. But if they are asked to describe its content in more precise terms, some degree of doubt and disagreement will inevitably emerge—*Quot homines, tot sententiae*!

---

[1] Bloustein, 'Privacy as an Aspect of Human Dignity' (1964) at 1001.

[2] Fish, *There's No Such Thing as Free Speech* (1994) p 102.

[3] On reasonable pluralism, see Rawls, *Political Liberalism* (1993).

P. O'Callaghan, *Refining Privacy in Tort Law*,
DOI 10.1007/978-3-642-31884-9_1,

This is not an essentialist argument in the Aristotelian sense. I do not claim that abstract concepts have an essence or a true meaning, for which we can provide an exhaustive definition.[4] How can we ever prove that we have found the truth of a concept if human fallibility means we are infinitely ignorant?[5] Moreover, once a scholar claims that he has found a concept's essence, he closes down dialogue and this leaves little room for reasonable disagreement. But abstract concepts must have content.[6] This is because these concepts are what Elias calls 'efficient instruments' that we have developed over the course of millennia. These instruments express what generations of people have 'jointly experienced' and 'wanted to communicate.'[7] I will argue that it is this shared experience which forms the content of an abstract concept.[8]

For more than a century, the ideal of a precise definition of another abstract concept, that of privacy, has lured lawyers into a privacy 'swamp', as one commentator has put it.[9] As we shall see, a search of the literature reveals a myriad of definitions ranging from the vague theories to the uncompromising taxonomies. But my thesis is that if we confine our task to *defining* privacy we risk entering the murky cave of Polyphemus searching for a definition, never to emerge again.[10] This first chapter provides a methodology for our study—this book's task is to refine privacy, to reflect upon our shared experience and, by means of critical rationalist thinking, to assess the methods of legal protection. But before we consider this task in greater detail, I must explain why privacy needs to be conceptualised in the first place.

---

[4] We must refrain from making essentialist arguments about the meaning of privacy as this leads to infinite regress. On this point, see Popper, 'Two Kinds of Definitions' (1987).

[5] Popper, *Conjectures and Refutations* (2002) p 38.

[6] Even anti-essentialists would admit that these concepts have content. Indeed, how could it be otherwise? Referring to terms such as 'democracy' and 'liberty', Popper says that they are 'much misused'. He implies, then, there are better ways of *using* these words. See Popper, 'Two Kinds of Definitions' (1987) p 96.

[7] Elias, *The Civilizing Process* (2000) p 8.

[8] Popper warns against becoming embroiled in an 'empty controversy about words'. On his account, this leads to verbiage—we end up substituting a 'merely verbal problem for a factual one.' See Popper, 'Two Kinds of Definitions' (1987) p 96. But often in law the verbal problem *is* the factual problem. If one party claims that he has suffered a legal wrong of invasion of privacy, the judge must know the scope of privacy as a legal right before she can pass judgment.

[9] Inness, *Privacy, Intimacy and Isolation* (1992) p 3. It is not just scholars who seek to provide a precise definition of privacy. In a recent parliamentary report on privacy, the committee sees the merits in providing a statutory definition of privacy (though they do not recommend it in the end). On their account, such a definition 'would have the advantage of perhaps creating more certainty in the law: editors might be able better to assess whether a proposed article is likely to infringe privacy or not.' See *House of Lords and House of Commons Report on Privacy and Injunctions* (2012).

[10] In his lectures on romanticism, Isaiah Berlin begins by stating that he 'does not propose to walk into the particular trap' of attempting to define romanticism. He calls it a 'dangerous and confused subject, in which many have lost. . .their sense of direction.' See Berlin, *The Roots of Romanticism* (2000) p 1.

1.2 Why Conceptualise Privacy?

1.2.1 Contemporary Context and Conceptual Confusion

In a recently published book on privacy law,[11] Carolan and Delany begin by quoting the philosopher Glenn Negley, who describes privacy as a 'distinctly contemporary' concept.[12] This is certainly a reasonable way to introduce the subject; it is, after all, a widely-held assumption. But is it accurate? A Google search of the word 'privacy', while perhaps not a scientifically sound method of ascertaining its contemporary relevance, can tell us something, nonetheless, about its place in our social milieu. A simple search of the word 'privacy' yields over 5.7 billion results. By contrast a search for 'liberty' results in 746 million hits, while 'dignity' provides 119 million. Searching 'privacy' with the Google timeline function, which tracks the years mentioned within web documents, produces an intriguing timeline graph indicating that the majority of these 5.7 billion privacy-related documents were produced during, or mention the years, 1990–2012. Documents produced during, or referring to the years, 1930–1950 have the fewest references to privacy, while references peak during the period 2001–2004.

We can debate these figures, of course. What about confounding factors? Should we not control, for instance, for the number of websites that have 'privacy policies', something that will inevitably contribute to the number of hits? We can also speculate about the figures. Does the peak during the period 2001–2004 point to increased concerns about individual privacy following government responses to the 11 September 2001 terrorist attacks? Some degree of debate and speculation is certainly possible but can we use these statistics to *prove* that privacy is a 'distinctly contemporary' concept?

We should bear in mind that statistical analysis provides us with a general overview only. Arendt reminds us that within this overview, acts and events can 'appear only as deviations or fluctuations' and these statistical peaks and troughs tell us almost nothing about the subject matter of the acts and events themselves.[13] The slightest deviation or fluctuation can often represent a profound act or event as 'the meaningfulness of everyday relationships is disclosed not in everyday life but in rare deeds, just as the significance of a historical period shows itself only in the few events that illuminate it.'[14] For Arendt, then, the application of the law of statistics to politics or history 'signifies nothing less than the wilful obliteration of their subject matter, and it is a hopeless enterprise to search for meaning in politics or significance in history when everything that is not everyday behavior or automatic trends has been ruled out as immaterial.'[15]

---

[11] Carolan & Delany, *The Right to Privacy* (2008).

[12] Negley, 'Philosophical Views on the Value of Privacy' (1966) at 319.

[13] Arendt, *The Human Condition* (1999) p 42.

[14] *Ibid.*

[15] *Ibid.*

In deciding whether privacy is 'distinctly contemporary', then, we must identify those deeds and historical events that have shaped our shared experience of privacy rather than make generalisations on the basis of statistics. This is the purpose of Chaps. 2 and 3 of this book. But, in the meantime, we should note that Negley described privacy as 'distinctly contemporary' in 1966, many years before the advent of the digital age. We find references to 'privacy' as a 'contemporary' idea in the nineteenth century—writing in 1890, Warren and Brandeis regarded the 'intensity and complexity of life' as sufficient reason for the establishment of a legal right to privacy in the United States.[16] Fifteen years later, Roscoe Pound referred to privacy as a 'modern demand'.[17] If by 'contemporary', we mean post-industrial revolution, then there is some truth to the notion that the right of privacy has gained 'currency' somewhat in recent years.[18]

The idea of 'invasion of privacy', then, (while not solely a concern of late modernity)[19] has undoubtedly gained traction of late. But this fact (if we can indeed refer to it as a fact) is not quite as revealing as it first appears—for it merely indicates that a particular word, 'privacy', has become particularly popular. Though privacy has a content (our shared experience), it does not necessarily follow that everyone who uses the word has a shared understanding of its meaning; in fact, the converse is possible—the more the word is used the more competing and conflicting meanings will emerge. This is because words are mobile; our understanding of them will vary with the context and time in which they are used. Indeed, as Oliver Wendell Holmes argued in one of his most famous judgments, a 'word is not a crystal, transparent and unchanged, it is the skin of a living thought and may vary greatly in color and content according to the circumstances and the time in which it is used.'[20] This may seem like an obvious point but it is an important one to stress nonetheless. All too often, the word 'privacy' is bandied about in contemporary debates without any real appreciation of its complexity—privacy, we are continually reminded, is an important political 'concern' or 'issue'. Those who use the word in this way seem to assume that there is some universal understanding of privacy. Of course, as Wacks points out, '[f]reedom, security, liberty and other values are, to a greater or lesser extent, vulnerable to similar criticism.' Vagueness, malleability and indeterminacy are permanent and unavoidable features of language but such obstacles should not prevent us from advancing knowledge. In this spirit, Wacks thus reasons that 'unless it is to be argued that subscribing to generalized values exhibits our commitment to [values such as privacy, freedom,

---

[16] Warren & Brandeis, 'The Right to Privacy' (1890) at 196.

[17] Pound, 'Interests of Personality' (1915) at 363.

[18] Carolan & Delany, *The Right to Privacy* (2008) p 1.

[19] As we will see in Chap. 3, since antiquity, every person has belonged to what Arendt calls 'two orders of existence'. For several centuries, at least, there has been a 'sharp distinction in [man's] life between what is his own (*idion*) and what is communal (*koinon*).' See Arendt, *The Human Condition* (1999) p 24.

[20] *Towne* v *Eisner* 245 US 418, 425 (1918) per Holmes J.

etc], it seems perverse not to attempt to refine the nature and scope of the problem, especially if this might engender more effective protection.'[21]

Wacks encourages us to think hard about the nature and scope of privacy rather than resort to vague generalisations. This is sound advice. But his argument that such work becomes more important if there is a chance that it 'might engender more effective protection' is less convincing. Further refinement of the nature and scope of a problem might 'engender', as he suggests, 'more effective protection' but, equally, further reflection might lead us to a different conclusion—we might discover that the perceived 'problem' is not in fact a problem after all and we may not even need to talk about 'protection' in the first place.

1.2.2 *To Define or to Refine?*

Yet, despite this criticism, Wacks' argument is of great consequence. Unlike many privacy scholars, by choosing the verb '*to refine*' he rejects definition. The act of *definition* is problematic for two reasons. First, the notion of precise definition itself is implausible. Those who employ a linguistic approach to words such as 'privacy' or 'law' face, as Raz suggests, 'the overwhelming problem that that word is used in a multiplicity of non-legal contexts'.[22] Definition is workable only when one assumption is made:

> That assumption is that the use of "law" [or "privacy" in this case] in all its contexts but one is analogical or metaphorical or in some other way parasitical on its core meaning as displayed in its use in one type of context and that that core meaning is the one the legal philosopher has at the centre of his inquiry.[23]

Thus, scholarship of this sort will always be agent-relative; we are simply directed to the 'core meaning' that the individual theorist has *selected* following *her* linguistic analysis.[24] But because this is presented as a definition, it demands universal acceptance and this leads us to the second problem with definition: its

---

[21] Wacks, *Law, Morality and the Private Domain* (2000) p 240. Ruth Gavison makes a similar point: 'Arguments for liberty, when examined carefully, are vulnerable to objections similar to the arguments we have examined for privacy, yet this vulnerability has never been considered a reason not to acknowledge the importance of liberty, or not to express this importance by an explicit commitment so that any loss will be more likely to be noticed and taken into consideration.' See Gavison, 'Privacy and the Limits of Law' (1980) at 468.

[22] Raz, 'The Problem About the Nature of Law' (1983) at 204.

[23] *Ibid.*

[24] This is, of course, a very old argument dating back to the sceptics of Ancient Greece. Kant explains that the standard understanding of truth is that it 'consists in the agreement of cognition with its object.' But 'since the object is outside me, the cognition in me, all I can ever pass judgement on is whether my cognition of the object agrees with my cognition of the object.' See Kant, *Lectures on Logic* (1992) pp 557–558. On agent-relativity, see also Nagel, *The View From Nowhere* (1986).

utopian characteristics. Definition is utopian in nature as it supposes finality, an end-state, a degree of preciseness and certainty that leaves no room for disagreement. Definition is akin to monologue as it demands universal acceptance; it pretends, in the words of the Russian literary theorist Mikhail Bakhtin, 'to be the ultimate word.'[25] More often than not, definitions act as an obstacle to the advancement of knowledge as they shut down the outside world.

Refinement, by contrast, is a process rather than an end-state. Of course, it also has its flaws. Like the act of definition, for instance, when we refine an idea or a concept we work from assumptions; but importantly, refinement is preferable because we refrain from making the ultimate utopian assumption that precise definition is possible. In refining a concept, first, we assume that the concept itself is capable of refinement and, second, we assume that we are faced with a complex question with more than one plausible answer (hence the need for refinement). We thus endeavour to filter competing and conflicting meanings; but as we lack a common scale to aid us, we can never pretend to be certain about the outcome.

In the natural sciences, refinement is commonly known as the *method of trial and error*. The method is more compatible with Rawls' conception of a 'realistic utopia', the idea of a 'social world [which] allows a reasonably just constitutional democracy existing as a member of a reasonably just Society of Peoples', accommodating, among other things, 'reasonable pluralism'.[26] Unlike the utopianism of definition, which is characterised by monologic thinking, the 'realistic utopia' is fundamentally dialogic. Rawls elucidates that '[b]y showing how the social world may realize the features of a realistic utopia, political philosophy provides a long-term goal of political endeavor, and in working toward it gives meaning to what we can do today'.[27] For a 'realistic utopia', like the process of refinement, is essentially about 'endeavor' rather than the declaration of a perfect end-state; we are not in possession of all the answers, and hard cases will continue to arise. But if we refrain from definition and monologue, we can, collectively in dialogue, work towards 'reasonable answers' and a 'realistic utopia'. As Rawls puts it, this idea 'describes what is possible and can be, yet may never be, though no less fundamental for that.'[28]

Refinement, then, is a preparedness to engage in dialogue. In contrast to definition, when we engage in refinement, we are also being intellectually humble, we are willing to accept that we 'might be wrong.'[29] We must appreciate the complexity of the content of privacy and think hard about potential competing and conflicting interpretations. This is not to say that those who use the word 'privacy' must first have developed an intricate philosophical understanding of it—that would be

---

[25] Bakhtin, *Problems of Dostoevsky's Poetics* (1984) pp 292–293.

[26] Rawls, *The Law of Peoples* (1999) pp 11–12.

[27] *Ibid* p 128.

[28] Rawls, *Political Liberalism* (1993) p 213.

[29] Sunstein, *Radicals in Robes* (2005) p 35.

absurd. But it is necessary that law-makers, at the very least, should engage with the concept and reflect on its content. While clarity is an important good in itself, law-makers have a special responsibility to ensure that the language they use is unambiguous (in so far as this is possible) and meets the demands of the rule of law. We will revisit this argument later.

There is at least one more reason why the conceptualisation of privacy is necessary. Abstract concepts and ideals are often associated with hypocrisy. We can suppose, without difficulty, that there are proponents of social justice in our community who routinely evade tax, for example, or outwardly pious individuals who flout their religion's moral code. Privacy is no different; the concept is laced with hypocrisy. Nagel, for instance, questions why in recent times 'along with a vastly increased tolerance for variation in sexual life we have seen a sharp increase in prurient and censorious attention to the sexual lives of public figures and famous persons.'[30] To Nagel, it appears that '[t]he culture seems to be growing more tolerant and more intolerant at the same time'.[31] We can identify further examples of hypocrisy quite readily. Increasing digitalisation and advances in information technology have allowed the state and private companies to access and store personal data about their citizens and customers. In a very real sense then, we live in a panoptic age where phrases such as 'Big Brother is watching' have become clichés. Privacy 'activists' relentlessly raise concerns about the invasion of personal privacy. A recent poll undertaken by *Zogby International* showed that the vast majority of Americans are 'concerned' about their online privacy.[32] Yet, despite these concerns, the majority (52 %) of the population over 12 years of age has a social networking profile,[33] voluntarily disclosing private information, providing details and images of their day-to-day activities to friends, friends of friends, and in some cases, to the world at large. According to a 2008 Ofcom report, while 48 % of adults restricted access to their personal profiles, almost as many, 44 %, allowed their profiles to be seen by anyone.[34] The Ofcom report found that despite intense media coverage of 'privacy and safety issues', users of social networking sites remained 'on the whole. . .unconcerned' about their privacy.[35] One does not need to be a statistician to grasp that there are significant discrepancies between the various survey results. It follows that some of those who on the one hand express concerns about a panoptic society appear to be less concerned about their personal privacy when using social networking websites.

There is no point in being overly-critical here. Whether one considers this to be hypocrisy or naivety, or both, it is, above all else, evidence of human frailty.

---

[30] Nagel, 'Concealment and Exposure' (1998) at 3.

[31] *Ibid.*

[32] Zogby International, *Polling/Market Research* (2010).

[33] See Edison Research Study, *The Social Habit* (2011).

[34] Ofcom, *Research Report on Social Networking* (2008).

[35] *Ibid* at 8.

But this example underscores the point that in order to better understand privacy we must think hard about the non-ideal shared experiences that form privacy's content rather than search in vain for its true meaning.

1.3 'Defining' Privacy

While the *method* of definition is problematic when scholars seek to establish truth in systems of thought, we can still gain instructive insights about privacy from scholarship of this sort. This is because we require at least some dogmatic thinking in scholarship. Definitions form reference points in scholarship; in other words they provide a framework for critical rationalist thinking. This framework 'allows us to approach a good theory in stages, by way of approximations'.[36] For this reason, before we move on to consider how a methodology of refinement might take shape, we must first pay attention to some of the various attempts at definition in the literature. These definitions will allow us to construct reference points in privacy scholarship for our critical rationalist enquiry.

Generally speaking, we can identify two main schools of thought in privacy scholarship. The first is the reductionist school, those scholars who believe that privacy represents a 'cluster' of freestanding interests, not necessarily related to one another in any significant way. The other school argues that privacy is a unitary, conceptually distinct right or interest. These latter scholars, for the most part, understand privacy as having a distinct moral value.

1.3.1 Reductionism

For reductionists, the right of privacy is too unwieldy a concept to serve any practical use in our laws. Understood in this way, these scholars seek to reduce the right to its 'true components'.[37] Yet, at the same time, it is not necessarily the case that reductionists fail to appreciate the moral value of privacy. Kalven, for instance, finds himself 'enmeshed with a paradox. Although privacy is for [him] a great and important value, tort law's effort to protect the right of privacy seems to [him] a mistake.'[38]

In the English-speaking world, Judith Jarvis Thomson is perhaps the most prominent reductionist. For her, the difficulties surrounding definition convey a

---

[36] Popper, *Conjectures and Refutations* (2002) p 64.

[37] Inness, *Privacy, Intimacy and Isolation* (1992) p 21.

[38] Kalven Jr, 'Privacy in Tort Law' (1966) at 327.

great deal about the right.[39] She advances the 'simplifying hypothesis' that privacy is in fact a 'cluster of rights' although not a 'distinct cluster', rather one which 'intersects' with other clusters, namely the cluster of rights concerning the person and the cluster of rights related to property ownership.[40] On this account, 'the right to privacy is everywhere overlapped by other rights'[41]; the rights in the privacy cluster also feature in other rights clusters.[42] For Thomson, then, conceptually and practically, we gain little by presenting privacy as a freestanding legal or moral right. In short, efforts to define privacy as a distinct concept are meaningless because:

> there is no need to find the that-which-is-in-common to all rights in the right to privacy cluster and no need to settle disputes about its boundaries. For if I am right, the right to privacy is "derivative" in this sense: it is possible to explain in the case of each right in the cluster how come we have it without ever once mentioning the right to privacy. Indeed, the wrongness of every violation of the right to privacy can be explained without ever once mentioning it.[43]

Thomson's reductionism should not be interpreted as an assault on the value of privacy. She does not suggest that privacy is meaningless, as some commentators attest,[44] but argues that the vague and indeterminate *right* of privacy need not enter the legal lexicon because privacy *interests*, in cases where they represent 'truly fundamental interests', are accorded sufficient protection by other clusters of rights.

Other reductionists employ a broadly similar line of argument though often have very different ideological starting-points.[45] Richard Posner, for instance, attempts to circumvent what he terms the 'definitional problem' of privacy by engaging in a reductionism informed by consequentialist thinking. It is perhaps no surprise that for Posner, we must engage in an economic analysis of privacy in order to better understand its purpose. In constructing his thesis, he focuses on those cases involving the 'withholding or concealment of information'.[46] On Posner's account, both 'prying' and privacy 'possess important attributes of intermediate goods'.[47] He suggests various instances in which invasions of privacy and protection of privacy can be justified on economic grounds but our decisions should always be informed by what is useful in a social context.[48]

---

[39] Thomson, 'The Right to Privacy' (1975).

[40] *Ibid* at 306.

[41] *Ibid* at 310.

[42] *Ibid* at 313.

[43] *Ibid* at 313.

[44] Carolan and Delany erroneously claim that for Thomson 'privacy has no meaning'. See Carolan & Delany, *The Right to Privacy* (2008) p 5.

[45] For a helpful discussion see Peikoff, 'The Right to Privacy' (2006).

[46] Posner, 'The Right of Privacy' (1978) at 393.

[47] *Ibid* at 394.

[48] *Ibid* at 400.

I emphasised 'English-speaking world' at the beginning of this section because we can draw parallels between the analyses of the reductionists and the legal treatment of privacy in several European legal systems, most notably Germany. As we will see later, in Germany, privacy is understood not so much a freestanding right (although it is considered an interest with a distinct moral value) rather one aspect of a more general personality right (*allgemeines Persönlichkeitsrecht*), encompassing those various 'rights over the person' to which Thomson refers in her essay. But in Germany privacy interests in certain contexts, such as the protection of image, are overlapped by property rights. In this way, privacy interests are *at once* an aspect of a general personality right *and* a classical property right. We shall pay greater attention to this understanding of privacy in Chap. 4.

1.3.2 Privacy as a Conceptually Distinct Right or Interest

Among privacy scholars, the reductionists, while influential, remain in the minority. Most scholars perceive privacy as a conceptually distinct interest or right, arguing that we lose something of 'moral importance' by engaging in reductionism.[49]

Edward Bloustein offers a *deontological* perspective, drawing on Warren and Brandeis' account of privacy as 'inviolate personality'.[50] For Bloustein, the inviolate personality principle '[posits] the individual's independence, dignity and integrity; it defines man's essence as a unique and self-determining being.'[51] He criticises Prosser's reductionism for being too elaborate—why do we need four principles when one suffices?[52] To this end, he argues that inviolate personality is the 'common thread of principle' weaving through all of Prosser's cases.[53] Bloustein stresses the personal and social importance of privacy: private space allows an individual to thrive while the absence of privacy is degrading. He contends that '[t]he man who is compelled to live every minute of his life among others and whose every need, thought, desire, fancy or gratification is subject to public scrutiny, has been deprived of his individuality and human dignity.'[54] Courts must, in his opinion, recognise inviolate personality as the underlying principle in privacy cases in order to achieve 'conceptual unity'.[55]

Most privacy scholars broadly agree with Bloustein's deontological thesis but some opt to focus on autonomy rather than dignity and advance a *control-based*

---

[49] Inness, *Privacy, Intimacy and Isolation* (1992) p 21.

[50] Bloustein, 'Privacy as an Aspect of Human Dignity' (1964).

[51] *Ibid* at 971.

[52] *Ibid* at 993.

[53] *Ibid* at 999.

[54] *Ibid* at 1003.

[55] *Ibid* at 1004.

account of privacy. Rachels, for example, argues that privacy is essential to the functioning of society because it allows us 'to maintain the variety of social relationships with other people.'[56] Our conduct varies from relationship to relationship; our behaviour at any given moment depends on the people we have around us. On this account, if 'we cannot control who has access to us, sometimes including and sometimes excluding various people, then we cannot control the patterns of behavior we need to adopt... or the kinds of relations with other people that we will have'.[57] Rachels regards this as a reason why privacy is a facet of liberty but he does not seek to engage in reductionism. Far from it—in fact, he criticises Thomson's account of privacy, emphasising that there is no easy answer.[58] Rather than focusing on the handful of distinctive cases, (in other words popular examples of invasion of privacy or examples from the case law), we need an 'account of the value [of] privacy [for the] many common and unremarkable cases as well.'[59] In fact, if we focus on the few special cases only, we miss 'something important' about the nature of the concept.[60]

For Rachels, that 'important something' is the control we exercise over our private lives. However, other authors, while acknowledging the value of this argument, refuse to entertain an account of privacy based solely on control. Ruth Gavison is one such scholar and also one of the fiercest critics of the reductionists. In an influential article, published in the *Yale Law Journal* in 1980, Gavison advances an account of privacy based on *accessibility*.[61] Like Rachels, she is critical of those who seek to define privacy by concentrating on case law alone. This is because there is a danger of paying attention to the 'desirable' features of privacy only. Understood in these terms, the control-based accounts of privacy also fall into that trap—privacy is understood as a form of control because this is a desirable feature. For Gavison, in order to truly 'understand' privacy we must look at it as a 'neutral concept' first.[62]

Gavison sees privacy as 'a complex' of 'three independent and irreducible elements: secrecy, anonymity, and solitude'.[63] Each element is independent because a 'loss or privacy may occur through a change in any one of the three, without a necessary loss in either of the other two'.[64] Yet, the concept is also coherent because all three elements fall under the umbrella of accessibility and may

[56] Rachels 'Why Privacy is Important' (1975) at 327.

[57] *Ibid* at 331.

[58] *Ibid* at 323.

[59] *Ibid* at 325.

[60] *Ibid* at 326.

[61] Gavison, 'Privacy and the Limits of Law' (1980).

[62] *Ibid* at 423.

[63] *Ibid* at 433.

[64] *Ibid* at 434.

all coexist in a given context.[65] Gavison claims that her 'neutral' conceptualisation of privacy embodies the meaning of the majority of privacy claims.[66] This means that her conceptualisation excludes some situations that are sometimes described as invasions of privacy, for example insult, harassment, presenting others in a false light and commercial appropriation of personality.[67] But this, she implies, is the price we pay for conceptual tidiness. For Gavison, 'if the concepts we use give the appearance of differentiating concerns without in fact isolating something distinct, we are likely to fall victims to this false appearance and our chosen language will be a hindrance rather than a help.'[68]

But for all the effort Gavison devotes to choosing the right methodology, we can subject her conceptualisation of privacy to the very same criticisms she raises of others. She suggests, for example, that her account of privacy is superior to that which regards privacy as a state of 'being let alone'. While she admits that the 'simplicity' of the definition 'gives it rhetorical force', it 'also denies it the distinctiveness that is necessary for the phrase to be used in more than a conclusory sense.'[69] On Gavison's account, many examples of 'not letting people alone' cannot be described as invasions of privacy.[70] She provides the examples of '[r]equiring that people pay their taxes or go into the army, or punishing them for murder'. On this account, the problem with the definition is that it 'gives an appearance of differentiation while covering almost any conceivable complaint anyone could ever make.'[71] But her conception of privacy does not fare any better as a great many instances of secrecy, anonymity and solitude have nothing to do with privacy either. I may be in a state of solitude if I fall into a well while walking alone in the countryside; it may also be a secret to everyone else but is it a privacy-related concern? While Gavison's formulation is more distinctive than the more general 'being let alone' test, it also has the potential to cover a great many conceivable complaints. Perhaps for this reason, Moreham proposes that we think in terms of 'desired inaccess'—that secrecy, anonymity or solitude must have been intended in the first place if a state of privacy is to exist.[72] But should intention always be a prerequisite? If, after several days in the well without food or water, I am rescued and the event is covered on live television, can we confidently say that these pictures do not constitute an invasion of privacy? Certainly, my solitude in the well was unintentional and my euphoric reaction to being rescued may have left me unconcerned about the presence of television cameras. But what if I become

[65] *Ibid.*

[66] *Ibid* at 428.

[67] *Ibid* at 436.

[68] *Ibid* at 437.

[69] *Ibid.*

[70] *Ibid* at 438.

[71] *Ibid* at 437–438.

[72] Moreham, 'Privacy in the Common Law' (2005) at 636.

distressed later that week when viewing recordings and reading accounts of the rescue? Undoubtedly, one of the enduring memories of the Chilean miners' rescue of October 2010 will be pictures of family members waiting and then, in turn, embracing their rescued loved-ones. But while this was a joyous occasion for Chile and the world at large, watching the raw emotion on our television screens, one could not help but feel that we were somehow prying on something very personal to the miners and their families. If, like Gavison, we are to approach our study with a 'neutral' understanding of privacy, I believe we must reject, at the outset, the argument that privacy exists only when it is desired.

Gavison's impressive article remains one the most influential and most cited essays about the right of privacy in the English-speaking world. Yet despite her rigorous efforts to construct a neutral methodology, she does not adequately justify why her account of privacy is more suitable than competing accounts. In the end, she faces the same problem that many others encounter when attempting to provide a universal definition of privacy: agent relativity. But there is some evidence in the essay that Gavison is conscious of this problem. In attempting to 'understand' privacy, she admits that we 'cannot avoid a functional analysis' and argues that the diverse values of privacy include a 'healthy, liberal, democratic and pluralistic society; individual autonomy'; mental health; creativity; and the capacity to form and maintain meaningful relations with others.'[73] But she treads carefully here. In the end, as there is no one theory concerning the nature of the person and relationships between persons, she acknowledges that 'the way in which we perceive privacy contributing to individual goals will itself depend on the theory of the individual we select.'[74] There is some indication here that Gavison is alert to the inherent difficulties involved in providing a universal 'solution' to our definitional problem. In our pursuit of true meaning, all scholars, whether we realise it or not, are faced with agent-relative impulses in our research. This is why I advocate intellectual humility and an adherence to the process of refinement. But before I begin this task, I wish to examine the views of a group of scholars who believe (albeit with one or two notable exceptions) that they have found a means of circumventing the problem of agent-relativity.

1.3.3 Taxonomies of Privacy Interests

For many creators of taxonomies, the value of a taxonomy lies in the 'fact' that it provides a complete and comprehensive account of a problem. If we ask a *sufficient* number of people, if we survey a *sufficient* number of cases, bills of rights, legal provisions and academic works, we will reach a point at which precise definition is

[73] Gavison, 'Privacy and the Limits of Law' (1980) at 442.

[74] *Ibid* at 445.

possible. Grounded in the tradition of empiricism, this might appear to be the most scientific method and, therefore, logically sound. But is it really a practical exercise? What constitutes a *sufficient* number in this context? Is it simply the point at which all *relevant* ideas and arguments have been recorded and the author cannot find any more? But who decides what is *relevant*? The taxonomist wants to achieve a complete understanding but, in the end, agent-relativity remains an obstacle that he cannot overcome.

Despite these criticisms, taxonomies of privacy interests remain valuable not because they provide a solution to our problem but because they provide a wealth of material for critical reflection and further refinement. Like definitions of privacy, taxonomies of privacy interests form reference points in scholarly debate and provide a framework for our reasoning. As long as we are alive to the problem of agent-relativity, we can learn a great deal from taxonomies. To this end, we now move on to consider some examples of taxonomies in privacy scholarship.

Perhaps the most famous privacy taxonomist is William Prosser. Following an examination of over three hundred cases, Prosser provided a definition of privacy that eventually formed the doctrinal basis of the present US privacy torts. On his account, there are four distinct types of invasion of privacy interests.[75] They are:

1. Intrusion upon the plaintiff's seclusion or solitude, or into his private affairs;
2. Public disclosure of embarrassing private facts about the plaintiff;
3. Publicity which places the plaintiff in a false light in the public eye;
4. Appropriation, for the defendant's advantage, of the plaintiff's name or likeness.

It is worth paying attention to each of these actions. Firstly, *intrusion*, in Prosser's sense, means something more than simple physical intrusion into one's private space. He argues that courts have extended it to eavesdropping by wire-tapping and the use of microphones.[76] Today, this encompasses intrusions of digital privacy such as email hacking and data-mining. Whatever the form of intrusion, in order to be actionable, it must be of a kind that is 'offensive or objectionable to a reasonable man.'[77] On Prosser's account, it is 'obvious that the interest protected [by this action] is primarily a mental one.' The second action results from *public disclosure of private facts*. Publicity is therefore key and the nature of the information must be such that the disclosure would be 'offensive and objectionable to a reasonable man of ordinary sensibilities'.[78] Prosser emphasises that this branch of the privacy tort is completely different from that of intrusion. This is because reputation is the protected interest, 'with the same overtones of mental distress that are present in libel and slander.'[79] Thirdly, the *false light* action seeks to ensure

[75] Prosser, 'Privacy' (1960) at 389.

[76] *Ibid* at 390.

[77] *Ibid* at 391.

[78] *Ibid* at 396.

[79] *Ibid* at 398.

that falsity will 'defeat the privilege of reporting news and other matters of public interest.'[80] Like the disclosure action, the interest protected here is one of reputation but the difference is that false light prevents or remedies the disclosure of false information rather than true facts.[81] Finally, the *appropriation* action concerns the 'exploitation of attributes of the plaintiff's identity. . .for the defendant's benefit or advantage.'[82] Prosser argues that the 'disarray' and 'confusion' exhibited by US courts in privacy cases results from a 'failure to separate and distinguish these four forms of invasion.' In short, it is a failure to comprehend that each form calls for a different approach.[83]

Prosser's influence, particularly on courts and legislators, has been immense.[84] He has also inspired legal academics to embark on similar projects. Among contemporary privacy scholars, Daniel Solove ranks as the most prominent taxonomist. Drawing on Wittgenstein's idea of family resemblances and the philosophy of pragmatism, Solove seeks to provide a taxonomy of privacy interests suited to the complexities of the twenty-first century. He focuses on problems, working from the bottom-up 'rather than trying to fit each situation into a rigid predefined category'.[85]

Solove places these privacy problems into four groups of 'harmful activities'—information collection, information processing, information dissemination and invasion.[86] They include:

1. *Information Collection*. This group consists of the potential wrongs of *surveillance* and *interrogation*; in other words, the act of gathering private information can be a wrongful act in itself.
2. *Information processing*. By this Solove means the wrongful storing or manipulation of private information. He identifies five types of processing. These include:

   - *Aggregation* ('the combination of various pieces of data about a person'),
   - *Identification* ('linking information to particular individuals'),
   - *Insecurity* ('carelessness in protecting stored information from leaks and improper access'),
   - *Secondary use* ('the use of collected information for a purpose different from the use for which it was collected without the data subject's consent'),
   - *Exclusion* ('the failure to allow the data subject to know about the data that others have about her and participate in its handling and use').[87]

---

[80] *Ibid* at 398.

[81] *Ibid* at 400.

[82] *Ibid* at 401.

[83] *Ibid* at 407.

[84] See generally McCarthy, *The Rights of Publicity and Privacy* (2008).

[85] Solove, *Understanding Privacy* (2008) p 44.

[86] *Ibid* p 103.

[87] *Ibid* p 104.

3. *Dissemination of private information.* Within this group, Solove identifies seven potentially wrongful activities:

   - *Breach of confidentiality, disclosure* ('revelation of truthful information' that impacts on reputation'),
   - *Exposure* ('revealing another's nudity, grief or bodily functions'),
   - *Increased accessibility* ('amplifying the accessibility of information'),
   - *Blackmail* (threatening to disseminate private information),
   - *Appropriation* (misuse use of an individual's identity),
   - *Distortion* ('disseminating false or misleading information about individuals').[88]

4. *Invasion.* This can take the form of *intrusions* that 'disturb one's tranquillity or solitude' or decisional interference ('incursion into the data subject's decisions regarding her private affairs').[89]

Solove's impressive taxonomy has a far greater range than Prosser's earlier attempt. In particular, it caters for a wide array of potential wrongdoing in a digital environment. He remains perhaps the leading privacy law scholar and his work is highly influential but taxonomising in this manner is also a popular pursuit elsewhere. In much of continental Europe privacy is understood to fall under the umbrella of personality rights.[90] While this *characterisation* is alien to most common law systems, the basic *idea* is familiar—apart from life, bodily integrity, freedom, ownership, property and economic interests, there are certain interests, connected to the personality of the individual, which warrant legal protection.[91] Following an analysis of the case law of the German *Bundesverfassungsgericht*/Federal Constitutional Court (*BVerfG*) and the *Bundesgerichtshof*/Federal Court of Justice (*BGH*), Brüggemeier identified five broad areas of protection contained within the multifaceted German general personality right under § 823 (1) *Bürgerliches Gesetzbuch* (BGB)[92]:

1. *Privacy* functions as a general heading for the protected area of conducting one's personal life (*persönlicher Lebensführung*) and anonymity, and includes the right to be let alone, the right to freedom from public exposure and the right to one's written and spoken word.
2. The *right to one's own image* is particularly relevant in the case of public figures. It also has a 'double nature' as a non-transferable personality right (right of privacy) and as a marketable property right (right to publicity).

[88] *Ibid* p 105.

[89] *Ibid.*

[90] See Brüggemeier, Colombi Ciacchi & O'Callaghan, *Personality Rights in European Tort Law* (2010).

[91] Zweigert & Kötz, *An Introduction to Comparative Law* (1998) p 685.

[92] Brüggemeier, *Haftungsrecht* (2006) pp 271–272.

3. The *Public Sphere* (*Öffentlichkeitssphäre*) concerns the protection of so-called persons of contemporary history (*Personen der Zeitgeschichte*). This is a peculiarity of German law and something that will be examined in more detail later on.
4. *Informational self-determination* or the right to one's own data is an independent aspect of privacy. It concerns the competence of the individual to decide whether information relating to his person is made accessible to private or state institutions, and under which circumstances.
5. *Personal honour* is a classical personal interest with a long tradition. It was protected primarily by criminal law following the introduction of the BGB. However, since the recognition of the general personality right, serious injuries to honour can be sanctioned with civil damages (*billige Geldentschädigung*).

We find that the German general personality right, as described here, encompasses a broad range of interests; but what is striking is that all of these interests fall within the scope of Bloustein's conception of privacy. What also emerges from Brüggemeier's taxonomy is that the German courts appear to have developed a highly elaborate legal framework regulating, among other things, the interaction between dignitarian and commercial interests (publicity right). We will analyse these points in more detail later.

What do we learn from these taxonomies of privacy interests? Can we identify commonalities that can act as reference points in our task of refinement? What is clear from this overview is that many of the same wrongs are emphasised, albeit they are sometimes expressed in different ways. First, we find a concern for individual *solitude*. This can mean protecting the physical private sphere (such as the home) against intrusion but it can also extend to the virtual private sphere of the internet. Second, the taxonomies highlight the wrong of *dissemination* of private information. This encompasses the well-known cases of media publication but can extend, in principle, to any form of unauthorised dissemination of information. Third, we find numerous references to *appropriation* of personality; in other words the misuse of the image or likeness of an individual (often for commercial gain). As we shall later see, here we are concerned with both dignitarian and commercial interests.

Taxonomists often seek to provide a complete definition of privacy but no matter how carefully they collect and arrange relevant cases, agent-relativity in the research will be inevitable and new problems and cases will continue to arise. Faced with this problem in his own analysis of personality interests a century ago, Roscoe Pound concluded that 'all classifications are more or less arbitrary'.[93] We should note that Solove is alert to this problem. He admits that his categorisation is 'not final and immutable' and that his 'own normative views are inescapably bound up in the framework'.[94] On his account, 'the primary function of [his] approach to

[93] Pound, 'Interests of Personality' (1915) at 349.
[94] Solove, *Understanding Privacy* (2008) p 105.

conceptualising privacy [is] to shift the kind of theoretical discussions we have about privacy.'[95] Understood in this way, the value of Solove's book is that it provides us with important material for further critical refinement.

Solove is right to highlight the dangers of the traditional methods of thinking about privacy. We must heed his advice and shift the theoretical discussion. In this book, I seek to contribute to this theoretical shift by engaging in refinement of privacy, albeit in the particular context of English tort law. But in order to do so we must first devise a method of refinement that is suited to law and legal scholarship.

1.4 Refining Privacy: The Method

What emerges from our overview of privacy scholarship is that the concept of privacy is more complex than generally assumed. This complexity means that refinement is necessary. But how do we even begin to distil the informing purposes or content of privacy when people understand it in so many different ways? I believe that the work of the philosopher of science, Karl Popper, is revealing here. Popper maintains that the theory of induction is illogical. This is because knowledge cannot start from a *tabula rasa*. In order to observe and engage in induction there must first be a 'point of view'. This point of view is 'as a system of expectations, anticipations, assumptions, or interests.'[96] What this means, in effect, is that agent-relativity is inevitable. But once we accept this to be the case, we need not wait 'passively for repetitions to impress or impose regularities upon us', rather 'we [can] actively try to impose regularities upon the world.' We apply our theories to the facts, but if we later discover flaws in these theories then we may discard them.[97] Consider how Popper replies to the question 'how do you know?:

> I do not know: my assertion was merely a guess. Never mind the source, or the sources, from which it may spring – there are many possible sources, and I may not be aware of half of them; and origins or pedigrees have in any case little bearing upon the truth. But if you are interested in the problem which I tried to solve by my tentative assertion, you may help me by criticizing it as severely as you can; and if you can design some experimental test which you think might refute my assertion, I shall gladly, and to the best of my powers, help you to refute it.[98]

In order to advance knowledge, then, we must test, we must 'do'. Hannah Arendt makes a similar point, arguing that '[n]othing indeed could be less trustworthy for acquiring knowledge and approaching truth than passive observation or mere contemplation. In order to be certain one [has] to make sure, and in order to

---

[95] *Ibid* p 172.

[96] Popper, *Conjectures and Refutations* (2002) p 59.

[97] *Ibid* p 60.

[98] *Ibid* p 35.

know one [has] to do.' The nature of knowledge is such that it must be 'tested only through more doing.'[99]

But what does all of this mean for our study? Most importantly, it means that we must avoid passive observation at all costs because this method does not encourage normative analysis. So, for example, in a study based on passive observation, the question and answer about the necessity of legal protection for privacy becomes:

Q: Why does privacy need legal protection?
A: Because Article 8 ECHR [or some other positive source of law] requires us to respect it.

When applying a method of passive observation, the lawyer tends to presuppose that origin and validity coincide. For Raz, this attitude stems from an 'unstated basic intuition [that the] law has to do with those considerations which it is appropriate for courts to rely upon in justifying their decisions'.[100] Because the lawyer operates at an executive level, his task is to make use of the relevant law (those 'authoritative positivist considerations') in order to manage the practical circumstances. As a rule, he accepts the validity of a legal proposition if its origin in positive law is identifiable and does not need to concern himself with the moral and political considerations that informed the deliberative stage. This is the 'lawyer's perspective', as Raz describes it—the 'unquestioning acceptance [of the basic intuition] as the starting point' for all discussion about a legal topic.[101]

But this is not a sound methodological stance.[102] For if we accept unquestioningly the 'basic intuition' as our starting point for conceptualising privacy, we obstruct necessary critical debate about the value and functions of privacy and, ultimately, the methods of protecting it. We must, as Raz advises 'stand back from the lawyer's perspective'[103] because even though one can identify law without 'resort[ing] to moral or any other evaluative argument,... it does not follow that one can defend the doctrine of the nature of law itself without using evaluative (though not necessarily moral) arguments.'[104] We must therefore adopt an 'institutional perspective', attempting to locate privacy in 'the wider perspective of social organization and political institutions generally.'[105] Privacy scholars should

---

99 Arendt, *The Human Condition* (1999) p 290. Following pragmatic philosophers, Solove reaches a similar conclusion about 'testing' and 'doing' and therefore opts to conceptualise privacy from the bottom up. See generally Solove, *Understanding Privacy* (2008).

100 Raz, 'The Problem About the Nature of Law' (1983) at 207.

101 *Ibid* at 208.

102 Raz writes that 'there is something inherently implausible in adopting the lawyer's perspective as one's fundamental methodological stance'. *Ibid* at 211.

103 *Ibid* at 212.

104 *Ibid* at 218. Note that Raz does not exclude moral arguments from the institutional perspective.

105 *Ibid* at 212.

therefore adopt a 'reflective critical attitude',[106] considering the value and functions of privacy before assessing the methods of legal protection.

But how does one adopt the 'institutional perspective' in privacy scholarship? How do we design an experimental test based on refinement for the social sciences? I believe we must begin by critically assessing the proposition that the value of privacy is such that it warrants legal protection in the first place. Rather than merely accepting this proposition without question, we must test it by considering two extremes. Drawing on existing theories and studies, I imagine a world in which privacy does not have any value and then the opposite: a world in which privacy is considered to be the most important and cherished value. By means of this contrast, I propose a number of *genuine conjectures* about privacy.

Popper regards 'genuine conjectures' as 'highly informative guesses about the world, although not verifiable (i.e. capable of being shown to be true)'.[107] The potential utility of conjectures in this sense extends beyond the so-called 'hard' sciences because conjectures, in every academic discipline, help advance knowledge. But conjectures have a particular value in the social sciences in helping to explore the 'limits of the practicably possible'. For Rawls, our problem 'is that the limits of the possible are not given by the actual.' On his account, we thus 'have to rely on conjecture and speculation, arguing as best we can that the social world we envision is feasible and might actually exist if not now then at some future time under happier circumstances.'[108]

The first step in our study, then, is to propose conjectures about the value and nature of privacy. If, as a result of this exercise, we conclude that privacy warrants some form of legal protection, we must then proceed to consider the possible means of protection. Here, I seek to test the methods of protecting privacy by putting each one forward tentatively and attempting to identify error. Popper was keen to point out that the 'method of trial and error is essentially a method of elimination.'[109] As such, if error is established, then the theory is eliminated. For Popper, the success of such a test 'depends mainly on three conditions, namely, that sufficiently numerous [...] theories should be offered, that the theories offered should be sufficiently varied, and that sufficiently severe tests should be made.'[110]

The methods of protecting privacy are certainly numerous and varied but how do we go about creating sufficiently stringent tests? Popper maintains that we test a theory 'by applying it to very special cases—cases for which it yields results different from those we should have expected without that theory, or in the light of other theories... [W]e try to select for our tests those crucial cases in which we

[106] Hart, *The Concept of Law* (1997) p 57.

[107] Popper, *Conjectures and Refutations* (2002) p 154.

[108] Rawls, *The Law of Peoples* (1999) p 12.

[109] Popper, *Conjectures and Refutations* (2002) p 421.

[110] *Ibid.*

should expect the theory to fail if it is not true.'[111] Against this backdrop, I construct my test by putting forward a select number of English privacy cases. I choose three hard cases: *Mosley* v *News Group Newspapers*, *Douglas* v *Hello*, and *Kaye* v *Robertson*. In each case the claimant is a celebrity but this reveals something important about English law. As we will later see, the claimants in successful privacy actions are almost always celebrities and this contributes to a skewed understanding among English tort lawyers of privacy's content.

The next step in our study is the comparative element. This involves testing the various methods of privacy protection in Germany against the special cases from English law. To this end, I consider how our hard cases might be decided by a German court. Again, I must emphasise that the aim here is to advance knowledge in the privacy field, rather than attempt to select a method which is supposedly correct or objectively true. But this does not prevent us from arguing that one method is better than the other. Clearly, one method is preferable to another if it withstands more attempts to falsify and refute it. But in assessing whether or not it is a sound method, we must also subject it to a further consideration: is the method in question consistent with the regulative ideals of justice and the rule of law?

1.4.1 The Rule of Law and Ideals of Justice as 'Regulative Ideals'

Popper explains that in science, objective truth acts as a *regulative ideal* (in the Kantian sense).[112] While we may not have a criterion of truth to hand, the 'very idea of error—and of fallibility—involves the idea of an objective truth as the standard of which we may fall short.'[113] Popper employs the metaphor of a mountain which is 'wrapped' in clouds.[114] The climber cannot see the summit and thus he can never be sure whether he has reached the main summit or a subsidiary peak. But this does not affect the summit's 'objective existence'.[115] When the climber says 'I doubt whether I have reached the actual summit', it follows that by implication he recognises its objective existence.[116] While the climber can never be sure that he

---

[111] *Ibid* p 150.

[112] Popper's notion of a 'regulative ideal' finds its origin in Kant's *Critique of Pure Reason*. For Kant, the regulative principle of reason contains 'nothing but...the pure schema of possible experience'. It 'postulates what we ought to do in the regress, but does not anticipate what may be given in the object prior to such regress.' See Kant, *Critique of Pure Reason* (2007) pp 252 & 448. Nussbaum argues that this 'regulative ideal [encompassing the categorical imperative] should be at the heart of both moral and political reflection and [it] supplies constraints upon what we may politically will.' See Nussbaum, 'Kant and Stoic Cosmopolitanism' (1997) at 12.

[113] Popper, *Conjectures and Refutations* (2002) p 311.

[114] *Ibid* p 306.

[115] *Ibid* pp 306–307.

[116] *Ibid* p 307.

has reached the summit (so long as it remains wrapped in clouds), sometimes it is possible for him to establish that he has *not* reached it; this is the case, for instance, when he encounters an overhanging wall. Understood this way, in systems of thought, while we can never be sure that we have found the absolute truth, we can edge towards it by means of critical rationalist thinking.

While truth is a goal of academic endeavour in all disciplines, we must keep in mind, as Rawls argues that '[j]ustice is the first virtue of social institutions, as truth is of systems of thought'. On this account:

> A theory however elegant and economical must be rejected or revised if it is untrue; likewise laws and institutions no matter how efficient and well-arranged must be reformed or abolished if they are unjust.[117]

Like objective truth in science, judges, when coming to decisions, use the rule of law and ideals of justice as *regulative ideals*; there is significantly more to their task than 'analogy mongering'.[118] As in Popper's metaphor of the climber who cannot see the summit of the mountain, even in those hard cases with no clear answer, judges do not doubt the existence of the rule of law and ideals of justice; these ideas are at the same time both a guide *and* a constraint in judicial decision-making. Even sceptics imply the existence of *regulative ideals*. Fish argues that in order to construct a 'persuasively told story',[119] judges must 'fashion [the story's] coherence out of materials [the story] is required to take into account.'[120] In this way, the law is 'constraining even if it is not, in the strict sense, a constraint'.[121] In our task of refining privacy and methods of protection, then, we face both centripetal and centrifugal pressures. But the method of trial and error demands that we must be bold and seek to explore the limits of the 'practicably possible' while remaining attentive to law's regulative ideals.

1.5 Concluding Remarks and a Reiteration

I have sought, in this first chapter, to outline the basic method of this study of privacy interests and to provide justifications for adopting this approach. This project differs from other work in the field in one major respect: its purpose. I do not seek to define privacy or taxonomise the legal wrongs; thus, I can draw a distinction between my project and Solove's recent work on privacy. Like Solove, I am also highly critical of the 'traditional method' in privacy scholarship, the

---

[117] Rawls, *A Theory of Justice* (1999) p 3.

[118] Unger, 'The Critical Legal Studies Movement' (1983) at 570.

[119] Fish, *There's No Such Thing as Free Speech and It's a Good Thing, Too* (1994) p 151.

[120] *Ibid.*

[121] *Ibid* p 152.

notion that one can 'conceptualize privacy by defining it per *genus et differentiam*'.[122] But unlike Solove, I do not propose a 'new understanding' of privacy in the form of a taxonomy. I hope the reader does not conclude as a result that my project lacks intellectual ambition but I believe that reflecting on our shared experience of privacy and critically evaluating existing theories and methods of protection is worthwhile. Not only can it provide us with important insights about how privacy laws are structured, as we will see in Chap. 5, a careful critical rationalist analysis can also reveal significant problems in our laws, particularly when we discover that the methods of protecting privacy are not fully aligned with the regulative ideals of justice and the rule of law.

Before we move on to the conjectures about the nature and value of privacy, I wish to emphasise one final point. Some readers might make the case that while I criticise agent-relativity, my approach in itself is entirely subjective for in proposing genuine conjectures, I *personally* select cases and ultimately sit as judge, testing the various methods of protection against these cases. In response, I would reiterate that the objective here is to not to solve the problems surrounding privacy once and for all but to advance knowledge in privacy scholarship (albeit within the confines of tort law). Agent-relativity is a hindrance to the former but necessary in order to achieve the latter (indeed, as Kant teaches us, how can it be otherwise?). It is necessary to view the same problem from as many different perspectives as possible, to propose conjectures and theories so that they can be falsified and refuted by others. Only in this way is knowledge truly advanced.

[122] Solove, *Understanding Privacy* (2008) p 14.

Chapter 2
Three Conjectures About Privacy

Im Eis der Einsamkeit wird sich der Mensch am unerbittlichsten zur Frage, und eben daher, da die Frage grausam sein Heimlichstes aufruft und ins Spiel zieht, wird er sich zur Erfahrung.

- Martin Buber

2.1 Introduction

We have seen that people understand privacy in many different ways and any scholar who sets out to define it per *genus et differentiam* ends up in a privacy 'swamp'. This is because the theory of induction is illogical. Moreover, in any attempt to provide a universal definition of privacy, agent-relativity remains an obstacle that the scholar cannot overcome. Our task therefore is to refine privacy—we must reflect on the shared experiences that make up its content. This task takes on added significance in legal scholarship because relatively little attention is paid in legal treatises to the value and nature of privacy.[1] Apart from occasional and often oblique references to the importance of autonomy and dignity, what emerges is that scholars often assume that the nature of privacy is such that it automatically warrants legal protection. But the reluctance to reflect on the content of privacy is unfortunate for it means that much of the legal discussion about privacy is often based on vague generalisations about its informing purposes. Clearly, laws based on generalisations are not always good laws. It would be more fruitful to pay close attention to privacy's content before we embark on any legal analysis. To this end, in this chapter I begin to refine privacy by proposing conjectures about its nature and value. These conjectures provide a conceptual framework for the legal analysis later in this book.

[1] There are exceptions. Solove, for instance, provides a thoughtful analysis of privacy's value. See Solove, *Understanding Privacy* (2009).

P. O'Callaghan, *Refining Privacy in Tort Law*,

DOI 10.1007/978-3-642-31884-9_2,

2.2 Assessing the Value of Privacy

In reflecting on privacy's content, I draw on the American sociologist Wright Mills' idea of a 'sociological imagination'. Wright Mills believed that the most instructive insights are often gained by thinking about extremes. This 'logically sound' method of establishing 'polar types' is an important part of the 'intellectual craftmanship' required to possess the sociological imagination.[2] In thinking about our shared experience of privacy, I propose imagining a world in which privacy does not exist in any form and a world in which privacy is understood as a value of paramount importance. This contrast will allow me to propose some *genuine conjectures* about privacy's content.

2.2.1 A World Without Privacy

Given that references to privacy are ubiquitous in our social milieu, how do we even begin to imagine a world without privacy? I suggest that historical accounts of privacy can help us glean instructive insights for our task. This is because for much of antiquity and the first millennium AD, governing classes and scholars viewed privacy negatively; in other words, they considered privacy detrimental to the wellbeing of the community. Once we reflect on these experiences, we are perhaps better placed to imagine a world without privacy.

According to Arendt, the ancient Greeks were unfamiliar with the idea of a private sphere. For them, privacy amounted to 'a state of being deprived of something.'[3] 'A man who lived only a private life', explains Arendt 'was not fully human'. The individual who spent his life in private, on his own (*idion*) was 'outside the world of the common', and thus 'idiotic'.[4] Similarly, in effect, the Romans did not distinguish between public and private or even between state finances and individual wealth; the 'grandeur of Rome was the collective property of the governing class and ruling groups of senators.'[5] The Romans frequently used the adjective 'private' (*privatus*)—holding public office, for instance, was considered 'an ideal of private behaviour'. But the 'private' was understood in a more negative sense, it 'characterized those things that an individual might do without

[2] See Wright Mills, *The Sociological Imagination* (2000) pp 213–214.

[3] Arendt, *The Human Condition* (1999) p 38.

[4] *Ibid*. Similarly, as Duby explains, in the Middle Ages, a person who willingly chose to be alone, to 'remove himself from the close and omnipresent conviviality. . .immediately became an object of suspicion', usually considered a criminal or a heretic. It was 'commonly believed that solitary wandering was a symptom of insanity.' Isolation made the person 'more vulnerable to the Enemy's attacks.' See Duby, 'Solitude' (1988) p 510.

[5] Veyne, 'The Roman Empire' (1987) p 95.

failing of the duties required of a man holding public office.'[6] In ancient Rome, private behaviour was frequently censored in public. Veyne explains that '[n]o one was exempt from justifying his private life before the bar of public opinion, not even emperors'.[7] This commitment to public life permeated Roman society. The head of the household, the *paterfamilias*, for example, would attempt to avoid public criticism by asking family and friends for advice on private matters, whether this involved marital problems or how to punish children.[8] The net effect was that the governing class ruled public life while 'private life [was ruled] by fear of what the governing class would say.'[9]

The early religious communities were suspicious of the notion of a private sphere for different reasons.[10] The religious literature from the second century BC onwards emphasises the 'need to mobilize the whole of the self in the service of a religious law'.[11] The law demanded full solidarity amongst the members of the community.[12] But it is clear from the literature that there was an 'unrelieved anxiety' that the members would fail in this enterprise and there was thus a 'sharp negative sense of the private.'[13] This is because the Jews and early Christians believed in the 'doubleness of heart', good and evil.[14] Hidden thoughts and feelings, the intimacies of the heart, were thus treated as 'possible sources of tensions', threatening the 'ideal solidarity of the community.[15] This ideal of religious solidarity—the 'total permeability of the private person to the demands of the community'[16] was to have a profound effect on Western thought up to the Enlightenment and found expression in utopian literature. Thomas More, for example, suggested that the ideal life was one in which one lives 'in full view of all'. In *Utopia*, 'nowhere is there any chance to loaf or any pretext for evading work; there are no wine-bars, or ale-houses, or brothels; no chances for corruption; no hiding places; no spots for secret meetings.'[17] In More's view, complete transparency of this sort would not only ensure economic efficacy but it would also root out evil and promote spiritual well-being generally.

---

[6] *Ibid* p 163.

[7] *Ibid* p 173.

[8] *Ibid.*

[9] *Ibid.*

[10] See Brown, 'Late Antiquity' (1987).

[11] *Ibid* p 253.

[12] *Ibid.*

[13] *Ibid* p 254.

[14] *Ibid* p 288. 'Singleness of heart' was thus the ideal. Later in his essay, Brown goes on to explain that the 'prestige of the monk lay in the fact that he was the 'lonely one'. He personified the ancient ideal of singleness of heart. He has renounced the world in the most starkly visible manner possible.'

[15] *Ibid.*

[16] *Ibid* p 254.

[17] More, *Utopia* (2002) p 59.

For More, pre-Enlightenment utopian thinkers, and the ancients, privacy was an impediment to achieving true social cohesion and economic efficacy. These are unfamiliar arguments in the twenty-first century but there are still some who choose to sacrifice privacy in order to participate in a particular community.[18] Solove quotes the psychologist Bruno Bettelheim who spent some time at an Israeli kibbutz. Bettelheim admits that there were some clear benefits arising from this sort of communal living. He notes, for example, that there was no crime or other forms of antisocial behaviour. Yet, Bettelheim admits that he 'felt suffocated by the lack of privacy.'[19]

The citizens of ancient Greece and Rome and the religious communities of late antiquity would not have been able to appreciate Bettelheim's feeling of suffocation. In Chap. 3, we will see that Bettelheim's reaction is a consequence of what Braunstein calls 'the invention of subjectivity',[20] a process of individualisation that began in the eleventh century and gathered pace with the urbanisation, industrialisation and secularisation of late-modernity. During the eleventh to thirteenth centuries it was primarily economic transformation through the acceleration of trade, combined with 'education through sermons' and the 'internalization of piety'[21] that 'liberated the individual.'[22] This period fundamentally altered what was meant by the word 'private'.[23] Duby writes that from this point on:

> Privacy meant being oneself among others, in one's own room, at one's own window, with one's own property, one's own purse, and one's own faults – recognised and pardoned – as well as one's own dreams, aspirations and secrets.[24]

[18] Apparently, there are also communities that do not have an understanding of any form of privacy in the first place. Räikkä, drawing on the work of Goncalves, provides the examples of the Paresi Indian communities in Brazil, in which brothers 'share' wives and the Yine Indian communities in Peru, in which 'strangers may touch a woman's breast in order to evaluate her ability to feed children.' See Räikkä, 'Is Privacy Relative?' (2008) at 535 citing Goncalves, 'A Woman between Two Men and a Man between Two Women' (2001).

[19] See Bettelheim, 'The Right to Privacy is a Myth', Saturday Evening Post, July 27, 1968, at 8, cited by Solove, Understanding Privacy (2009), p 81.

[20] Braunstein, 'Toward Intimacy' (1988) p 536.

[21] Duby explains that at the beginning of the Middle Ages, members of the community 'entrusted their deliverance from civil to delegated representatives' e.g. monks would pray for the souls of the community. But over the course of the thirteenth century, in particular, 'private devotion' became more common. The Fourth Lateran Council Declaration of 1215 illustrates this point. Until 1215, confession used to be 'rare and public.' But the Lateran Council required every person, peer and commoner alike, to study his own soul and confess his intimate sins in private to a priest. This combined with the practice of consuming the body of Christ for 'an intimate encounter' had the effect of 'magnif[ing] the human person' as an individual. See Duby, 'Solitude' (1988) pp 528–531.

[22] Duby, 'Solitude' (1988) p 533.

[23] *Ibid.*

[24] *Ibid.*

So, from the thirteenth century, privacy is understood as something that the individual possesses or enjoys rather than something that the community abhors. This is an understanding of privacy that is more familiar to us.

At its extreme, then, a world without any form of privacy is a world in which others have access to all of our thoughts, desires and feelings or the 'sheer tropical luxuriance of the inner life', as Nagel puts it.[25] It is a world in which all others have an unlimited right of entry and access to our property, our email accounts and our homes. But this world is clearly at odds with what we now consider to be fundamental interests and demands, most notably human dignity and autonomy. 'The man', as Bloustein argues, 'who is compelled to live every minute of his life among others and whose every need, thought, desire, fancy or gratification is subject to public scrutiny, has been deprived of his individuality and human dignity.'[26] This person 'merges with the mass' and, 'although sentient, [he] is fungible; he is not an individual.'[27] It is for this reason that James Griffin has argued that autonomy is at risk where there is no privacy.[28] But the lack of autonomy that results from a denial of privacy creates other problems. A world in which the individual exercises little or no control over his own life is at odds with the Millsian idea that '[t]he only freedom that deserves the name, is that of pursing our own good in our own way so long as we do not attempt to deprive others of theirs, or impede their efforts to obtain it.'[29] In a very real sense, then, without individual autonomy, liberal democracy and society (as we know it) are not feasible and it is for this reason that Nagel considers concealment 'a condition of civilisation'.[30]

2.2.2 A World in Which Privacy Is the Ultimate Value

The social order of liberal democracies is based on what Vlastos terms an 'equalitarian community'.[31] The basic premise of this community is that each individual has the 'capacity to choose and to pursue [their] conception of a worthwhile life' (in other words, 'normative agency').[32] If we agree that normative agency is not possible without respect for human dignity, a world without privacy, then, is clearly undesirable.[33] But what about a world in which privacy is considered to be of

---

[25] Nagel, 'Concealment and Exposure' (1998) at 4.
[26] Bloustein, 'Privacy as an Aspect of Human Dignity' (1964) at 1003.
[27] *Ibid.*
[28] Griffin, *On Human Rights* (2008) p 225.
[29] Mill, *On Liberty* (1863) pp 28–29.
[30] Nagel, 'Concealment and Exposure' (1998) at 4.
[31] Vlastos, 'Justice and Equality' (1984) p 50.
[32] Griffin, *On Human Rights* (2008) p 45.
[33] On normative agency see generally Griffin, *On Human Rights* (2008).

paramount importance, so much so that it trumps all other values? There are numerous arguments against absolute privacy, almost all of them emphasising the social and economic cost and potential damage to the community.

First, in considering some of the 'virtues and vices' of privacy, Solove makes the point that privacy 'lessens a society's ability to detect and punish disobedience, which makes it harder to enforce laws and norms'.[34] Clearly, a world in which privacy was the overarching value would provide fertile ground for all sorts of crime and illicit behaviour. Second, while some degree of privacy is required in order to develop the individual personality and maintain intimate relationships, too much privacy leads to a lack of trust with the potential to seriously damage relationships.[35] Concealment of information and a lack of transparency also have negative implications for economic bargaining and the market economy generally.[36] Third, absolute privacy would stifle freedom of expression, the 'very life-blood of a democracy'.[37] Without freedom of expression, not only would it be difficult to maintain checks on government and officialdom, civic discourse and social cohesion would be threatened. Emerson advocates the 'safety-valve' function of freedom of expression[38]; on his account, open discussion allows for adaptability and stability in the community.[39] It maintains 'the precarious balance between healthy cleavage and necessary consensus'.[40] Generally, the individual is willing to accept decisions, even those that may ultimately disadvantage him, if he feels he has participated in the decision-making and deliberative process. Clearly, a state of absolute privacy endangers this balance.

Like a world without privacy, absolute privacy would fundamentally change the nature of society and the economy. Liberal democracy, as we know it, would not be possible. A system based on absolute privacy would rank the interests of the individual over those of the community. But it does not follow that having complete attention afforded to individual interests is necessarily beneficial to individual wellbeing. Some psychologists have suggested that absolute privacy may lead to a tendency towards 'self-concealment'; in other words, cases where an individual attempts to hide negative or painful personal information from others.[41] Numerous studies have shown an association between 'self-concealment' and adverse

[34] Solove, *Understanding Privacy* (2008) p 81.

[35] Solove quotes the sociologist Steven Nock who argues that '[t]rust and the ability to take others at their word are basic ingredients in the social order.' See Nock, *The Costs of Privacy* (1993) cited by Solove, *ibid* p 81.

[36] Posner, 'The Right of Privacy' (1978).

[37] *R (Simms)* v *Secretary of State for the Home Department* [2000] 2 AC 115, at 126 (per Lord Steyn).

[38] See Emerson, *The System of Freedom of Expression* (1970).

[39] Emerson, 'Toward a General Theory of the First Amendment' (1963) at 884.

[40] *Ibid.*

[41] Larson & Chastain, 'Self-concealment' (1990).

physiological and psychological outcomes.[42] Arendt argues thus that the men who 'become entirely private... have been deprived of seeing and hearing others, of being seen and being heard by them.'[43] Absolute privacy ensures that we all become 'imprisoned in the subjectivity of [our] own singular experience'.[44] This sort of psychological imprisonment is deeply damaging to the well-being of both the individual *and* the community.

2.2.3 Contrasting the Extremes

In contrasting these extremes, it becomes evident that neither is in itself desirable but the contrast reveals some important features about privacy's content. First, it demonstrates that privacy is essential to the human *personality*, particularly basic interests in autonomy and dignity. We cannot fully develop our personalities, or arrive at an *ichbewusstsein*[45] or a self-identity, without some enjoyment of privacy. Second, a link between privacy and property emerges. Not only has the home been the central feature of private life since antiquity, once we accept the argument that privacy is essential to *ichbewusstsein* we are further faced with potential property-related questions. To what extent, for instance, does one 'own' one's reputation? As we will see later in this chapter, this raises complex questions about human personhood and commodification.

The contrast also highlights the complex relationship between individual interests and those of the community. Even though personhood emphasises the centrality of human dignity and autonomy, the person and the community remain interdependent. We need some form of social interaction, a wider *community*, in order to construct our self-identity and to 'flourish' as the German idealists might have put it. The German philosopher and psychiatrist, Karl Jaspers, understood personality as 'that mode of being oneself which, in its very nature, cannot be alone; it is something related, must have something else apart form it: persons and nature.'[46] As social beings, not only do we seek acceptance from others, we also use others as reference points in constructing our individual identities, much in the same way that a child learns to play a game.[47] With this in mind, Nagel argues, '[t] he awareness of how one appears from outside is a constant of human life, sometimes burdensome, sometimes an indispensable resource.'[48]

---

[42] Cole *et al*, 'Elevated physical health risk among gay men who conceal their homosexual identity' (1996).

[43] Arendt, *The Human Condition* (1999) p 58.

[44] *Ibid.*

[45] On *ichbewusstsein* see Jaspers, *Allgemeine Psychopathologie* (1913).

[46] Schilpp, *The Philosophy of Karl Jaspers* (1957) p 263.

[47] Mead, *Mind, Self, & Society* (1934).

[48] Nagel, 'Concealment and Exposure' (1998) at 18.

For these reasons, I propose the following three conjectures about privacy's content or, in other words, our shared experience:

1. Privacy is an essential constituent of personhood; an absence of privacy threatens basic interests in dignity and therefore normative agency.
2. If we accept this to be the case, it follows that we are required to consider potential proprietary aspects of privacy for, as Kant and Hegel emphasise, private property is vital for autonomy.
3. Personality (and therefore privacy) is ontologically dependent on the community. Moreover, an absence of privacy also threatens the very existence of our equalitarian community.

It should be apparent that these conjectures are not intended to be analytically distinct—they overlap to a considerable degree and therefore privacy cannot be reduced to one or the other. In fact, the central theme in what follows is that personality, property and the community are conceptually-interdependent. I now move on to consider each of these conjectures in turn.

2.3 Privacy and Personality

Personality is a thick concept not least because it remains a subject of study in psychology, the biological sciences and economics on the one hand *and* moral philosophy on the other, but also because it does not lend itself very easily to analysis—how can something so intrinsic to the individual be studied?[49]

2.3.1 *Identity, Human Dignity and Rank*

The difficulty associated with potential scientific objectification throws light on the concept itself. Personality implies individuality. In that it distinguishes one individual from the other, it is, as one of the earliest social psychologists George Herbert Mead writes, 'the most precious part of the individual'.[50] Yet, personality, Mead suggests, also 'implies that the individual has certain common rights and values obtained in him and through him.'[51] Personality, thus, embodies all of those features that make us human but also those peculiarities that define our

---

[49] Kateb argues that we are doomed to an 'incomplete and imperfect understanding of the human psyche and hence of human life because of human inwardness.' See Kateb, *Human Dignity* (2011) pp 157–158.

[50] Mead, *Mind, Self, & Society* (1934) p 324.

[51] *Ibid.*

individuality. It represents *at once* 'commonness and distinctiveness'.[52] In this way, *personality* is associated with *identity*. Through it, we become conscious of the unique identity of the human species as a whole and the uniqueness of each human individual. This is what Kateb calls the 'truth of personal identity' but this 'truth' is endangered when:

> any individual is treated as if he or she is not a human being like any other, and therefore treated as more or less than human. The truth of identity is also at stake when a person is treated as if he or she is just one more human being in a species, and not, instead, a unique individual who is irreplaceable and not exchangeable for another.[53]

Similarly Dworkin writes that the 'vague but powerful idea of human dignity… supposes that there are ways of treating a man that are inconsistent with recognizing him as a full member of the human community [and] such treatment is profoundly unjust.'[54] A failure to take personal identity seriously is a denial of human uniqueness. Personality demands respect or attention in the sense of *Achtung*. It is for this reason that ideal theories of personality, dating back to *der Kategorische Imperativ*, emphasise human dignity and autonomy. Within the Categorical Imperative, Kant draws our attention to commonness and distinctiveness when he emphasises the 'humanity in our person'; the 'principle of humanity' and each individual person is to be treated as ends only and never as means to an end.[55]

What all of this means, in effect, is that we cannot appreciate personality in isolation. The obvious but indubitable fact is that each individual not only lives in common with others but also shares basic traits with the rest of humanity. The reader will note in Chap. 3 that the notion of social rank or standing is a recurring theme in the history of personality rights. The history of personality rights is a history of what Whitman calls a 'levelling up' of rank so that individuals are considered to be equal in rank in contemporary democratic societies.[56] In a similar manner, Jeremy Waldron draws our attention to this core idea of 'rank' when he offers an 'interpretive account' of dignity, arguing that it 'has its roots in the thick reality of historically existing schemes of rank and nobility.'[57] He elaborates further: 'Once associated with hierarchical differentiation of rank and status, "dignity" now conveys the idea that all human persons belong to the same rank and that rank is a very high one indeed.'[58]

---

[52] Kateb refers to 'commonness and distinctiveness' in writing about personal identity. Even though he says they 'seem to go in opposite directions', 'they cooperate in constituting the idea of equal individual status.' See Kateb, *Human Dignity* (2011) p 10.

[53] *Ibid.*

[54] Dworkin, *Life's Dominion* (1993) p 236.

[55] Kant, *Groundwork of the Metaphysics of Morals* (2011) p 45.

[56] See generally Whitman, 'The Two Western Cultures of Privacy' (2004).

[57] Waldron 'Dignity and Rank' (2007) at 230.

[58] *Ibid* at 201.

Humanity is accorded the highest rank of all species and each individual person is equal in rank within this scheme.[59] But while equal rank means that each person should be treated in the same way (as ends only), it does not mean that persons are indistinguishable from one another. Personality stands for the uniqueness of humanity as a species *and* the uniqueness of each individual member. Respect for human dignity is a commitment to preserve this uniqueness but it is not the only basic human interest to which we must pay close attention.

2.3.2 Autonomy and Self-Realisation

Ideal theories of personality emphasise autonomy alongside dignity. We associate autonomy with the Rousseauian 'moral freedom... which alone makes man truly the master of himself.'[60] Taken at face value, this conception of autonomy suggests the capacity for more or less unrestricted action but, as Baynes explains, Rousseau grappled with the question of social dependence: 'how is it that an individual can be autonomous despite his inevitable dependence on others'?[61]

While Kant's concern was moral freedom, a conception of freedom as self-realisation was a significant feature of the late eighteenth and early nineteenth century German idealist writing on autonomy. Drawing on the work of Rousseau, the idealists emphasised the place of self-determination and rationality in human autonomy.[62] Freedom as self-realisation has its roots in Christian Humanism and the writings of Leibniz and Erasmus but it can be further understood as a nineteenth century opposition to determinism and a reaction to liberalism.[63] Hegel, in particular, paid a great deal of attention to autonomy and sought to address the question posed by Rousseau—how is autonomy possible if we are dependent on society?[64] Two oft-cited sentences are revealing. In the *Philosophy of Right*, Hegel writes: 'Be a person and respect others as persons'[65] and in *Logic*, he notes that freedom is 'being at home with oneself in another.'[66] Underlying these ideas was a particular take on freedom as a concept. Singer explains that Hegel viewed liberal conceptions of freedom as superficial because they do not question 'why individuals make the

[59] This is because every member of humanity 'deserves to be treated in a manner consonant with the high worth of the species.' See Kateb, *Human Dignity* (2011) p 3.

[60] Rousseau, *The Social Contract* (1997) p 54.

[61] Baynes, 'Freedom and Recognition in Hegel and Habermas' (2002) at 2.

[62] See generally Leuze, *Die Entwicklung des Persönlichkeitsrechts im 19. Jahrhundert* (1962).

[63] Whitman, 'The Two Western Cultures of Privacy' (2004) at 1181.

[64] Baynes, 'Freedom and Recognition in Hegel and Habermas' (2002) at 2.

[65] Hegel, *Grundlinien der Philosophie des Rechts*, § 36.

[66] Hegel, *Logic* (1975) 24A quoted by Baynes, 'Freedom and Recognition in Hegel and Habermas' (2002) at 1.

choices they do'.[67] Real freedom does not arise from merely being let alone but by taking control. In classical liberal thought, we must accept that our freedom is limited by the 'conflicting wills' of others.[68] Hegel, however, argued that we can resolve this problem by recognising that the ability to reason is common to all human beings. If a community is constructed on a rational basis, everyone will accept it as an expression of his own individual rational will.[69] In this way, we avoid the Kantian 'perpetual conflict between duty and interest', as in a truly rational community, duty and interest would coincide because our duty is based on reason and our interest is to be truly rational.[70]

Whitman notes that unlike Anglo-American theorists, the 'paradigmatic free actor' for German philosophers 'was commonly the artist more than the consumer'.[71] Writers such as von Humboldt argued that self-realisation and human flourishing could not be provided by the market alone.[72] Freedom did not merely encompass the superficiality of being let alone or engaging in market transactions but allowing each individual to fully realise his own potential. Whitman argues that Germans consequently put less emphasis on 'consumer sovereignty' than individuals in Anglo-American countries and more on the 'unfettered creation of the self, on the fashioning of one's image and the realization of one's potentialities.'[73] Whitman's account provides us with an important insight about the German experience and, as we shall later see, this throws light on how German privacy laws are structured.

2.3.3 Personality, Worth and Ideal Theory

The two constituents of ideal theories of personality—dignity and autonomy—feature quite prominently in privacy scholarship. As we noted earlier, deontologists such as Bloustein stress the central role of human dignity and the grave injury that stems from an invasion of privacy. Moreover, in control-based accounts of privacy we find references to the idea of freedom based on self-realisation: the notion that an agent has the capacity to take control of his or her private life and decide its parameters. But while we can identify points of correlation between ideal theories of personality and privacy theories, we should perhaps ask what relevance ideal theories of personality based on dignity and autonomy have for a non-ideal world?

[67] Singer, 'Hegel' (1995) p 341.

[68] *Ibid.*

[69] *Ibid.*

[70] *Ibid.*

[71] Whitman, 'The Two Western Cultures of Privacy' (2004) at 1181.

[72] *Ibid.*

[73] *Ibid* at 1182.

With this in mind, Radin refers to the 'dynamism' present within the concept of personhood—for her, contextuality is key.[74]

A non-ideal theorist may argue that abstract theories of dignity and autonomy do not reveal what personality means to 'real' people and, ultimately, they do not adequately identify threats to personhood in the 'real' world. My response, drawing on Rawls, is that ideal theory helps us to refine privacy because it creates reference points for further reflection and critical refinement. When thinking about privacy and our non-ideal reality, it is useful to make use of the standard of a 'well-ordered society', in Rawls' sense, in which '[e]veryone is presumed to act justly and to do his part in upholding just institutions.'[75] As Rawls explains, in 'beginning with ideal theory [we obtain] the only basis for the systematic grasp of . . . more pressing problems'.[76] Understood in this way, instructive insights emerge at the confluence of the ideal and the non-ideal.

Legislators and courts in both civilian and common law systems often use the ideal standard in their reasoning. In Germany, for example, Articles 1 and 2 of the Constitution (*Grundgesetz*), encompassing human dignity and the 'free development of personality', are considered to be the foundational principles of the constitutional order.[77] In explaining the importance of these principles, the Constitutional Court has contrasted (in effect) the ideal of a 'well-ordered society' with the harsh realities of National Socialism:

'Dem Grundgesetz liegen Prinzipien der Staatsgestaltung zugrunde, die sich nur aus der geschichtlichen Erfahrung und der geistig-sittlichen Auseinandersetzung mit dem vorangegangenen System des Nationalsozialismus erklären lassen. Gegenüber der Allmacht des totalitären Staates, der schrankenlose Herrschaft über alle Bereiche des sozialen Lebens für sich beanspruchte und dem bei der Verfolgung seiner Staatsziele die Rücksicht auch auf das Leben des Einzelnen grundsätzlich nichts bedeutete, hat das Grundgesetz eine wertgebundene Ordnung aufgerichtet, die den einzelnen Menschen und seine Würde in den Mittelpunkt aller seiner Regelungen stellt.'[78]

'The principles of state-formation underlying the Basic Law can be explained only by the historical experience and the spiritual-moral confrontation with the previous system of National Socialism. Compared to the omnipotence of the totalitarian state, its unlimited control over all aspects of social life in order to pursue its national objectives, treating the lives of individuals as if they meant nothing, the Basic Law has constructed a value-bound order in which the individual person and his or her dignity/worth is at the centre of all rules and regulations.'

German scholars refer to the *Ausstrahlungswirkung* (radiating effect) of these basic rights and entitlements in that they radiate through the legal system as a

[74] Radin, *Contested Commodities* (2001) pp 60–78.

[75] Rawls, *A Theory of Justice* (1999) p 8.

[76] Our non-ideal reality becomes 'more tractable in the light of [the ideal theory].' *Ibid* pp 8–9.

[77] See Kumm, 'Who's Afraid of the Total Constitution?' (2006).

[78] BVerfGE 39, 1, 67 = NJW 1975, 573 573 (*Schwangerschaftsabbruch I*).

whole.[79] Respect of *Würde* is of such paramount importance for a 'well-ordered society' that scholars have termed it a *Basisgrundrecht* (the right at the basis of all fundamental rights).[80] Eberle argues that Kantian morality is clearly envisioned in modern German law where humans are viewed as 'spiritual-moral beings who act freely, but their actions are bound by a sense of moral duty.'[81] Actions, he argues, are guided by a 'sense of social need, personal responsibility, and human solidarity.'[82] Evidence of Kantian morality is ubiquitous but perhaps most obvious in the recent Constitutional Court decision on the constitutionality of the Aviation Security Act.[83] Following the terrorist attack on the Twin Towers in New York in 2001, the German parliament enacted legislation authorising the air force to shoot down any airplane that had been hijacked by terrorists if it could 'be assumed' that their intention was to use the airplane 'against human life'. According to the Court, while the State has a duty under the *Grundgesetz* to protect the lives of potential victims, the idea that this duty allows the State to infringe the 'supreme value' of the Constitution, namely human dignity, is 'inconceivable'. Under no circumstances should the helpless victims on the plane be treated as mere 'objects'. The Court explained that:

'Eine solche Behandlung missachtet die Betroffenen als Subjekte mit Würde und unveräußerlichen Rechten. Sie werden dadurch, dass ihre Tötung als Mittel zur Rettung anderer benutzt wird, verdinglicht und zugleich entrechtlicht; indem über ihr Leben von Staats wegen einseitig verfügt wird, wird den als Opfern selbst schutzbedürftigen Flugzeuginsassen der Wert abgesprochen, der dem Menschen um seiner selbst willen zukommt.'[84]	'Such treatment does not take into account the status of the persons in question as subjects who possess dignity and inalienable rights. In that their killing is used as a means to save the lives of others, they are being treated as objects without rights; in that the State unilaterally disposes of their lives, those persons on the airplane (themselves, as victims, requiring protection) are denied the value owed to each individual being.'

Habermas contends that the 'echo of Kant's categorical imperative is unmistakable in these words... The respect for the dignity of every person forbids the state to dispose of any individual merely as a means to another end, even if that end be to save the lives of many other people.'[85]

But references to 'dignity' or 'personhood' in the ideal sense are not limited to German case law; they also feature in common law judgments. In the US case of

---

[79] Beckmann *et al*, 'Germany' (2010) p 266.

[80] *Ibid* p 259.

[81] Eberle 'Human Dignity, Privacy, and Personality in German and American Constitutional Law' (1997) at 973.

[82] *Ibid.*

[83] BVerfGE 115, 118 = NJW 2006, 751 (*Luftsicherheitsgesetz*).

[84] *Ibid.*

[85] Habermas, 'The Concept of Human Dignity and the Realistic Utopia of Human Rights' (2010) at 465.

Rosenblatt v *Baer*,[86] frequently cited by American courts in defamation cases, Justice Stewart stressed that:

> [t]he right of a man to the protection of his own reputation from unjustified invasion and wrongful hurt reflects no more than our basic concept of the essential dignity and worth of every human being—a concept at the root of any decent system of ordered liberty. The protection of private personality, like the protection of life itself, is left primarily to the individual States under the Ninth and Tenth Amendments. But this does not mean that the right is entitled to any less recognition by this Court as a basic of our constitutional system.

We can draw parallels between the 'decent system of ordered liberty', as understood by Justice Stewart, and the Rawlsian idea of a 'well-ordered society'. Again, I must emphasise here that by contemplating the 'nature and aims of a perfectly just society' we gain (at the confluence of the ideal and the non-ideal) a deeper understanding of personality and, ultimately, privacy's content.[87] We will return to this idea later but for now we must consider our second conjecture about our shared experience of privacy.

2.4 Privacy as Property

While dignity and autonomy are central to personality, ordinary language reveals a latent side to the concept. In English, we speak of the wrong of *appropriation of personality*, the French talk about *les biens de la personnalité*, while German lawyers treat personality as a *Rechtsgut*.[88] Each of these expressions hints at possession but to what extent can we say that privacy has proprietary characteristics? And even if we establish this to be the case, how can we reconcile potential proprietary characteristics of personality, assuming exclusivity, transferability and universality, with human dignity and uniqueness?

Such questions are highly relevant to the debate on universal commodification—the idea that everything of value should be treated as if it were property. In her seminal book, *Contested Commodities*, Margaret Jane Radin argues that scholars who advance this view use 'market rhetoric [to] extend the market, metaphorically at least, beyond what we are conventionally comfortable with.'[89] For Radin, commodification 'implies a strong form of value commensurability'[90] because once everything of value is reduced to money, 'sums of money, in turn, can be compared consistently in a linear way.'[91] But commensurability 'cannot

[86] 383 US 75, 92 (1966) (Stewart, J, concurring).

[87] Rawls, *A Theory of Justice* (1999) p 9.

[88] Reiter, 'Personality and Patrimony' (2002) at 674.

[89] Radin, *Contested Commodities* (2001) p 4.

[90] *Ibid* p 9.

[91] *Ibid* p 8.

capture—and may debase—the way humans value things important to human personhood.'[92] We now turn to consider some of the questions raised by Radin in her book and examine their implications for privacy.

2.4.1 *The Subject/Object Dichotomy*

The liberal desire to neatly delineate inalienable political rights and alienable property rights has its roots in the Kantian and Hegelian subject/object dichotomy.[93] Kant's *Würde* is a rejection of the Hobbesian view that 'the value or worth of a man is... his price'.[94] In his *Grundlegung zur Metaphysik der Sitten*, Kant insists that:

> in the kingdom of ends everything has either a price or a dignity [*Würde*]. What has a price can be replaced by something else as its equivalent; what on the other hand is raised above all price and therefore admits of no equivalent has a dignity [...] that which constitutes the condition under which alone something can be an end in itself has not merely a relative worth, that is, a price, but an inner worth, that is, *dignity*.[95]

In this passage Kant draws a distinction between external things and 'inner worth'. This distinction between inner and outer, inalienability and alienability was adopted by the idealists, including Hegel. For Hegel, property is alienable because:

> ...it is mine only in so far as I put my will into it. Hence I may abandon... anything that I have or yield it to the will of another... provided always that the thing in question is a thing external by nature.[96]

Radin argues that Hegel distinguishes between alienable and inalienable things in this passage. For Hegel, 'substantive characteristics of the personality' are inalienable because they are not innately external things. Radin explains that these include 'personality as such', 'universal freedom of will', 'ethical life' (*Sittlichkeit*), and 'religion.' They are inalienable because they constitute the 'personality itself and the essence of self-consciousness.'[97]

However a difficulty arises here. Kant and Hegel stressed that both private property and contract were crucial in order to achieve freedom as self-actualisation.[98] But if property is alienable because 'I put my will into it', then

---

[92] *Ibid* p 9.

[93] *Ibid* pp 34–40.

[94] Hobbes, *Leviathan*, pt I, ch 10.

[95] Kant, *Groundwork of the Metaphysics of Morals* (2011) p 42.

[96] Hegel, *Philosophy of Right*, para 65, quoted by Radin, *Contested Commodities* (2001) p 35.

[97] *Ibid* p 35.

[98] Kant, *The Doctrine of Right*, pp 68–71; Hegel, *Philosophy of Right*, pp 41–71, cited by Radin, *Contested Commodities* (2001) p 35.

am I not entitled to treat my own person as property? For Kant, the answer is obvious: the basic principle is that '[m]an cannot dispose over himself because he is not a thing. . . . [I]t is impossible to be a person and a thing, the proprietor and the property'.[99] Similarly, as Radin explains, Hegel proposes an argument that is a 'contradiction'—'if I relinquish my personhood, then no "I" remains to have done the relinquishing.'[100] For Kant and Hegel, then, there is a 'bright line' between alienable external things and the inalienable personality.[101] Kant was so adamant about this point that not only did he regard the sale of sexual services as being prohibited, he also insisted that this prohibition extended to the selling of teeth.[102] Understood in Radin's terms, the Kantian and Hegelian argument posits *complete commodification* against *non-commodification*. Things 'external by nature' can (and perhaps should if we are to achieve self-actualisation) be completely commodified, while it is not possible to commodify personhood and 'inner worth'. But a necessary question follows: even if we accept the value of the external things/inner worth distinction, is a complete commodification/non-commodification dichotomy desirable in a non-ideal world?

2.4.2 Publicity as an Example of 'Incomplete Commodification'?

Radin's conception of 'incomplete commodification' is highly relevant here. She argues that we need to think about market-inalienability in a different way. In particular, we must try to avoid the subject/object dichotomy.[103] She stresses contextuality, arguing that a theory 'should not be too far divorced from the realities of needs, capacities, and circumstances that shape personal development in practice in the world'.[104]

Say, in a particular case, we find the abstract idea of complete commodification to be abhorrent but the context reveals that the practical circumstances are such that non-commodification is unfeasible and/or undesirable? Rather than frame the debate as a choice between complete commodification on the one hand and non-commodification on the other, we should embrace 'incomplete commodification'. Radin argues that '[a] more accurate way to see our situation with respect to commodification... is to modify the hypothetical of universal commodification and instead think of commodification as a matter of degree.'[105]

---

[99] Kant, *Lectures on Ethics*, p 165, quoted by Radin, *ibid* at 36.

[100] *Ibid* p 40 citing para 66R of Hegel, *Philosophy of Right*.

[101] *Ibid* p 40.

[102] Radin, *Contested Commodities* (2001) p 234.

[103] *Ibid* p 54.

[104] *Ibid* p 63.

[105] *Ibid* p 115.

Understood in these terms, while we may be willing to accept a degree of commodification in a given case, 'incomplete commodification' ensures 'special non-market significance' for the value in question.[106] Consider privacy and personality. Complete commodification of the personality is objectionable because it would infringe human dignity. But the non-commodification alternative is equally problematic as it would interfere with basic interests in autonomy. Personality rights, in practice, are an example of 'incomplete commodification' in Radin's sense. These rights remain deontological constructs, ensuring respect for human dignity, but for well over a century, legislators and courts have treated certain personality interests as having proprietary characteristics. As we shall see in Chap. 3, the notion of a subjective alienable economic right emerged in a rapidly industrialising nineteenth century Germany, resulting in intellectual property rights and proprietary rights to one's own name (§ 12 BGB) and image (§ 22 KUG). Similarly, in the US, Prosser admitted that his fourth tort of appropriation was profoundly different to the others saying that the 'interest protected is not so much a mental as a proprietary one, in the exclusive use of the plaintiff's name and likeness as an aspect.'[107] This raises pertinent questions for a contemporary culture in which public figures and celebrities have free rein to market their persona as a product, deciding how, when and where their images are used. These celebrities may well argue that they 'own' their persona and are entitled to exploit it commercially or grant a licence to a third party to do the same. In a similar way, one's reputation can be understood as a form of intangible property, comparable to goodwill.[108] Post explains how an individual can build up a reputation through the exertion of particular skill or ingenuity and any injury to this reputation can cause pecuniary loss. The value of reputation 'is determined by the marketplace in exactly the same manner that the marketplace determines the cash value of any property loss.'[109] Individuals are connected to one another through the institutions of this 'market society.' Post suggests that this image of reputation explains much about the law of defamation, for example, why commercial entities can sue for defamation.[110] He argues that reputation as property is 'deeply imbedded' in our understanding of defamation law.[111]

A system of 'incomplete commodification' of personality, then, allows for the coexistence of dignitarian and proprietary interests. But practical concerns remain. How do we classify the legal wrongs? For instance, if a third party makes use of a celebrity's image without her consent and we accept that dignitarian and proprietary interests can co-exist, can the celebrity then sue for invasion of privacy or

[106] *Ibid* p 112.

[107] Prosser, 'Privacy' (1960) at 406.

[108] Post, 'The Social Foundations of Defamation Law' (1986) at 692.

[109] *Ibid* at 694.

[110] *Ibid* at 696.

[111] *Ibid.*

an infringement of a property-related right or entitlement? As we shall see later, this remains an unresolved question in English law, not least because the remedies for the two infringements are so different. But for now, we must turn our attention to the third conjecture about privacy.

2.5 Privacy and Community

We have seen how dignity and autonomy are informing purposes of privacy and how, through a system of 'incomplete commodification', proprietary interests are accommodated. The final conjecture relates to the enabling context of the community—the idea that we cannot begin to refine privacy without paying attention to the dynamic relationship between the individual and the community.

2.5.1 Personal Honour and Esteem

The idea of personal honour may seem like a peculiar starting-point for our discussion in this section but I believe that an appreciation of the historical and conceptual roots of personal honour is key to understanding the relationship between the individual and her community.

Honour exists, as Post puts it, where 'an individual personally identifies with the normative characteristics of a particular social role and in return personally receives from others the regard and estimation that society accords to that role.'[112] In contrast to reputation, the individual does not generally 'build up' honour. Society itself confers honour on the individual through his particular social role—whether that is nobility, military or clergy, for example. In describing the 'essential characteristics of honour', Post quotes the anthropologist John Davis:

> [F]irst ... it is a system of stratification: it describes the distribution of wealth in a social idiom, and prescribes an appropriate behaviour for people, at the various points in the hierarchy; it entails acceptance of superordination and subordination. Second it is an absolute system... each competitor occupies a unique system within the hierarchy. One of the weapons in such discrimination is the distinction between honour-virtue and honour-status... Third, it does not seem to be characteristic of honour that it is associated with integrity: the whole man is contemplated.[113]

Reputation as a form of property 'presupposes' that everyone is equal in the marketplace, but honour assumes everyone is unequal because they exercise

---

[112] *Ibid* at 699–700.

[113] *Ibid* at 700 quoting Davis, *People of the Mediterranean: An Essay in Comparative Social Anthropology* (1977) p 98.

different social roles.[114] It encompasses the 'whole man' and unlike reputation in the marketplace, it cannot be destroyed and built up again. Dishonour is 'a fall from grace in the most comprehensive sense – loss of face in the community, but also loss of self and separation from the basic norms that govern human life.'[115] Hence, as Cairns emphasises, 'those who have considerable reserves of esteem will be most concerned to avoid the risk of losing it.'[116]

Within a system of honour, social roles are so well-established that they provide the 'point of reference both for the ascription of social status and for the normative standards of personal conduct.'[117] It is a 'deference society'.[118] In a market society, reputation is merely an individual interest and has no special claim to legal protection. By contrast, honour in a deference society is created by 'shared social perceptions that transcend the behaviour of particular persons.'[119] Honour is owned not by the individual but by the public. 'An insult to the king involves not only injury to the king's personal interests, but also damage to the social status with which society has invested in the role of kingship.'[120]

While legislative provisions and judges sometimes make reference to the concept of honour, particularly in the common law of defamation, it does not feature prominently in contemporary legal discourse. Post argues this is a consequence of our 'commitment to egalitarianism'.[121] Western societies have experienced a 'levelling-up' of honour in Whitman's sense. In communities, in which there are still rigidly defined social roles, personal honour remains of consequence (the same is true of religious or military institutions). But honour has had a formative role in the history of personality interests and it may even throw light on aspects of contemporary privacy law. Do deep-rooted notions of personal honour help explain, for example, why an injured party often feels that an award of damages is an unsuitable remedy in a case of invasion of privacy, especially if the individual feels that he has suffered a fall from grace or loss of esteem? If so, it echoes a much older theme. Writing in the early sixteenth century, Jean de Mille, provost of Paris, declared that a 'loss of property or patrimony is always reparable in one way or another, but never a loss of honour or life.'[122] We will revisit this argument but for now we must turn to consider other aspects of the dynamic relationship between the individual and her community.

---

[114] Post, 'The Social Foundations of Defamation Law' (1986) at 700.

[115] *Ibid* at 701 quoting Berger, Berger & Kellner, *The Homeless Mind: Modernization and Consciousness* (1973) p 90.

[116] Cairns, 'Honour and Shame' (2011).

[117] Post, 'The Social Foundations of Defamation Law' (1986) at 701.

[118] *Ibid* at 702.

[119] *Ibid*.

[120] *Ibid*.

[121] *Ibid* at 707.

[122] Farge, 'The Honor and Secrecy of Families' (1989) p 579.

2.5.2 Independence and Dependence

I have argued that privacy is an essential constituent of human personhood. It follows, therefore, that privacy is also essential to the community as personality and the community are ontologically interdependent. Hegel provides the most compelling explanation for this association. According to Hegel, 'self-consciousness achieves its *Befriedigung* (satisfaction) only in another self-consciousness', becoming *ein Anerkanntes* (an acknowledged).[123] In other words, self-consciousness requires a social context; the individual is not ontologically autonomous but is constituted by the community.[124] This idea underlies Hegel's thoughts on language. On his account, the 'power of speech':

> is the real existence of the pure self as self; in speech, self-consciousness, qua independent separate individuality, comes as such into existence, so that it exists for others. Otherwise the "I", this pure "I", is non-existent, is not there.[125]

Understood in these terms, as Forster explains, language allows conceptual thought (and individual identity depends on the ability to engage in conceptual thought) but it requires that the individual participates in a 'linguistic community'.[126] Consequently, the very identity of an individual depends on participation in such a community. The individual and the community are inseparable and so we can speak of 'the I that is We and We that is I'.[127] Similarly, Mead argues that in the process of self-realisation, the individual attempts to distinguish himself from others, emphasising that which 'makes him what he is.'[128] But in so doing, Mead explains, the individual:

> asserts himself over others in some peculiar situation which justifies him in maintaining himself over against them. If he could not bring that peculiarity of himself into the common community, if it could not be recognized, if others could not take his attitude in some sense, he could not have appreciation in emotional terms, he could not be the very self he is trying to be.[129]

In other words, while we associate self-realisation with the thoughts and actions of the independent individual, *ichbewusstsein* is at the same time dependent on the community. In the course of self-realisation, it falls to others recognise the individual personality—in a very real sense, then, the community (rather than the individual) confirms the uniqueness of the personality. The German courts frequently highlight this relationship of independence and dependence. In the *Mephisto* case,

---

[123] Hegel, *Phenomenology of Spirit* (1977) para 178.

[124] A similar argument has been advanced by the social historian Amos Funkenstein. See Funkenstein, *Perceptions of Jewish History* (1993) p 5.

[125] Hegel, *Phenomenology of Spirit* (1977) para 508.

[126] Forster, *Hegel's Idea of a Phenomenology of Spirit* (1998) p 84.

[127] Hegel, *Phenomenology of Spirit* (1977) para 177.

[128] Mead, *Mind, Self, & Society* (1934) p 324.

[129] *Ibid.*

the Constitutional Court stressed that the human person is 'an autonomous being developing freely within the social community.'[130] In similar vein, in the *Lebenslange Freiheitsstrafe* case, the Court noted:

'Diese Freiheit versteht das Grundgesetz nicht als diejenige eines isolierten und selbstherrlichen, sondern als die eines gemeinschaftsbezogenen und gemeinschaftsgebundenen Individuums.'[131]	'The *Grundgesetz* understands this freedom as not that of an isolated and self-regarding individual rather that of an individual who is related to and bound to the community.'

Eberle argues that passages of this sort demonstrate a consensus on morality and community in Germany and, in contrast to common law systems, the law is informed by more stable 'core values'.[132] But we can object to his view because it ignores the place of community in common law reasoning. In classical common law theory, the common law was understood to be the 'accumulated wisdom of the ages',[133] giving expression to the mores of the community. According to this view, the 'community' was *Gemeinschaftlich*, it was the source or 'bank' of collective knowledge and wisdom,[134] the sum of multiple voices and thus achieved a type of 'multeity in unity' in Coleridge's words.[135] The notion of 'community' has retained significance in the common law and nowadays finds expression in the 'reasonable person' and notions of 'what is fit and proper.' A similar argument has been advanced by Robert Post who argues that the common law regards the individual as both independent and socially dependent.[136] Interests attached to the human personality such as reputation and privacy, for example, are socially contingent, i.e. the individual might experience wounded feelings in the event of injury to these interests but their worth and the success of any civil action is also dependent on the views and assessments of others.[137] Consider the traditional tests used to ascertain whether a statement was defamatory: did the statement subject the individual to ridicule or contempt, did it lower the individual in the eyes of right-thinking members of society or cause the individual to be shunned or avoided?[138] Each

[130] BVerfGE 30, 173, 193 = NJW 1971, 1645 (*Mephisto*).

[131] BVerfGE 45, 187, 227 = NJW 1977, 1525 (*Lebenslange Freiheitsstrafe*).

[132] Eberle 'Human Dignity, Privacy, and Personality in German and American Constitutional Law' (1997) at 975. Eberle argues that it is not the community but the individual autonomous person who determines the 'norms and values' of the American social order. He argues that the best example of this is the concept of free speech. But given that *ichbewusstsein* is only possible when the community recognises it, can we not respond to Eberle's argument by saying that free speech is an expression of the general will in the United States?

[133] Postema, *Bentham and the Common Law Tradition* (1986) p 63, quoting Blackstone (1 Comm 442).

[134] *Ibid* p 66.

[135] On this point see O'Callaghan, 'Monologism and Dialogism in Private Law' (2010).

[136] Post, 'The Social Foundations of Defamation Law' (1986).

[137] Gibbons, 'Defamation Reconsidered' (1996) at 592.

[138] McNamara, *Reputation and Defamation* (2007).

test is dependent on the moral judgement and core values of the community and it is for this reason that Post suggests defamation law 'presupposes an image of how people are tied together, or should be tied together in a social setting.'[139]

On this account, defamation law concerns itself not only with corrective justice but also with distributive justice, as both reputation and free speech are 'social primary goods' in the Rawlsian sense.[140] As we will see in Chap. 4, we also find reference, albeit implicitly, to both corrective and distributive justice in recent privacy case law, particularly in the construct of the 'reasonable expectation of privacy' test in English law.[141] In the event of an unauthorised disclosure of private facts, courts first consider whether, on a subjective level, the aggrieved individual felt she had a reasonable expectation of privacy in the case at hand. But even if she insists that this expectation was present, it does not follow that she will be entitled to a remedy. For the court must also consider, on a more general and objective level, whether the community agrees with her. And so we are faced with a question of distributive justice. Among other things, this ideal maintains that the law should not compensate trivial claims because, as Pound noted, a reciprocal sharing of the benefits and burdens of society or 'give and take' is the unavoidable consequence of the way in which we choose to live. When weighing competing interests, the 'oversensitive must give way.'[142]

If the communitarian 'embeddedness' thesis is correct,[143] then the community, although it does not feature in modern discourse as prominently as it did in classical law theory, will always inform judicial decision-making. In determining what is 'fit and proper' or in 'balancing' privacy and freedom of expression, courts have regard to the *Sitten* of the community.[144] We will consider this process of reasoning in Chap. 4.

---

[139] Post, 'The Social Foundations of Defamation Law' (1986) at 693.

[140] Rawls, *A Theory of Justice* (1999) pp 90–95.

[141] See *Campbell* v *MGN* [2004] 2 AC 457. See also Moreham 'Privacy in the Common Law' (2005).

[142] Pound, 'Interests of Personality' (1915) at 354.

[143] Caney, 'Liberalism and Communitarianism' (1992).

[144] In liberal democracy there is tension between interests in privacy and freedom of expression. But though they are frequently portrayed as opposites, privacy and free expression are interdependent. Westin makes this point: 'This development of individuality is particularly important in democratic societies, since qualities of independent thought, diversity of views, and non-conformity are considered desirable traits for individuals. Such independence requires time for sheltered experimentation and testing of ideas, for preparation and practice in thought and conduct, without fear of ridicule or penalty, and for the opportunity to alter opinions before making them public.' See Westin, *Privacy and Freedom* (1967) p 34.

2.6 Concluding Remarks

What do we learn about privacy's content from this analysis? When we imagine a world without privacy and a world in which privacy is the absolute value, what emerges is that neither in itself is desirable. We might draw here on Aristotle's 'doctrine of the mean' and say that both an 'excess and deficiency' of privacy 'destroys' its purpose. But the 'mean preserves it.'[145] The mean is revealed when we contrast the two extremes and three conjectures about privacy's purpose materialise. First, I suggest that privacy is essential to *ichbewusstsein*; in other words, normative agency cannot be exercised without privacy. Second, privacy also has proprietary aspects. Thus, if we value autonomy, we must also value privacy. Although we must pay careful attention to the Kantian and Hegelian subject/object dichotomy, publicity (as an aspect of privacy) is an example of incomplete commodification in Radin's sense. Finally, privacy is ontologically dependent on the community and any analysis of privacy must take this enabling context into account.

Perhaps influenced by Bakhtinian centripetal forces, in other words a desire to bring about coherence,[146] scholars sometimes treat personality, property and the community as being conceptually distinct. But we have seen in this chapter that personality, property and the community—though often portrayed as being very different—are ontologically dependent on one another (the same can be said of the privacy/free speech relationship). This interdependence, then, reveals something vital about privacy as a concept. If we neglect even one of these informing purposes in our laws, we are failing in our task to probe the Rawlsian 'limits of the practicably possible'.

Having proposed conjectures about the nature and value of privacy, I now turn to consider the genealogy of privacy—we must of course pay close attention to the past if we are to come to a better understanding of our shared experience of privacy.

[145] *Ibid.*

[146] See O'Callaghan, 'Monologism and Dialogism in Private Law' (2010).

2.5 Concluding Remarks

Chapter 3
A Privacy Curve

> *Wer kann was Dummes, wer was Kluges denken, das nicht die Vorwelt schon gedacht?*
> *- Johann Wolfgang von Goethe*

3.1 Introduction

In the introduction to his seminal work, *The Civilising Process*, Norbert Elias notes that we can separate mathematical concepts from those who use them. Triangles, he adds, 'may be explicable without reference to historical situations'. But concepts such as civilisation or *Kultur*, Elias argues, are not. He goes on:

> It may be that particular individuals formed [these concepts] from the existing linguistic material of their group, or at least gave them new meaning. But they took root. They became established. Others picked them up in their new meaning and form, developing and polishing them in speech or writing. They were tossed back and forth until they became efficient instruments for expressing what people had jointly experienced, and wanted to communicate.[1]

Like the concepts of civilisation and *Kultur*, privacy is real; it has taken root. But the process of development and polishing of the concept is on-going. So, while we must pay attention to the historicality of privacy, as an expression of what people throughout history 'have jointly experienced', we must also be mindful of privacy's potentiality (its 'multiplicity of possibilities') or *Seinkönnen* in the Heideggerian sense.[2]

If we are to take proper account of both the historicality and *Seinkönnen* of privacy, I believe we must reject traditional forms of historical analyses in legal treatises. One such approach is the attempt to provide a 'comprehensive' account of

[1] Elias, *The Civilizing Process* (2000) p 8.

[2] See Heidegger, *The Concept of Time* (1998).

P. O'Callaghan, *Refining Privacy in Tort Law*,
DOI 10.1007/978-3-642-31884-9_3, © Springer-Verlag Berlin Heidelberg 2013

the history of privacy. We must reject this utopian and potentially monologic method for the reasons given in Chap. 1. The second approach seems less ambitious on first glance, but is equally problematic. This is the idea that we can 'trace' the origin of a concept. I believe that this approach is similarly precarious because it leads to infinite regress. But why do scholars routinely try to establish the historical origin of concepts? The reason for this is rooted in what Elias terms the psychological reasons motivating us to search for origins.[3] He explains that traditional ways of thinking means that we are continually faced with 'static alternatives'. This means that when surveying the past we think of points on a timeline with 'separate abrupt changes, or no change at all.' Consequently, we find it difficult to appreciate that we are 'located in a gradual, continuous change with a particular structure and regularity'.[4] In his study, Elias does not attempt to identify the origin of civilisation or *Kultur*, rather he pays close attention to subtle changes in behaviour and identifies a 'civilizing curve' over the course of the centuries.

Following Elias, I suggest that since antiquity there has been a privacy curve. As the curve inclines, the individual slowly emerges from the collective and, simultaneously, concern for privacy becomes more pronounced. In laws and legal literature on personality rights and privacy, we find increasing emphasis being placed on human dignity, autonomy, ownership and, particularly from the nineteenth century onwards, the conceptual relationship between individual privacy and the interests of the community. Thus we find within the curve support for the proposition that the three conjectures outlined in Chap. 2 shed light on privacy's content.

My immediate task in this chapter is to identify inclining gradients in the privacy curve. I will argue that during classical and late antiquity and for a large part of the Middle Ages, the curve remains relatively linear but begins to steepen around the period of the Renaissance and continues to do so right up to late modernity. Four points must be emphasised here. First, the following is not a historiography in the sense of remaining faithful to the 'pastness of the past'; rather I attempt here to outline a 'usable past', demonstrating how the privacy curve has shaped not only our laws but also our shared experience of privacy.[5] Second and as a consequence of the first point, the gradients do not necessarily follow in chronological order; very often, they overlap. Third, the privacy curve plots our increasing concern for privacy rather than the actual level of privacy we enjoy. Finally, the curve can

---

[3] Elias, *The Civilizing Process* (2000) p 403.

[4] *Ibid* p 403.

[5] See Susman, 'History and the American Intellectual' (1964). In any case, the idea that we can remain 'faithful to the pastness of the past' is 'naive' according to Gadamer. He argues that '[t]rue historical thinking must take account of its own historicality.' By this he means that we must not try to 'overcome' temporal distance (at least for the purposes of hermeneutics). Distance in time is a 'positive and productive possibility of understanding. It is not a yawning abyss, but is filled with the continuity of custom and tradition in the light of which all that is handed down presents itself to us.' See Gadamer, *Truth and Method* (1975) pp 264–265. For Gadamer, temporal distance is therefore necessary in order to interpret a text and identify the 'true' and 'false' prejudices.

perhaps be better understood as a fractal curve—it has no end point; reflecting privacy's *Seinkönnen*, it goes on forever.

In what follows, I will argue that there are six principal *inclining gradients* in the privacy curve of Western history: 'the Fall of Rome', 'the Sacralisation of Personality', 'the Emergence of the Individual', 'the Levelling-Up of Rank', 'Between the Home and the State' and the 'Challenges of Late Modernity'. Within each section, I seek to provide evidence of an incline through references to law and legal literature on personality rights and privacy. We now turn to consider each of these gradients in turn.

3.2 The Fall of Rome

The dialectical relationship between the emphasis on *res publica* in Rome and the *res privata* among the Germanic tribes constitutes the first gradient in the privacy curve. We will see that paying close attention to the laws of Rome and the early Germanic laws throws light on the foundations of contemporary privacy laws in both Germany and England.

3.2.1 The Res Publica

We noted in the last chapter that the ancient Romans did not distinguish between public and private spheres, at least in the same manner we do today. This is because citizens of Rome were chiefly concerned with their status and rank in the *bios politicos*. In contributing to public life, one ensured that one's *dignitas* was 'enhanced'.[6] Dignity, in the 'interpretive community' of Rome, was 'an ideal of glory'. But dignity could be 'won or lost'—the exiled Cicero despaired when he lost his dignity as he was 'reduced to nothing'.[7] These ideas of dignity and rank were so central to the Roman mind-set that anyone who was outside the *bios politicos* was considered 'less than a man, a person of no account'.[8] Thus any man who refused to serve the emperor or city was deemed 'idiotic' and ostracised. For this reason, we find few references to notions of a private sphere or a private life in the literature of classical antiquity.

What do we learn from the laws of classical Rome? Unsurprisingly, perhaps, given the emphasis on the *bios politicos*, we find that the laws of classical antiquity gave expression to an understanding of dignity as rank. This insight is vital to our

[6] Veyne, 'The Roman Empire' (1987) p 101.
[7] *Ibid* p 101.
[8] *Ibid* p 106.

efforts to understand contemporary privacy laws for the drafters of the liability clauses of several European civil codes, such as Article 1382 *Code Civil* or § 823 (1) *Bürgerliches Gesetzbuch* drew inspiration from classical Roman law.

Since classical antiquity, civilian legal scholars have argued that the protected legal interests in the law of delict are related either to property or the person.[9] On one hand, the *lex Aquilia* allowed recovery from a defendant who either intentionally or negligently inflicted unlawful damage (*damnum iniuria datum*) to a claimant's property, but Roman law also afforded protection to some non-economic interests under the *actio iniuriarum*.[10] The older understanding of *iniuria* related primarily to matters of bodily integrity (*corpus*) such as a beating with one's fist or a club but also extended to insults such as suggesting that a man was insolvent or composing or publishing defamatory verses.[11] In the later Republic, the praetorian formally recognised that the remit of *iniuria* extended to other non-physical aspects of the personality, including insult.[12]

The formal recognition of insult as an *iniuria* is significant as it indicates a shift in the remit of the action from bodily integrity to protection of feelings. By all accounts, Labeo was the first to equate insult (*contumelia*) with *iniuria*[13] and by the time of Ulpian, Paulus and Gaius, the perceived humiliation that had been suffered by an injured party was central to the action.[14] As Leage puts it, the essence of the delict was 'a contemptuous disregard of another's dignity tending to cause loss of repute, and deliberately intended to produce this result.'[15]

A loss of dignity was an existential threat to the citizens of ancient Rome. A citizen, who had been insulted by a *contumelia,* suffered a grave loss of face but he could not retreat to a private sphere lest he risk even more humiliation. For this reason, those who, through no fault of their own, suffered a loss of *dignitas* sought public reaffirmation of their status within the *bios politicos*. The praetors responded to these developments with a more elaborate legal framework, introducing four

[9] Brüggemeier, *Haftungsrecht* (2006) p 197; See further Nicholas, *Introduction to Roman Law* (1962); Wolff, 'The Historical and Constitutional Background of Roman Law' (1951).

[10] The origin of *actio iniuriarum* can be traced to Tab 8, 4 of the XII Tables. See Zimmermann, *The Law of Obligations* (1992) pp 1050–1094.

[11] Leage, *Roman Private Law* (1954) p 376. Some of the remedies provided by the XII Tables included retaliation for broken limbs, a fine of 200 asses (Roman copper coin) for broken bones, and a fine of 25 asses for other types of injury. See Sohm, *The Institutes* (1901) p 437. As the Roman economy developed, the fine of 25 asses was deemed to be an insufficient deterrent, as perhaps demonstrated by the famous story of an L Veratius who wandered the streets of Rome slapping unsuspecting passers-by in the face—he was followed by his loyal slave who carried pockets full of asses to distribute to those unfortunate citizens injured by his master. See further Leage, *Roman Private Law* (1954) p 377.

[12] Zimmermann, *The Law of Obligations* (1992) p 1052; see also Wittmann, 'Entwicklungslinien der klassischen Injurienklage' (1974); Hagemann, *Iniuria* (1998).

[13] See Ulp D 47, 10, 15, 46. On this point, see Hagemann, *Iniuria* (1998) p 65.

[14] *Ibid.*

[15] Leage, *Roman Private Law* (1954) p 376.

specific edicts, which could give rise to an *actio iniuriarum*—*convicium, adtemptata pudicitia, ne quid infamandi causa fiat* and *servum alienum verberare*.[16] For our purposes, the most important edicts were *convicium* and *ne quid infamandi causa fiat*, to which we now turn.[17]

Convicium was the oldest form of *iniuria*, originating from the XII Tables of the early Republic where it prohibited acts of *occentare*, the utterances of hurtful magic charms.[18] Following the reforms of the praetorian during the later Republic, scholars came to understand *convicium* as abusive speech uttered within earshot of others,[19] although it was not necessary that the targeted individual be present.[20] An act fell under the remit of the edict only if it was *adversus bonos mores* (contrary to public morals)[21]; it was further differentiated from abuse in written form.[22] The second relevant edict, *ne quid infamandi causa fiat*, prohibited acts that brought another person into hatred or contempt.[23] One of the best known examples of a prohibited act under this edict was a display of mourning by an individual who was not entitled to be in mourning.[24] Ulpian lists other examples of prohibited acts.[25] These included cases where individuals offered to influence the outcome of legal proceedings, thereby putting the honour and reputation of the judge into disrepute.[26] Other cases related to creditworthiness and sanctioned individuals who gave the false impression that a party was unable to honour his debts[27] or where a

---

[16] Raber, *Grundlagen klassischer Injurienansprüche* (1969) p 7. See generally Zimmermann, *The Law of Obligations* (1992) pp 1053–1062.

[17] *De adtemptat pudicitia* concerned the protection of the moral reputation of those who still wore the toga praetexta while *servum alienum verberare* concerned the beating or torturing of another person's slave. See Zimmermann, *The Law of Obligations* (1992) pp 1054–1056.

[18] See the unpublished thesis of Beckmann (1923) cited by Zimmermann, *ibid* p 1054. See also Lindsay, 'Defamation and the Law under Sulla' (1949); Hendrickson, 'Verbal Injury, Magic, or Erotic Comus?' (1925); Hendrickson, 'Convicium' (1926).

[19] See Ulp D 47, 10, 15, 2; Mommsen defines it 'im ursprünglichen Sinn, die jemand mit öffentlicher Zusammenrottung vor seinem Hause zugefügte Schmähung'. See Mommsen, *Römisches Strafrecht* (1899) p 794.

[20] Ulp D 47, 10, 15, 7.

[21] Ulp D 47, 10, 15, 5.

[22] See Smith, 'The Law of Libel at Rome' (1951) at 172.

[23] Ulp D 47, 10, 15, 25. See further Zimmermann, *The Law of Obligations* (1992) pp 1056–1059.

[24] Ulpian describes the common signs of mourning as the wearing of mourning attire and keeping an unkempt beard and untidy hair. See Ulp D 47, 10, 15, 27. While it was appropriate to behave in this way when a close relative had died or was in an *iudicium publicum* (where an individual was publicly charged with a crime), under the edict of *ne quid* it was unlawful for an individual outside the circle of close relatives to behave as if he were in mourning. In the case of the *iudicium publicum*, such behaviour was understood as a slur on the reputation of the prosecutor. See Wittmann, 'Entwicklungslinien der klassischen Injurienklage' (1974) at 323.

[25] The following examples are detailed in Hagemann, *Iniuria* (1998) pp 75–81.

[26] Ulp D 47, 10, 15, 30.

[27] Ulp D 47, 10, 15, 31–33.

creditor took a debtor's property into his possession when he knew that the property was not owed to him.[28]

These examples encapsulate the essence of *iniuria*: it emphasised the importance of one's place in the *bios politicos* and ensured respect for social rank. This conclusion is supported by the distinction made in Roman law between serious and less severe infringements of legal interests protected by the *actio*.[29] The praetors could reject a claim if the injury was only a minor infringement of another person's legal interests.[30] Examples of a serious infringement included insult in public, such as in the theatre or in the forum, especially if the injured party was insulted by someone of a lower social rank.[31] So an insult directed at a freeman by a slave was always considered sufficiently serious, even where the insult itself was not objectively serious.[32]

This brief account of the Roman history of the *actio* is instructive for a number of reasons. First, it highlights some similarities between classical Roman law and civil actions for invasion of privacy in late modernity. Humiliation or insult was central to the *iniuria* action as was the requirement that the behaviour had to be *adversus bonos mores*, in the sense that it had to be at odds with the morals of the community or *civitas*. Second, and perhaps most significantly, *iniuria*, as a legal mechanism, ensured respect for rank and status within the *bios politicos*. In effect, it reinforced the social gulf between freemen and 'lesser men' who were not entitled to participate in public life. It is for this reason that the gravest *iniuria* of all was the slave who insulted his master. While these ingredients can be considered foundation stones in the legal protection of personality interests, later developments, to which we now turn, have had a more profound impact on contemporary law and our understanding of privacy.

3.2.2 The Res Privata

In ancient Rome, a strong commitment to the *res publica* was evident, so much so that anyone who retreated into a private sphere was considered by the wider community to lack *dignitas*. What emerges from the fragmentation of the Roman Empire, however, is a shift to an emphasis on the *res privata*. Unlike Rome, where participation in public life was an 'ideal of glory', for the Germanic tribes glory meant the accumulation of personal wealth. Rouche argues that for the Germanic

28 Ulp D 47, 10, 15, 31.

29 Herrmann, *Der Schutz der Persönlichkeit in der Rechtslehre des 16.-18. Jahrhunderts* (1968) p 12 *et seq.*

30 *Ibid.*

31 *Ibid.*

32 *Ibid.*

tribes 'practically everything fell within the private domain'.[33] In his *History of the Franks*, Gregory of Tours is at pains to draw a distinction between the Eastern Roman Empire as a republic (*res publica* or 'public thing') and the 'barbarian' German tribes.[34] On Rouche's account, 'what held [the Germanic tribes] together was not, as in Rome, the idea of public safety and the common good, but private interests, joined together in a provisional partnership perpetuated by victory.'[35] Feudalisation thus represented what Duby calls a 'privatization of power'.[36]

We find evidence of this shift in the laws of the Germanic tribes. Roman law applied to all citizens of the Empire, but in the Germanic *Lex Salica* of 511 only eight of the seventy-eight provisions concerned public law.[37] Among these provisions, we find references to the protection of interests in reputation, but unlike Roman freemen, the drafters of the Germanic laws were demonstrably more concerned with monetary compensation rather than the restoration of *dignitas*.[38] Disgrace or dishonour were the core elements in almost every cause of action at this time.[39] If the defendant had beaten the plaintiff, he was entitled to a certain sum of shillings for the damage itself, but received far more for the dishonour caused.[40]

Equally revealing is the concern for the home in the *Lex Salica*. Provision 34, 1 criticises 'those who break enclosures (saepes)'. Duby explains that that the barrier or hedge was a 'sign' of privacy.[41] Everything within the walls of the enclosure were under the jurisdiction of the 'head of household' rather than public law.[42]

The early Germanic laws thus drew a sharp distinction between public and private. But it is important to emphasise that while these laws gave expression to a *private space* based on the idea of a man's home as his castle, this was a property-based understanding of privacy. The notion of a *private sphere*, or a right to be let alone, was a completely alien idea. Feudal houses, for instance, whether they took the form of rural huts, urban dwellings or castles, were invariably overcrowded. Only the very wealthy did not have to share sleeping quarters with several others. Moreover, acts, which would today be considered private, frequently

---

[33] Rouche, 'The Early Middle Ages in the West' (1987) p 415.

[34] *Ibid* p 419.

[35] *Ibid* p 420.

[36] Duby, 'Introduction' (1988) p 8.

[37] Rouche, 'The Early Middle Ages in the West' (1987) p 422.

[38] Veeder, 'The History and Theory of the Law of Defamation I' (1903) at 548. If a man called another a 'wolf' or a 'hare', he had to pay three shillings; if a woman was falsely imputed as unchaste, a fine of forty-five shillings was payable. See *Lex Salica,* tit. 30. The earliest Anglo-Saxon laws demonstrate similar concerns, often punishing the wrongdoer with excision of the tongue. On this point, see Plucknett, *A Concise History of the Common Law* (1956) p 483.

[39] Veeder, *ibid* at 549.

[40] *Ibid.*

[41] Duby, 'Introduction' (1988) pp 11–12.

[42] *Ibid* p 13.

took place in public; openly urinating in public was common, for example.[43] In fact, as in classical antiquity, the solitary individual was viewed with great suspicion—it was thought that walking on one's own (unless done for religious reasons) was evidence of insanity.[44] For these reasons, even as late as the fifteenth century, solitariness remained a *vilain mot*, leading the Italian statesman Francesco Guicciardini to speak of an 'idle life, devoid of dignity and perfectly private'.[45]

3.3 The Sacralisation of Personality

The first gradient on the privacy curve, then, is the fragmentation of the Roman Empire and the resulting Germanic emphasis on private property rather than the interests of the *res publica*. The second major gradient in the privacy curve is what I call the sacralisation of personality, in other words the impact of the Church on the collective understanding of the distinction between private and public. The increasing influence of the Church can be seen in the laws relating to what we today call defamation. The Anglo-Saxon laws on reputation were safeguarded by the local secular courts.[46] Kiralfy argues that the courts were 'essentially concerned to maintain some sort of peace in the community where they functioned.'[47] Defamatory words were more often than not accompanied by 'more violent acts.'[48] But following the Norman conquest of England, more serious instances of attacks on reputation gradually came to be considered by the Church courts.[49] The Church considered defamation a sin and claimed jurisdiction in order to correct 'the sinner for his soul's health.'[50] Language which had the effect of damaging one's good fame became known as 'diffimation' and was understood as a branch of the Roman law of *iniuria*.[51] The Church would 'stay the tongue' of the wrongdoer, *pro custodia morum* of the community and *pro salute animae* of the defamer.[52] The usual remedy or penance was to admit the 'baselessness of the imputation' in front of clergymen and to apologise to the injured party.[53]

---

[43] Elias, *The Civilizing Process* (2000) p 118.

[44] Duby, 'Solitude' (1988) p 510.

[45] Braunstein, 'Toward Intimacy' (1988) p 537.

[46] Kiralfy, *Potter's Historical Introduction to English Law and its Institutions* (1962) pp 430–431.

[47] *Ibid* p 431.

[48] *Ibid.*

[49] Veeder, 'The History and Theory of the Law of Defamation I' (1903) at 549; Helmholz, *The Oxford History of the Laws of England, Vol I* (2004) p 567.

[50] Veeder, *ibid* at 550–551.

[51] *Ibid.*

[52] *Ibid.*

[53] *Ibid.*

While the Church was the dominant force in those early years and exercised extensive jurisdiction, secular courts were allowed limited jurisdiction. The statute of *Circumspecte Agatis* 1285 permitted the church courts to punish defamation as a sin but the statute excluded claims for monetary damages from ecclesiastical jurisdiction, requiring such claims to be heard by the local or temporal courts.[54] Despite the statute, the jurisdiction of the ecclesiastical courts remained wide-ranging. Even as late as the fifteenth and sixteenth centuries, judges understood defamation as representing an ecclesiastical matter. Fineux CJ, for example, opined in 1497 that 'the case of defamation is entirely a spiritual offence.'[55]

And so we return to our central theme: through its rules on defamation, the Church emphasised individual responsibility. But these rules must be considered alongside other ecclesiastical developments during the Middle Ages, which helped distinguish the individual from the collective. Over the course of the thirteenth century, in particular, private devotion became more common. The Fourth Lateran Council Declaration of 1215 illustrates these developments. Up until that point confession used to be 'rare and public' but the Lateran Council required every person, peer and commoner alike, to study his own soul and confess his intimate sins in private to a priest.[56] This, combined with the practice of consuming the body of Christ for 'an intimate encounter', had the effect of 'magnif[ing] the human person' as an individual.[57]

The Church, then, by means of the sacralisation of personality, helped the individual emerge from the collective. But the late scholastics were to provide a conceptual basis for these developments.[58] Gordley argues that the ideas of Aristotle and Aquinas on distributive and commutative justice were at the foundation of late scholastic legal theory. According to commutative justice, when a person deprives another of personal property, he is obliged to 'restore an equivalent', he must make 'restitution' in the terminology of Aquinas.[59] The late scholastics thus regarded the distinctions between *iniuria*, the *lex Aquilia* and other Roman actions as a 'mere matter of Roman positive law'[60] and proposed a general principle that the defendant should be liable whenever he, through his own fault, deprived another of his property. Dignity and reputation were considered to 'belong' to the person and so restitution had to be made for their loss.

Integrating the classical Roman concepts of *iniuria, dignitas* and *fama* with the works of Aristotle and Thomas Aquinas, the late scholastics considered that there

[54] See Plucknett, *A Concise History of the Common Law* (1956) p 485.

[55] YB 12 Hen VII, T, f 24, pl 2 cited by Kiralfy, *Potter's Historical Introduction to English Law and its Institutions* (1962) p 431.

[56] Duby, 'Solitude' (1988) p 531.

[57] *Ibid* p 531.

[58] See Gordley, *Foundations of Private Law* (2006) ch 11.

[59] *Ibid* p 222.

[60] *Ibid* p 219.

were two ways in which personal dignity (*dignitas personae*) could be injured.[61] These were detraction (*detractio*) and insult (*contumelia*). Detraction involved 'impairing another's reputation (*fama*) ... in secret'.[62] Insult involved 'dishonouring someone' by doing 'that which is contrary to his honour in the presence of himself and others'.[63] The late scholastics thus differentiated between *honour* and *reputation* under the umbrella of *personal dignity*, with each concept very much grounded in Aristotelian theory: they were of worth because they pertained 'to human perfection' and enabled one 'to do good'.[64] In drawing this distinction between honour and reputation, Gordley explains that the late scholastics were able to include the revelation of true but embarrassing facts about another person under the remit of the *actio iniuriarum*.[65] In Gordley's description of the late scholastics' standpoint: 'Having an undeserved reputation, like having an undeserved fortune, is still of value because of the good it enables a person to do. ... [I]t would be a violation of commutative justice to deprive a person of an undeserved reputation.'[66]

Aristotle's influence on the work of the late scholastics is also apparent in their writings on remedies for injury to honour and reputation.[67] Under Roman law, a successful action for *iniuria* resulted in the payment of damages. But Aquinas incorporated the views of Raymond of Penafort so that in order to make restitution, the defendant should either publicly announce that he had made an erroneous statement or apologise.[68] In this way, under commutative justice, the injured party could be restored to his original position.[69] If honour or reputation could not be restored to an appropriate level, then the defendant would have to pay damages.[70]

Professor Gordley's research into the writings of the late scholastics is of immense importance because it bridges the gap between the classical Roman understanding of *iniuria* and the *usus modernus* of the action. Two observations in particular are to be noted. First, the conceptual distinction between *honour* and *reputation* has, to one degree or another, remained a part of civilian legal traditions. Second, the recognition that an individual could also claim *iniuria* for the revelation of true facts forms one of the foundations for a modern understanding of a right of privacy.

---

[61] *Ibid.*

[62] *Ibid* citing Aquinas, *Summa theologiae* II-II, Q 73, a 1.

[63] *Ibid* citing Aquinas, *Summa theologiae* II-II, Q 72, a 1.

[64] *Ibid* p 221.

[65] *Ibid.*

[66] *Ibid* citing Aquinas, *Summa theologiae* II-II, Q 62, a 2 ad 2; Q 73, a 1 ad 3.

[67] *Ibid* p 222.

[68] *Ibid* citing Raimundus de Penafort, *Summa de poenitentia* (Ochoa, X and Diez, A (eds) (1976) lib 2, tit 5, no 42.

[69] *Ibid* p 223.

[70] *Ibid* p 224 citing Aquinas, *Summa theologiae* II-II, Q 62, a 2, ad 1; ad 2.

The ecclesiastical influence on our privacy curve is thus highly significant. It is within this gradient that we see the first indications of a shift in focus from the collective and civil society to the individual. But, as we shall see, this was just the beginning of a long process of individualisation.

3.4 The Emergence of the Individual

Perhaps the steepest gradient in the privacy curve is what I call the *emergence of the individual*. I must first clarify what I mean by 'emergence': I do not mean, as is sometimes portrayed in the literature, that, as a consequence of the Renaissance, Europeans *suddenly* recognised each other as distinct individuals (and not as merely belonging to a particular tribe or clan) and that later, as a consequence of the Enlightenment, Europeans *suddenly* became rational autonomous agents. This historical narrative is a fundamentally mistaken view for two reasons. First, it paints a picture of humans as passive agents, moulded by grand narratives that have somehow (perhaps through the work of great thinkers and artists) come into existence. In actuality, the Renaissance and the Enlightenment were reflections of an already existing trend of individualisation in Western Europe.[71] Second, this view implies a neat shift to individualisation and rationalism whereas, in reality, this was a gradual process that transpired over the course of many centuries.

How do we explain the process of individualisation? Elias argues that the trend results from medieval court life. Here the 'human self-image developed.' Through competition for social advancement, members of court closely observed each other's conduct and 'self-control' became a basic prerequisite 'for the preservation of one's social position'.[72] But there are other ways we can explain the process of individualisation. It was further encouraged, for instance, by a new form of reading, which became popular during the Middle Ages: reading silently. Chartier argues that the 'privitization' of reading was one of the most important 'cultural developments' of the Middle Ages.[73] It 'created an air of intimacy that separated the reader from the outside world.'[74] Indeed, developments in literature generally are illustrative of the trend of individualisation. Consider that medieval literature

[71] Elias makes a similar point. He criticises those who seem to believe that the 'change from magical-traditional to rational forms of thinking in the history of the West, had its cause in the emergence of a number of geniuses and outstanding individuals.' In fact, Elias argues that these great individuals 'gave comprehensive and exemplary expression to what their contemporaries experienced in their daily actions without being able to grasp it clearly in thought'. These great men were 'interpreters and spokesmen of a social chorus' but they were not the 'originators of the type of thought... prevalent in their society'. See Elias, *The Civilizing Process* (2000) p 413.

[72] *Ibid* p 400.

[73] Chartier, 'The Practical Impact of Writing' (1989) p 125.

[74] *Ibid* p 143.

was, for the most part, community-based; writers remained anonymous.[75] But the sixteenth century can be understood as a 'period of transition'. Ronsard and the poets known as *la pléiade* invented what we now call 'lyrics poetry'; the poetry of private feelings.[76] At the same time, diary-writing and *Ich-Erzähler* (first-person) novels became popular. The cultural shift was such that Goulemot argues we can see how much we have moved away from the medieval commune by the eighteenth century because there is a 'persistent regret of the more joyous forms of community' evident in the literature of that century.[77]

During the Middle Ages, then, we find the beginnings of a very obvious social trend of individualisation. In what follows, I pay close attention to the laws and legal literature of the period between the Middle Ages and late modernity. This material is instructive because it illustrates this gradient's steep incline. I focus on German law and make relatively few references to English law. This is because we find in the German literature of the time a much more intricate discussion about individualisation and personality rights.

3.4.1 The Individualisation Trend in Law and Legal Literature

Individualisation was expressed in law and the legal literature through references to human reason. Jurists such as Grotius, Pufendorf, Thomasius and Wolff worked to refine legal thought by drawing on 'the law of reason'.[78] The law of reason, as Wieacker points out, was one aspect of the 'law of nature',[79] hence the tendency to refer to the prominent jurists of this time as natural lawyers.[80] Enlightenment

---

[75] Goulemot, 'Literary Practices' (1989) p 364.

[76] *Ibid* p 368.

[77] *Ibid* p 375 citing Rousseau's *La Nouvelle Héloïse* (1761).

[78] Wieacker argues that the Law of Reason and the Enlightenment are 'not quite one and the same.' He argues that the law of reason 'consisted of a reformulation of a social philosophy which had been in continuous existence in the West since ancient times' (he argues that Aristotle's view of man as of the *polis* provided the 'anthropological basis' for the social contract). The Enlightenment, according to Wieacker, was a 'moral, ultimately religious break-through to a new attitude to life, which was to produce a vast change in public thought and enormous reforms in public life.' He goes on to say that '[t]he two movements are closely connected, however, both in their origins, for the systematic Law of Reason was rendered possible only by the thinkers of the early Enlightenment such as Galileo and Descartes, and in their effects, since it was on the Law of Reason that enlightened thinkers based their humanitarian demands for the abolition of torture, corporal punishment, and the crime of witchcraft.' See Wieacker, *A History of Private Law in Europe* (1995) p 249.

[79] *Ibid* p 199.

[80] Berlin writes: 'When seventeenth- and eighteenth-century authors say "nature", we can translate that into "life" perfectly easily. The word "nature" was as much a commonplace in the eighteenth century as the word "creative" is now, and had about as precise a meaning.' See Berlin, *The Roots of Romanticism* (2000) p 23.

theorists believed that the correct use of reason could answer all questions about man and his place in this world. As Isaiah Berlin puts it: '[i]n the eighteenth century there was a fairly wide consensus that what Newton had achieved in the region of physics could surely also be applied to the regions of ethics and of politics.'[81]

As early as the sixteenth century, Donellus had argued that private law was a system of material subjective rights, of which personality rights protected by the *actio iniuriarum* were a part.[82] Donellus, a 'convinced Calvinist', thought that God had 'gifted' life to individuals and personality interests were 'inseparable' from this gift.[83] In a sense, then, Donellus sought to find a way to bring this conviction 'into harmony' with established Roman law, in particular the *actio iniuriarum*.[84] Later, natural law scholars such as Grotius and Pufendorf accepted the principle that a person could receive damages under the general law of delict if his reputation and honour were negligently or intentionally harmed.[85] In Chapter II, subsection 1 of Pufendorf's *De jure natuerae et gentium*, he writes:

> Besides that affection which every man maintains for his own life, and body, and possessions, by which he cannot but resist and repel whatever threatens destruction to those dear concerns; we may discover likewise deeply rooted in his Mind, a most tender *Esteem* and *Value* for himself; which if any one endeavour to impair he is seldom less (and sometimes much more) incensed, than if a mischief had been offered to his person, or to his estate. This passion, though it may be heightened and improved by various external causes, yet seems to lay its first foundations in the very constitution of human nature. The word man is thought to carry somewhat of dignity in its sound; and we commonly make use of this, as the last and most prevailing argument against a rude insulter, *I am not a Beast, a Dog, but I am a Man as well as yourself*. Since then human nature agrees equally to all persons, and since no one can live a sociable life with another, who does not own and respect him as a man; it follows as a command of the law of nature, *that every man should esteem and treat another as one who is naturally his equal, or who is a man as well as he*.[86]

According to Pufendorf, natural law requires men to respect and treat each other as equals. Each individual is ranked on the same level by virtue of nature. On his account, the impairment of a man's esteem and value (or dignity) can often result in a more serious injury than damage to his property or personal injury. Indeed this was a common refrain among the natural lawyers; an individual's dignity was as deserving of protection as his life, body and possessions.

Natural law scholarship inspired codifications in Prussia (*Allgemeines Landrecht* of 1794), France (*Code Civil* of 1804) and Austria (*Allgemeines Bürgerliches Gesetzbuch* of 1811).[87] While Hobbes, Locke and Rousseau, along with the no

---

[81] *Ibid.*

[82] Leuze, *Die Entwicklung des Persönlichkeitsrechts im 19. Jahrhundert* (1962) pp 12–15.

[83] *Ibid* p 14.

[84] *Ibid.*

[85] Gordley, *Foundations of Private Law* (2006) p 221 citing Grotius, *De iure belli ac pacis libri tres* (1625); Pufendorf, *De iure naturae ac gentium libri octo* (1688).

[86] von Pufendorf, *Of the Law of Nature and Nations* (1729).

[87] See Kelly, *A Short History of Western Legal Theory* (1992) pp 258–277.

small matter of the French Revolution, undoubtedly tempered the political climate, it was perhaps Christian Wolff, more so than any other jurist, who shaped German legal scholarship during the eighteenth century.[88] His influence, particularly his theory of *jura connata* (innate rights including freedom, honour and reputation) was evident in the Prussian *Allgemeines Landrecht* (ALR).[89] §83 ALR, for example, made reference to the 'general rights of the person', which are based on 'natural freedom', although the ALR did not expand on this point in any great detail.[90] Commentators such as Koch[91] argued that this provision protected personality rights, as elaborated by Donellus, namely '*vita, incolumitas corporis, libertas, existimatio*'.[92] But while the scope of personality rights protection in the new Prussian Civil Code remained uncertain, legal scholars, under the influence of the natural lawyers, nonetheless accepted the *actio iniuriarum* as a private action. Weber, for example, proclaims in 1820 that no more 'evidence' is needed to establish that the *actio* is a private penalty (note the empiricist language).[93]

Though the Romanticists[94] and later Kant were critical of Wolff's efforts, the autonomous individual person was also central to their work. So, Kant argues that there is only one overarching innate right, that of freedom[95]; it is the 'one original right that belongs to every human being by virtue of his humanity'.[96] On this account, rights to equality and honour are simply subsumed under this overarching original right (*Urrecht*).[97] In contrast to the philosophy underlying the Prussian Civil Code, Kant believed that a necessary consequence of the *Urrecht* was that

[88] See Leuze, *Die Entwicklung des Persönlichkeitsrechts im 19. Jahrhundert* (1962) pp 20–27.

[89] While the ALR arguably incorporates Wolff's distinction between *status moralis* and *status naturalis* it did not regard each individual as being equal in law (*Rechtsfähigkeit*/Legal Capacity). Para 1(1) of the ALR bluntly set out: 'Der Mensch wird, insofern er gewisse Rechte in der bürgerlichen Gesellschaft genießt, eine Person genannt' ('An individual will be called a person, insofar as he enjoys certain rights of civil society'). Leuze shows that legal capacity depended on an individual's position within civil society, with the nobility possessing most of these privileges. See Leuze, *Die Entwicklung des Persönlichkeitsrechts im 19. Jahrhundert* (1962) p 25.

[90] *Ibid* p 24.

[91] *Ibid* citing Koch, *Kommentar zum Allgemeinen Landrecht für die Preußischen Staaten* 1. Teil, 1 Bd (1852) p 80.

[92] Leuze, *Die Entwicklung des Persönlichkeitsrechts im 19. Jahrhundert* (1962) p 24.

[93] Moosheimer, *Die actio injuriarum aestimatoria im 18. und 19. Jahrhundert* (1997) citing Weber, *Über Injurien und Schmähschriften* (1820) p 45.

[94] Friedrich Schiller had ridiculed Wolff's *jura connata*: 'Jahre lang schon bedien ich mich meiner Nase zum Reichen. Hab ich denn wirklich an sie auch ein erweisliches Recht' ('For many years my nose has served me for smelling. Do I then have a legally provable right?') See Schiller, *Sämtliche Werke* (1958) p 299 cited by Leuze, *Die Entwicklung des Persönlichkeitsrechts im 19. Jahrhundert* (1962) p 22.

[95] *Ibid* citing Kant, *Einleitung in die Metaphysik der Sitten* (1798) p XLV.

[96] *Ibid*.

[97] *Ibid* p 29.

every human being had *Rechtsfähigkeit* (legal capacity), dismissing the notion of varying degrees of capacity.[98]

This particular philosophy influenced the drafters of the Austrian Civil Code (ABGB).[99] In fact, the father of the Civil Code, Franz von Zeiller, was a self-proclaimed Kantian.[100] In his seminal work, *Das natürliche Privatrecht*, von Zeiller refers to the *Urrecht* as the 'right of personality, that is the right to affirm the dignity of a rational, free-acting being [*Wesen*] or the right to legal freedom'.[101] Von Zeiller labels these rights 'material rights'. Under this heading, he includes the right to independence: more specifically, 'independence from constraint by every external choice of another' ('*seine Person von jeder äußeren nötigenden Willkür freizuerhalten*'.)'[102] According to von Zeiller, personality rights make up 'inner being or property of the person and the individual enjoys the right to be respected (*Recht der Unbescholtenheit*). Leuze argues that von Zeiller's account of personality rights is almost identical to the German understanding post-World War II. Understood in these terms, the integration of von Zeiller's personality right and Kant's *Urrecht* helped provide the conceptual foundations for the post-War general personality right.[103]

For Leuze, the new 'epoch', in which personality rights became an integral part of the legal order, began with Gareis who understood copyright law as a *Recht der Persönlichkeit*.[104] Unlike Windscheid, he believed that such rights were protected by the legal order and developed his theories with reference to *Individualität*: the private law system recognises the individuality of its actors.[105] Gareis divided such rights into three groups[106]:

---

[98] *Ibid* p 32. In Germany, Kantian-inspired efforts to construct a legal personality right culminated in Otto von Gierke's work. This work can be understood as the *Vollender* of the efforts to establish a personality right. On this point, see Götting, 'Geschichte des Persönlichkeitsrechts' (2008) p 32. Of the nineteenth century authors, we can conclude that von Gierke comes closest to describing a 'personality right' in terms that we would instantly recognise today. But other important commentators were instrumental in establishing the dogmatic framework, namely Neuner, Gareis and Kohler. See further Leuze, *Die Entwicklung des Persönlichkeitsrechts im 19. Jahrhundert* (1962) pp 60–121.

[99] Leuze, *ibid* p 33.

[100] *Ibid* p 34.

[101] *Ibid* citing Von Zeiller, *Das natürliche Privatrecht* (1812).

[102] *Ibid* p 36 citing Von Zeiller, *Das natürliche Privatrecht* (1812). In translating this phrase, I draw on Matthias Kaufmann's translation of Kant's phrase 'Unabhängigkeit von eines anderen nötigender Willkür.' See Kaufmann, 'Rational Egoism, Morality and Human Rights' (2008) p 110.

[103] In 1911, Wellspacher highlighted the significance of this integration of ideas. See Wellspacher, *Das Naturrecht und das ABGB* (1911) pp 187–188 cited by Leuze, *ibid* p 34.

[104] See Gareis, 'Das juristische Wesen der Autorrechte, sowie des Firmen-und Markenschutzes' (1877) cited by Leuze, *ibid* p 93. Leuze later explains (p 95) that Gareis decided on this term because 'person' was synonymous with 'legal subject' and *Persönlichkeit* on its own synonymous with legal capacity.

[105] *Ibid*.

[106] *Ibid* p 95.

- The right of the individual to 'preserve' his existence
- The right to be recognised as an individual (right to one's name and the right to honour)
- All types of author's rights (literary and artistic).

The legal order, Gareis argues, recognises the 'abstract and simultaneously concrete "I" (metaphysically: the will) of a person (*'abstrakte und zugleich konkrete Ich (metaphysisch: der Wille) einer Person'*).[107] The Hegelian influences are obvious: each individual has to right 'to control' his personality and the legal order should afford appropriate protection.

Though Gareis' work was highly influential, it was von Gierke who introduced the term *'Allgemeine Recht der Persönlichkeit'* into German legal discourse.[108] He defines the general personality right in the following way:

'"Persönlichkeitsrechte" nennen wir Rechte, die ihrem Subjekte die Herrschaft über einem Bestandteil der eigenen Persönlichkeitssphäre gewährleisten. Mit diesem Namen werden sie als "Rechte an der eigenen Person" gekennzeichnet und somit durch den Hinweis auf die Besonderheit ihrer Objektes von allen anderen Rechten unterschieden. …Das Recht der Persönlichkeit ist ein subjektives Recht und muss von jedermann anerkannt und geachtet werden. Es ist das einheitliche subjektive Grundrecht, das alle besonderen subjektiven Rechte fundamentiert und in sie alle hineinreicht, das dahe so gut die öffentlichen Rechte wie die Privatrechte und so gut die Rechte und Sachen wie die Rechte an Personen trägt und begleitet. Inwieweit aber aus ihm besondere Rechte herauswachsen oder in ihm der Stoff zu solchen Rechten unausgeschieden stecken bleibt, darüber entscheidet die rechtsgeschichtliche Entwicklung. Um diese Entscheidung ist gerade hinsichtlich der Rechte an der eigenen Person in römischen und in unserem Rechte ungleich ausgefallen.'[109]

'"Personality rights" are those rights which ensure that their subjects have control over a part of their own personal sphere. With this name they are characterised as "rights over one's own person" and thus in this way their special nature vis-à-vis all other rights is demarcated. The right of personality is a subjective right and must be recognised and respected by all others. It is the unitary subjective fundamental right, which lies at the base of all other subjective rights and into which they extend. So for this reason it sustains and supports public laws and private laws as well as property law and personal rights. However, the extent to which special rights emanate from it or it has the capacity to do such must be decided by legal-historical development. In respect of this decision, we must especially concern ourselves with how the rights over one's own person differ in Roman law compared to our own laws.'

In this passage, von Gierke argues that the right of personality is 'a subjective right' and must be recognised and respected by everyone. He calls it the 'the unitary subjective fundamental right', which forms the basis of all special subjective rights and into which all of these rights extend. Its influence stretches across public law and private law. While the drafters of the new BGB excluded this right from its

[107] Gareis 'Das Recht am menschlichen Körper' in *Festgabe der Juristischen Fakultät zu Königsberg für ihren Senior Johann Theodor Schirmer* (1900) p 74 cited by Leuze, *ibid* pp 96–97.

[108] Götting 'Geschichte des Persönlichkeitsrechts (2008) p 32.

[109] von Gierke, *Deutsches Privatrecht* (1895), pp 702–704, cited by Götting, *ibid* p 32.

remit, this passage from von Gierke's work demonstrates that this 'deficit stimulated and provoked a contrary view in the academic literature'.[110] As we will later see, this contrary view became the dominant view after World War II.

In our examination of this gradient, it is clear that the 'emergence of the individual', the autonomous rational being, had a profound impact on German law. The literature on personality interests in English law during this period is not quite as revealing, but we can infer that a similar trend towards individualisation shaped English law. This is exemplified in the writings of Starkie.[111] McNamara traces the various editions of Starkie's *Treatise on Slander and Libel*, highlighting the subtle (and not so subtle) changes in the text as the nineteenth century progressed. In the second edition of 1830, Starkie argues that we must regard reputation as a 'civil right' on the same level as rights 'to the enjoyment of life, liberty, health, property and all the comforts which appertain to a state of civil society...'.[112] By 1897 and the sixth edition of Folkard's *Starkie on Slander and Libel*, McNamara suggests that there is an element of 'historical revisionism' present.[113] Folkard writes:

> By common law of England, reputation is acknowledged as an inherent personal right: the character and good fame of individuals are placed under protection... Character and reputation are...absolute individual rights, and have always been recognised as such.[114]

Also in nineteenth century England, then, we find a shift in thinking about interests of honour and reputation. The gradient of individualisation has inclined to such as extent that these interests are no longer regarded as fundamental to keeping the peace in the community rather they are inherent in the person, above all else.[115] Understood in this way, the individual had finally emerged from the collective.

In this overview of the law and legal literature of the period between the Middle Ages and the nineteenth century, we find clear evidence of a steep inclining

---

[110] *Ibid* p 33.

[111] McNamara, *Reputation and Defamation* (2007) pp 91–94 citing Starkie, *A Treatise on the Law of Slander, Libel, Scandalum Magnatum and False Rumours* (1813); (2nd edn, 1830). The work was revised by Henry Coleman Folkard in the latter part of the nineteenth century. See Folkard, *The Law of Slander & Libel*, founded upon the Treatise of the late Thomas Starkie (3rd edn, 1869); (4th edn, 1876); (5th edn, 1876); (6th edn, 1908).

[112] Starkie, *ibid* (2nd edn, 1830) viii, xxii.

[113] McNamara, *Reputation and Defamation* (2007) p 94.

[114] *Ibid.*

[115] Signs of increasing individualism were prevalent during the nineteenth century. Despite the Church's opposition, we find, for example, a wider variety of first names being used rather than those relatively few referenced in the bible. Corbin explains that this was motivated by a desire to differentiate between generations as well as between individuals. Moreover, increasing urbanisation meant that individuals were at risk of mistaking one person for another. Corbin points to other signs of individualisation such as the increased use of mirrors and self-portraits. This trend of individualisation even continued after death. The use of individual epitaphs on gravestones became widespread and individual burials became increasingly common. On these points, see Corbin, 'The Secret of the Individual' (1990).

gradient of individualisation. The natural lawyers were the 'spokesmen' and 'interpreters' of a 'social chorus' that emphasised the individual rational agent.[116] The early natural lawyers sought to find ways to merge these new ideas with the existing Roman law. Understood in this way, the natural lawyers argued that the law was in fact as system of subjective rights, of which personality rights (given effect through *iniuria*) were an essential part. We should note that personality here did not yet explicitly incorporate interests in privacy though von Zeiller's *Recht der Unbescholtenheit* was certainly broad enough to have done so. Before we move on to examine the first references to privacy as a legal interest, we must first consider a gradient that overlaps in many ways with our discussion about individualisation: the 'levelling-up of rank.'

3.5 The Levelling-up of Rank

3.5.1 Bourgeoisification

The next significant gradient in the privacy curve is the levelling-up of rank. Alongside the emergence of the individual from the collective, during the sixteenth and seventeenth centuries, Europe witnessed what Elias calls the 'slow rise of the middle classes.'[117] In much of Europe, but especially in France, the class system underwent a 'fairly slow process of transformation, of bourgeoisification, which, at least up to 1750, went hand in hand with a simultaneous courtization of bourgeois elements'.[118] This resulted in a 'new upper class' derived from 'diverse social origins'.[119]

But what does Elias mean by a simultaneous transformation of bourgeoisification and courtization? Increasing urbanisation and trade during this period led to the rise of the bourgeoisie; cities and towns in much of Europe gained communal rights and rich merchants began to form guilds.[120] As a result, the volume of money in circulation increased, leading to inflation. This came as a devastating blow to the nobility, who were financially dependent on inherited wealth and the income from their estates. Those nobles who could not adapt to the changing economic circumstances were left 'impoverished'.[121] But as the bourgeoisie gained increasing influence in society, they sought to adopt the practices and behaviour of the

[116] Elias, *The Civilizing Process* (2000) p 413.

[117] *Ibid* pp 29–30.

[118] *Ibid* p 88.

[119] *Ibid* p 68

[120] *Ibid* pp 330–334.

[121] *Ibid* p 334.

nobility in order to differentiate themselves from the lower classes.[122] The *homme d'honneur* of the aristocratic court, that model of 'refined proper social behaviour' became something to which the wealthy middle classes sought to aspire.[123]

For the nobility and the 'ambitious bourgeoisie' who 'aped' the manners of the *homme d'honneur*,[124] there was a constant fear of 'social degradation', of 'lapsing into inferiority'[125] and the 'sense of what to do and what not to do in order not to offend or shock others became subtler'.[126] This became especially prevalent as the 'functional dependence' between the various groups in society increased. A 'permanently smouldering fear' of social degradation of this sort has profound implications because it:

> also constitutes one of the most powerful driving forces of the social control that every member of this court upper class exerts over himself and other people in his circle. It is expressed in the intense vigilance with which members of court aristocratic society observe and polish everything that distinguishes them from people of lower rank: not only their speech, their gestures, their social amusements and manners. The constant pressure from below and the fear it induced are, in short, one of the strongest driving forces – though not the only one – of that specifically civilized refinement which distinguishes the people of this upper class from others and finally becomes second nature to them.[127]

In what follows, I select examples of statutes and cases from English and German law that provide grounds for arguing that a fear of social degradation was also one of the 'driving forces' in the legal protection of personality rights. At the same time, as a consequence of various social and economic factors, we also find a levelling-up of rank in much of Western Europe. This is significant for two reasons. First, it shows how rights that were initially confined to the nobility were gradually extended to all. Second, it highlights some idiosyncratic elements of German law. This is because the German history of levelling-up is very different to that of the rest of Europe. In fact, for much of the eighteenth and nineteenth centuries, the reaction among Germans to egalitarian movements elsewhere was wholly negative. For this reason, much of pre-World War II German law can be explained, at least in part, by disapproval among scholars of the levelling-up of rank in other countries. We now turn to consider these points in greater detail.

---

[122] Erasmus' book on good manners, *de civilitate morum puerilium* of 1530, was particularly influential in this context and was used in Lutheran and Calvinist schools across Europe. Revel suggests that as a consequence of this influence '[t]he inner man was viewed solely as an object to be manipulated, to be brought into conformity with a model based on the notion of a happy medium, a rejection of all excess'. The ideal of 'true civility' involved 'ridding oneself of all idiosyncratic gestures and using only those recognised and accepted by the majority of people'. Revel, 'The Uses of Civility' (1989) p 170.

[123] *Ibid* p 192.

[124] *Ibid* p 424.

[125] *Ibid* p 415.

[126] *Ibid* p 69.

[127] *Ibid* p 424.

3.5.2 *The Scandalum Magnatum and the Closing Gap Between Classes*

The history of the English *scandalum magnatum* of 1275 is a neat illustration of how a fear of social degradation influenced the law of personality rights.[128] This remarkable statute prohibited 'false statements which might cause discord or scandal (esclaunder) between the King, magnates and people, to the detriment of the nation.'[129] What this meant, in effect, was that the spreading of false information about 'great men of the realm'[130] fell under the jurisdiction of the common law courts. The purpose of the statute was to prevent civil unrest during periods of political instability and to afford the nobility a means to defend their honour without resorting to violence.[131] Nonetheless, the statute lay dormant for a few hundred years[132] as it appears that the 'great men' preferred to solve such disputes in their own way.[133]

It was naturally in the interests of civil society to ensure that such claims were heard in court rather than have the parties resort to the sword. There is some evidence that the statute was used in 1498[134] but the first record of the *scandalum magnatum* in case law can be found in *Lord Lisle* v *William Debenham* in 1535 where the defendant accused Lord Lisle of encouraging 'contumacy' and disobeying the law 'in contempt of the King and against the form of the Statute.'[135]

By the time of *Lord Cromwell's Case*[136] in 1578, the action had been enrolled as an action of Trespass on the Case[137] and an additional clause on 'seditious words' was added.[138] Furthermore, by the middle of the sixteenth century, it was possible

[128] See McNamara, *Reputation and Defamation* (2007) pp 75–79.

[129] Kiralfy, *The Action on the Case* (1970) p 115.

[130] Referred to as 'magnates' in the first statute but glossed as peers, prelates, justices and various named officials in the re-enactment in 1378. See Plucknett, *A Concise History of the Common Law* (1956) p 486.

[131] Lassiter, 'Defamation of Peers' (1978) at 217.

[132] *Ibid.*

[133] Speaking in 1677, Sir Francis Pemberton explains why the statute was originally introduced: 'The state of the kingdom, at the time of the making of this statute, being considered, will tend much to the understanding the meaning of it. And for that we must know, that the state of the kingdom at that time was military; their tenures, yea their very recreations were military, and the sword was the usual means of attaining titles and dignities; and then the use was, that if any of the great men received a provocation, they presently betook themselves to their swords for their vindication; and that was the reason of making this and other statutes against riots and liveries.' See *Lord Townsend* v *Dr Hughes* (1676) 1 Freeman 220, at 220–221.

[134] Kiralfy, *The Action on the Case* (1970) p 116, citing *Lord Beauchamp* v *Croft* (1498) Dyer 285a, Keilw 26.

[135] *Ibid*, citing CP roll Hil 26 Hen VIII, m 526.

[136] *Ibid*, citing 4 Rep 12b, QB roll Trin 20 Eliz M 28.

[137] *Ibid.*

[138] Plucknett, *A Concise History of the Common Law* (1956).

to attain damages for breaches of the statute, even though the statute itself did not provide a civil remedy.[139] Between 1660 and 1700, we see a sharp increase in the number of actions brought under the statute.[140] Plucknett argues that this is explained in part by the re-enactments of the sixteenth century but Lassiter has a more persuasive argument. He contends that the *scandalum magnatum* became popular because it 'perpetuated in law a distinction between peers and commoners which was in fact becoming obscured at the upper levels of English society during the century or so preceding the outbreak of the civil war in the 1640s.'[141] By the second half of the seventeenth century, the mercantile class in England had gained power and influence and in this way the 'gap' between the classes 'was closing'.[142] The nobility suffered a loss of military and political influence and a loss of income through inflation.[143] Lassiter goes on to explain that the 'immediate result was an alarming erosion of the social and economic barrier which separated peers (*nobilitas major*) from gentry (*nobilitas minor*) and along with it the deference which had once been the most gratifying proof of its existence.'[144] The sudden popularity of the *scandalum magnatum* was a direct consequence of this loss of respect and 'an attempt by the legal system itself to compensate for that loss by awarding damages and punishing those guilty of disrespect.'[145] We should also note that 1660 marked the beginning of the Restoration under Charles II, perhaps reinforcing the desire among the gentry to reinstate the old social boundaries.

The case law of the 1600s demonstrates that the distinction between peer and commoner was foremost in the minds of plaintiffs and the judiciary. In *Earl of Lincoln* v *Roughton*, the defendant accused his Lord of being a 'base earl, and a paltry lord' and keeping 'none but rogues and rascals like himself.'[146] The Court awarded the Earl compensation, holding that the words:

> touched him in his honour and dignity; and to term him "base earl" and "paltry lord," is matter to raise contempt betwixt him and the people, or the King's indignation against him; and such general words in case of nobility will maintain an action, although it will not in case of a common person.[147]

That a peer was able to maintain an action in such circumstances was considered by the courts to be perfectly reasonable response. The wrath of the courts lay in store for commoners who had the audacity to compare themselves to nobles.

---

[139] *Ibid.*
[140] See Lassiter, 'Defamation of Peers' (1978).
[141] *Ibid* at 219.
[142] *Ibid* at 220.
[143] *Ibid.*
[144] *Ibid.*
[145] *Ibid.*
[146] *Earl of Lincoln* v *Roughton* (1606) Croke, Jac 196.
[147] Lassiter, 'Defamation of Peers' (1978) at 196.

In *Earl of Marlborough* v *Thomas Bennett*,[148] the Earl successfully sued Bennett who had claimed 'to be as good a gentleman as the Earl' and insisted that 'his family was as good as the Earl's [and had] taxed the Earl with baseness and base dealing.'[149] The Earl was awarded £1000 and Bennett fined a further £1000.[150]

From 1700, there were fewer documented actions under the *scandalum magnatum*. But it remained a cornerstone of defamation law for years to come. In 1768, Blackstone, made reference to the statute, defining it as:

> Words spoken in derogation of a peer, a judge, or other great officer of the realm, which are called *scandalum magnatum* [slander of the nobles], are held to be still more heinous; and, though they be such as would not be actionable in the case of a common person, yet when spoken in disgrace of such high and respectable characters, they amount to an atrocious injury: which is redressed by an action on the case founded on many ancient statutes; as well on behalf of the crown, to inflict the punishment of imprisonment on the slanderer, as on behalf of the party, to recover damages for the injury sustained.[151]

Though Blackstone thought it important to emphasise the distinction between peer and commoner, Lassiter shows that actions under the *scandalum magnatum* became less frequent during the eighteenth century.[152] We see a degree of levelling-up in that a man's 'quality' was 'less and less an acceptable criterion for determining whether he was entitled to damages in cases of defamation.'[153] More significantly, however, the eighteenth and nineteenth centuries were relatively politically stable periods and the traditional social hierarchies remained intact, thus reducing the need for the nobility to set themselves apart in law from the lower classes.

3.5.3 The Pursuit of Das Rein Geistige

While claims under the *scandalum magnatum* became less frequent during the eighteenth century, we encounter a very different trend in Germany. Elias writes that the social context of seventeenth to nineteenth century Germany was in 'complete contrast' to that of France and England, where the new upper classes were more concerned about achievements in business and politics.[154] He explains:

> What legitimised this eighteenth century [German] middle-class intelligentsia to itself, what supplied the foundation of its self-image and pride, was situated beyond economics and politics. It existed in what was called for precisely this reason *das rein Geistige*

[148] *Earl of Marlborough* v *Thomas Bennett* (1637) Calendar of State Papers, Domestic 472 cited by Lassiter, 'Defamation of Peers' (1978) at 222.

[149] *Ibid.*

[150] *Ibid.*

[151] Blackstone, *Commentaries on the Laws of England, Book the Third* (1768) p 123.

[152] Lassiter, 'Defamation of Peers' (1978) at 233.

[153] *Ibid* at 234.

[154] Elias, *The Civilizing Process* (2000) p 24.

(the purely spiritual), in books, scholarship, religion, art, philosophy, in the inner enrichment, the intellectual formation (Bildung) of the individual, primarily through the mechanism of books, in the personality.[155]

For the aspiring German bourgeoisie, then, their objective was the pursuit of *das rein Geistige*, rather than money or aristocratic status (which was confined, at any rate, almost exclusively to families with a military tradition). Such sentiments found expression in the law of the time. During the *usus modernus*, the *actio iniuriarum* was considered a criminal law action.[156] Most commentators opined that a private and public action dealing with the same injury to the same legal interests were simply incompatible with each other.[157] They also used the assessment formula (*Schätzungseid*) of the glossators as a justification. It read:

'[e]r wolle vor solchen Schimpff nicht 100 Thlr. nehmen, ... er wolle lieber 1000 Thlr. aus seinem bereitesten Vermögen verliehren als solche Beschimpffung erdulden...'[158]	'he did not want to accept 100 Thaler following such a dishonour... he would rather have lost 1000 Thaler from his whole property than withstand such contumeliousness...'

By contrast, the commentators accepted that the *actio legis Aquiliae* had a compensatory character and thus could exist in parallel to a criminal action.[159] As noted earlier, under the influence of the natural lawyers, the *actio iniuriarum* operated as a private action for a brief period in the early 1800s. At the same time, however, some authors began to question the necessity and purpose of the *actio iniuriarum*. Gradually, over the course of the nineteenth century, such concerns became commonplace and the remedy was abolished in several German territories,[160] culminating with the coming into force of the *Reichsstrafgesetzbuch* in 1871, unifying the criminal law protection of personality in the whole *Reich*.[161] In 1877 the procedural rules were introduced and § 11 I EGStPO expressly stated that actions for insults could only be taken as part of a criminal action.[162] Despite the efforts of von Jhering, who argued that the private action should be retained for certain situations,[163] 1877 signalled the end for the *actio* as a private action.

[155] *Ibid.*

[156] See Herrmann, *Der Schutz der Persönlichkeit in der Rechtslehre des 16.-18. Jahrhunderts* (1968) p 60 citing *inter alia* Struve, *Syntagmatis juris civilis*, vol III (1719) Exerc 48, lib 47, tit10, n 60; Berger, *Oeconomia juris* (1734) lib 3, tit 9, para 15, n 2ff; Lauterbach, *Collegium theoretico-practicum* (1763) lib 47, tit 10, para 30.

[157] *Ibid.* Herrmann uses Stryk as an example, *Continuatio quarta Usus moderni* (1729) lib 47, tit 10, para 21.

[158] *Ibid* citing Berger, *Oeconomia juris* (1719) lib 3, tit 9, para 15, n 6.

[159] *Ibid* citing Stryk, *Continuatio quarta Usus moderni* (1729) lib 47, tit 10, para 21.

[160] See generally Moosheimer, *Die actio injuriarum aestimatoria im 18. und 19. Jahrhundert* (1997). Prussia had already abolished its *Duellmandat* in 1713.

[161] Halfmeier, *Die Veröffentlichung privater Tatsachen als unerlaubte Handlung* (2000) p 46.

[162] *Einführungsgesetz zur Strafprozessordnung* 1877.

[163] von Jhering, 'Rechtsschutz gegen injuriöse Rechtsverletzungen' (1886) p 233 *et seq.*

Consequently, the drafters of the new BGB in 1896 refused to provide civil protection for personality rights.[164]

Several plausible reasons can be advanced as to why the *actio* was moved from private to criminal law. The first explanation relates to culture, or to be more precise, the culture of the Prussian nobility.[165] As we have seen, it was commonly regarded as disreputable to attach a monetary value to one's honour and therefore persons of standing would rarely make use of the *actio iniuriarum*.[166] This can be contrasted with Article 1382 *Code civil*:

'Tout fait quelconque de l'homme, qui cause à autrui un dommage, oblige celui par la faute duquel il est arrivé, à le réparer.'	'Any act of man that causes damage to another, obliges the one who is at fault to compensate it.'

The general liability clause of the French Civil Code emphasises the natural law ideal of equality in *Rechtsfähigkeit*, something which the Prussians refrained from emulating in their code despite its natural law connotations. Writing in 1888, Hartmann contrasts German law with French, describing the French system as 'completely alien' ('*absolut fremdartig*'). He goes on to argue that it is:

'dem tiefern deutschen Sinn widerstrebend, die heiligsten Gefühle in schnödem Mammon abzumessen, und jede schuldhafte Kränkung derselben durch eine Geldleistung aufwägen zu lassen'.[167]	'abhorrent to the deep German soul[168] to measure cherished feelings in filthy lucre, and to allow every culpable slight to the same to be calculated as a sum of money.'

Hartmann quite clearly believed that the German Volksgeist was a profoundly different creature to the French Geist. There were undoubtedly many deep-rooted and complex prejudices underlying such a belief. First, these prejudices must be understood within the context of the new wave of nationalist pride in a 'reunited' German Empire. A newly formed state often defines itself by *what it is not* rather than what it is.[169] It is possible that the nobility helped construct the identity of the new German Empire by contrasting it, in what they saw as a favourable light, with its powerful neighbour. A second and related point is that the relationship between Germany and post-Revolution France was nothing short of tumultuous. The German upper classes were horrified by the social unrest in France following the Revolution and were even more appalled by Napoleon and his plans for a French

[164] Brüggemeier, *Haftungsrecht* (2006) pp 265–267.

[165] Moosheimer, *Die actio injuriarum aestimatoria im 18. und 19. Jahrhundert* (1997) p 122.

[166] *Ibid.*

[167] Hartmann, 'Der Civilgesetzentwurf, das Aequitätaprincip und die Richterstellung' (1888) p 364. Gordley translates this as 'base mammon'. See Gordley, *Foundations of Private Law* (2006) p 229.

[168] *Sinn* in this context is difficult to translate. Possible alternatives to 'soul' are 'mind' or 'sense'.

[169] Hanafin, *Constituting Identity* (2001). Consider also Freud's theory of reaction formation. On this point see Freud, *Drei Abhandlungen Zur Sexualtheorie* (1905).

Europe. But underlying all of this ill-feeling was, as Isaiah Berlin puts it, 'a huge national inferiority complex.'[170] The French had humiliated the Prussians and the Austrians on the battlefield; French national icons dominated science and the arts with, according to Berlin, 'a kind of arrogance and success unexampled hitherto.'[171] Perhaps one of the best forms of retaliation was to reject all things French and in legal scholarship this meant discrediting Article 1382 *Code civil.*

Taken together, nationalist pride and anti-French feeling, inevitably led German legal scholars to seek an *Ausgangspunkt* (point of departure) for a purely German legal scholarship, rather than relying on the French *philosophes* as legislators as the southern European states had done. The *Ausgangspunkt* was Friedrich Karl von Savigny's *System des heutigen Römischen Rechts.* In constructing their thesis, Savigny and the historical school rejected the notion that law was based solely on *Vernunft.*[172] Wieacker argues that the 'Kantian concept of law' is at the basis of Savigny's system: 'law [is] an "independent entity" which empowers the individual to be independently ethical, but does not force him to be so.'[173] All law 'arises out of and seeks to fulfil the inherent moral freedom of human beings'.[174] Under the influence of Hegelian thought, Savigny placed the person at the 'centre of private law'.[175] Individuals should be afforded free and secure *raum* (scope/space), within which they can exercise free will.[176] Savigny writes:

'Das Wesen des Rechtsverhältnisses ist bestimmt als ein Gebiet unabhängiger Herrschaft des individuellen Willens'.[177]	'The character of a legal relationship is defined as the area of independent control of the individual will'.

What emerges from Savigny's work is a focus on control of individual will and possession of property. Private autonomy, in this sense, concerned subjective alienable economic rights (*Vermögensrechte*), rather than the *jura connata.* As Brüggemeier emphasises, the natural law concept of a basic right to personality

[170] Berlin, *The Roots of Romanticism* (2000) p 35.

[171] *Ibid.*

[172] The historical school believed that law could not be extracted from reason but from the *Volksgeist* of a nation, which requires careful historical study. For Germany, this meant reverting to the principles of Roman law. Legal disputes should be decided by scientific deduction from these principles. See Posner 'Savigny, Holmes and the Law and Economics of Possession' (2000) at 537. See also Whitman, *The Legacy of Roman Law in the German Romantic Era* (1990).

[173] Wieacker, *A History of Private Law in Europe* (1995) p 315.

[174] Brüggemeier, 'Constitutionalisation of Private Law' (2006) p 60.

[175] Leuze, *Die Entwicklung des Persönlichkeitsrechts im 19. Jahrhundert* (1962) p 46.

[176] *Ibid* p 47.

[177] Savigny, *System des heutigen Römischen Rechts*, Vol 1 (1840) p 334, cited by Leuze, *Die Entwicklung des Persönlichkeitsrechts im 19. Jahrhundert* (1962) p 47.

based on dignity and freedom was discarded.[178] The person was 'reduced to an aspect of legal capacity (§ 1 BGB), the subjects of legal relationships'.[179]

The 'levelling-up of rank' is a highly significant gradient in our privacy curve for two reasons. First, it helps explain how ideas of respect, dignity and privacy, eventually permeated society as a whole. As a consequence of unique cultural factors, the German history of levelling-up is very different to that of the rest of Europe (as we shall see below, it occurs much later) and this helps explain some of the idiosyncratic elements of current German law on privacy. Second, because jurists were highly critical of egalitarianism elsewhere in Europe they sought a purely German *Ausgangspunkt*. Thus, we discover how Savingy's ideas became influential. As we will see in the next chapter, this also goes some way towards explaining some of the more unusual features of contemporary German law.

3.6 Between the Home and the State

The next gradient on the privacy curve concerns the expanding role of the state and the corresponding importance ascribed by the individual to the home. This trend was common to all Western European states during the long nineteenth century (in Hobsbawm's sense) but the French experience is particularly revealing because of the centralised nature of the state from the reign of Louis XIII onwards.[180] The French revolutionaries of 1789 sought to bring an end to the absolutist form of government. Through new laws such as *l'inviolabilite du domicile*, under Article 184 of Penal Code, the new Republic formally recognised a private sphere. But at the same time the revolutionaries emphasised the Republican ideal of *l'espirit publique*, which demanded a commitment to transparency and openness in personal and financial affairs.[181] The devotion to this ideal clearly became overbearing for some and encouraged a 'romantic withdrawal into the self.'[182] Even Rousseau recommended solitary walks, as 'an exaltation of privacy [is] the ground of philosophical truth'.[183] The commitment to equality and the newly drafted family laws of the French Republic further ensured that 'in the long run ... the French revolution sharpened the distinction between the public and private spheres, emphasised family values, and led to a differentiation of sexual roles'.[184]

---

178 Brüggemeier, *Haftungsrecht* (2006) p 265.

179 *Ibid.*

180 Ariès, 'Introduction' (1989) p 3.

181 Hunt, 'The Unstable Boundaries of the French Revolution' (1990) p 13.

182 *Ibid.*

183 Goulemot, 'Literary Practices' (1989) p 389.

184 Perrot, 'Introduction' (1990) p 9.

This trend continued into the nineteenth century. During this period, politicians throughout Europe became increasingly interventionist in social matters; this despite the commitment to *laissez faire* in the economic context.[185] In the newly unified German Empire, Bismarck introduced social security insurance, while in France, industrialists and public health officials proposed new housing policies to reduce overcrowding.[186] Across Europe, a recurring theme was the importance of the family home; the home as a 'moral entity' but also a 'political one.'[187] At the same time, individuals were compelled to provide central government with more sensitive personal information, through a government census for example.[188] As cities grew in size and the state became more interventionist and centralised, the upper classes sought to 'hide themselves away from the masses', 'fearful of the ignorance and filth.'[189] It is during this time that 'semi-private spaces' such as gentlemen's clubs, lodges, gaming rooms, cafés and cabarets became popular.[190]

Understood in these terms, it comes as no great surprise that a significant number of privacy cases in the nineteenth century concerned physical intrusions into the private sphere. In England, this was expressed by an understanding of privacy as an aspect of property.[191] This was inspired, most notably, by Blackstone's understanding of the right to property as that which 'excludes everyone else but the owner from the use of it.'[192] As early as 1604, in *Semayne's Case*,[193] Sir Edward Coke prohibited a sheriff from gaining entry to the plaintiff's house, holding that the 'house of every one is his castle'.[194] Over the course of the eighteenth century, the maxim became a firmly established common law principle and a remedy was available in trespass.[195] By the nineteenth century, the courts were applying 'the trespass remedy to all unwelcome intrusions, howsoever motivated.'[196] While privacy was equated with property in such cases, at times the courts made reference to civil mores. In *Merest* v *Harvey* (1814), for example, the defendant had trespassed on the plaintiff's land and 'spoiled the plaintiff's grass.'[197] On whether exemplary damages should be awarded for this 'insult', Gibbs CJ stated:

---

[185] Perrot, 'The Family Triumphant' (1990) pp 99–100.

[186] Perrot, 'At Home' (1990) p 351.

[187] *Ibid* p 343.

[188] Seipp, 'English Judicial Recognition of a Right to Privacy' (1983) at 342.

[189] Perrot, 'At Home' (1990) p 342.

[190] *Ibid* p 341.

[191] Seipp, 'English Judicial Recognition of a Right to Privacy' (1983).

[192] Blackstone, *Commentaries on the Laws of England, Book the Second* (1770), ch I, p 8.

[193] *Semayne's Case* (1604) 5 Coke Reports 91a.

[194] *Ibid.*

[195] See, for example, *Wilkes* v *Wood* (1763) Lofft 1, 98 ER 489; *Bruce* v *Rawlins* (1770) 3 Wils KB 61, 95 ER 934; *Bostock* v *Saunders* (1773) 2 WBl 912, 96 ER 539.

[196] Seipp, 'English Judicial Recognition of a Right to Privacy' (1983) at 335.

[197] *Merest* v *Harvey* (1814) 5 Taunton 442.

> I wish to know, in a case where a man disregards every principle which actuates the conduct of gentlemen, what is to restrain him except large damages? To be sure, one can hardly conceive worse conduct than this. What would be said to a person in a low situation of life, who should behave himself in this manner? I do not know upon what principle we can grant a rule in this case, unless we were to lay it down that the jury are not justified in giving more than the absolute pecuniary damage that the Plaintiff may sustain.[198]

Gibbs CJ compared this conduct to a man who 'intrudes and walks up and down before the window of [a gentleman's] house, and looks in while the [gentleman] is at dinner.'[199] In other words, the defendant's behaviour fell short of the expected standard of social conduct that had emerged from the social processes of individualisation and levelling-up.

Following the urbanisation and population growth of the nineteenth century, householders who, as Seipp puts it, 'had long enjoyed freedom from curious eyes sought legal protection…when neighbours opened windows overlooking them.'[200] Actions based on the doctrines of ancient lights[201] and nuisance were routinely successful but by the 1860s, the 'courts' attitude had hardened' against such claims.[202] In *Jones* v *Tapling* (1865),[203] the plaintiff complained that the defendant's window overlooked his grounds and argued that this was an invasion of privacy. In addressing this claim, Baron Bramwell stated that it is well established that 'privacy is not a right. Intrusion on it is no wrong or cause of action.'[204] Seipp argues that the absence of a privacy action meant that by the end of the nineteenth century, the 'English householder…was at the mercy of curious and resourceful neighbours.'[205] He cites the example of a 1904 case in which a Balham dentist failed in his complaint against his neighbours 'who had arranged large mirrors in their garden in order to observe all that went on in [the plaintiff's] study and operating room.'[206] While to

---

[198] *Ibid* at 443.

[199] *Ibid.*

[200] Seipp, 'English Judicial Recognition of a Right to Privacy' (1983) at 336.

[201] See *Cherrington* v *Abney* (1709) 2 Vernon's Cases in Chancery 646, 23 ER 1022, at 1023: 'Where an old house is pulled down, wherein were ancient lights, and a new one is built; the lights in the new house must be in the same place, and of the same dimensions, and not more in number than the lights in the old house.' In this case, the windows could not be altered 'as if before so high, as they could not look out of them into the yard, shall not make them lower and the like; for privacy is valuable.'

[202] Seipp, 'English Judicial Recognition of a Right to Privacy' (1983) at 336.

[203] *Jones* v *Tapling* (1862) 12 Common Bench Reports (New Series) 826, 142 ER 1367. Affirmed in House of Lords (1865) 11 HLC 290; 11 ER 1344.

[204] *Ibid* at 850.

[205] Seipp, 'English Judicial Recognition of a Right to Privacy' (1983) at 337.

[206] *Ibid* citing Editor's Note in Kenny, *A Selection of Cases Illustrative of the English law of Tort* 367 (4th edn, 1926).

varying degrees, nuisance,[207] trespass[208] and criminal law[209] provided remedies to individuals who claimed invasion of the physical private sphere, by the end of the nineteenth century, the notion that a right of privacy was not available in English law was firmly fixed in the common law mind-set.

We find in the nineteenth century, then, the first significant references to privacy as a legal interest. This was a consequence of the changing nature of society, most notably urbanisation and the introduction of new forms of housing. For this reason, individuals were concerned with privacy of property, echoing much older themes about a man's home being his castle. But as the nineteenth century progressed, we see the emergence of different privacy concerns, to which we now turn.

3.7 The Challenges of Late Modernity

The final gradient in our privacy curve consists of the implications of what can be identified as the 'challenges of late modernity'. Two points must be emphasised here. First, while I use the term 'late modernity', I do not use it in Anthony Giddens' sense[210]—I survey here a period from the late nineteenth century to the present and 'late modernity' serves as a convenient label. Second, in what follows there are potentially several different gradients: *misuse of private information* (especially by an increasingly active and intrusive press), *the appropriation of personality* and *totalitarianism*. But for reasons of space, I shall keep them under the broad umbrella of this single gradient.

3.7.1 Misuse of Private Information and Appropriation of Personality

As noted earlier, it is during the nineteenth century that we see the first significant references to 'privacy' as a *legal* interest. Apart from cases involving physical intrusion into private space, the most common privacy claims during the late nineteenth to early twentieth century were for the misuse of private information and appropriation of personality. This can be explained, at least in part, by an increasingly active press and developments in technology such as the invention of photography. But, in both English and German law, courts were at first hesitant to

207 See *Walker* v *Brewster* (1867) LR 5 Eq 25.

208 *Harrison* v *Rutland* [1893] 1 QB 142; *Hickman* v *Maisey* [1900] 1 QB 752.

209 Seipp, 'English Judicial Recognition of a Right to Privacy' (1983) at 337 gives examples of 'longstanding prohibitions against peeping Toms and eavesdroppers'.

210 Giddens, *Modernity and Self-Identity* (1991).

recognise actions based on 'injuries to feelings' so much so that for some time an understanding of privacy as property continued to find expression. As we will see, even in informational privacy cases, the interests at stake were presented as an aspect of property, usually intellectual property rights. We now consider developments in English and German law.

3.7.1.1 English Law

The understanding of privacy as property is most apparent in English law. In *Gee* v *Pritchard*, for example, the defendant intended to publish letters sent to him by the plaintiff, without obtaining the former's consent.[211] The Court of Chancery granted an injunction against publication on the grounds that unpublished letters constituted literary property. But previous authority had suggested that there was no property in letters.[212] Eldon LC distinguished these decisions as the courts had not 'inquire[d] whether the intention of the writer was or was not directed to publication.'[213] The recipient of the letter only has rights over the letter for the certain qualified purpose for which the letter was sent.[214] The plaintiff had also made reference to her 'wounded feelings' but the Lord Chancellor emphasised that this was not within the jurisdiction of the Court.[215] While privacy was arguably the underlying interest, the decision was based 'upon the idea of property in the thing published, as being the product of the mind of the sender.'[216]

As such, the most troublesome actions for nineteenth century judges concerned unpublished private information disclosed to a third party. These actions were troublesome for two reasons. First, because they concerned unpublished information, they did not fall under the remit of the Statute of Anne (1710) and second, the

[211] *Gee* v *Pritchard* (1818) 2 Swanston 402.

[212] *Pope* v *Curl* 2 Atk 342, and *Thompson* v *Stanhope* Amb 737.

[213] (1818) 2 Swanston 402, at 414.

[214] *Ibid* at 415–416 (per Lord Chancellor Eldon): '…that by sending the letter, the writer had given, for the purpose of reading, and, in some cases, of keeping it, a property to the person to whom the letter was addressed, yet, that the gift was so restrained, that *ultra* the purposes for which the letter was sent, the property was in the sender. If that is the principle, it is immaterial whether the publication is for the purpose of profit or not. If for profit, the party is then selling, if not for profit, he is giving, that, a portion of which belongs to the writer.'

[215] *Ibid* at 426 (per Lord Chancellor Eldon): 'The doctrine is thus laid down, following the principle of Lord *Hardwicke*: I do not say that I am to interfere because the letters are written in confidence, or because the publication of them may wound the feelings of the Plaintiff; but if mischievous effects of that kind can be apprehended in cases in which this Court has been accustomed, on the ground of property, to forbid publication, it would not become me to abandon the jurisdiction which my predecessors have exercised, and refuse to forbid it.'

[216] *Prince Albert* v *Strange* (1849) 2 De Gex & Smale 652 (per Knight Bruce VC at 666).

courts of equity did not have jurisdiction to consider mere injury to feelings, as property was 'the sole ground of equitable interference.'[217] In hard cases such as these, judges sought, in so far as they could, to equate privacy with property.[218] But this argument was sometimes difficult to sustain. Consider *Prince Albert* v *Strange* (1849).[219] In that case, the defendant obtained, published in a 'Descriptive Catalogue', and intended to sell copies of private etchings created by the Prince Consort and his family.

The plaintiff claimed 'protection for the privacy of his property'[220] but counsel for the defendant argued that privacy and property were distinct notions:

> It has been argued that privacy is the essence of property, and that the deprivation of privacy would make it, in fact, cease to be property. But the question here is not of that kind; the question is not, what is right and fitting to be done, but what is the law of the land. The notion of privacy is a notion altogether distinct from that of property. That a thing belongs to a man constitutes property; that another man should or should not see it is not property. There is no such property as the exclusive right of seeing and talking about property.[221]

Counsel for the defendant suggested that the plaintiff was using property rights as a means to protect interests that did not find expression in the 'law of the land.' As such, the plaintiff complained 'of an offence not against law, but against manners'; in other words, the 'order and well-being of life depended greatly on things not within the cognisance of laws and can in very many instances not be protected or vindicated by them.'[222] While the actions of the defendant may have been repugnant to civil mores, there was nothing in law to prevent such actions. Vice-Chancellor Knight-Bruce admitted that he agreed with this contention but attempted to ascertain whether this case was an example of a breach of good manners that is also a breach of the law.[223] In doing so, he faced two major hurdles. First, as noted above, the courts did not concern themselves with mere 'wounded feelings', there had to be special damage. But the Vice-Chancellor observed that such pain 'is not always disregarded in Courts of Justice.'[224] He gave the example

---

[217] See *Southey* v *Sherwood* (2 Mer 437).

[218] See, for example, *Millar* v *Taylor* (1769), in which the strained language of stretching the law is evident: 'Suppose a man, with or without leave to peruse a manuscript work, transcribes and publishes it; it is not within the Act of Queen Ann.; it is not larceny; it is not trespass; it is not a crime indictable; (the physical property of the author, the original manuscript, remains:) but it is a gross violation of a valuable right. Suppose the original, or a transcript, was given or lent to a man to read, for his own use; and he publishes it; it would be a violation of the author's common law-right to the copy. This never was doubted; and has often been determined.' *Millar* v *Taylor* (1769) 4 Burrow 2303 at 2330 (per Willes J).

[219] *Prince Albert* v *Strange* (1849) 2 De Gex & Smale 652.

[220] *Ibid* at 674.

[221] *Ibid* at 680–681.

[222] *Ibid* at 688.

[223] *Ibid* at 689.

[224] *Ibid* at 690.

of a trespass to property, which is 'barely appreciable and is only nominally compensated'. But if this trespass is 'accompanied by circumstances of oppression or malignity, insolence, affront or reproach, which by themselves could not be made the subject of an action', these may ultimately be 'considered in the suit for the trespass, and swell the damages to a heavy amount.'[225] The second difficulty was equating privacy with property. Knight-Bruce VC reasoned that the etchings were the 'produce of mental labour, thoughts and sentiments', an example of intellectual property.[226] As such, the creator of this property, whether 'famous or obscure' has the right to prevent publication or disclosure to third party.[227] This is because: '[u]pon the principle... of protecting property... the common law... shelters the privacy and seclusion of thoughts and sentiments committed to writing, and desired by the author to remain not generally known.'[228]

The Vice-Chancellor stated that this principle also applied, by analogy, to other products of mental labour. But despite the interference with property, fundamentally the actions of the defendant amounted to:

> an intrusion – an unbecoming and unseemly intrusion – an intrusion not alone in breach of conventional rules, but offensive to that inbred sense of propriety natural to every man – if, intrusion, indeed, fitly describes a sordid spying into the privacy of domestic life – into the home (a word hitherto sacred among us)...[229]

The injunction was upheld on appeal but Cottenham LC held that the outcome did not depend 'solely upon the question of property, for a breach of trust, confidence, or contract, would of itself entitle the plaintiff to an injunction.'[230] This statement is considered to be authority for the grant of an injunction for breach of confidence.[231]

Chancery, then, did not have jurisdiction to grant an injunction unless there was injury to property.[232] But early in the nineteenth century, Chancery had indicated that it was willing to grant injunctions in cases where libel caused injury to business

[225] *Ibid* at 690–691.

[226] *Ibid* at 695.

[227] *Ibid* at 694.

[228] *Ibid* at 695.

[229] *Ibid* at 313.

[230] *Prince Albert* v *Strange* (1849) 1 Macnaghten & Gordon 25 at 44.

[231] Toulson & Phipps, *Confidentiality* (2006) p 10.

[232] See *Emperor of Austria* v *Day* 45 ER 861; (1861) 3 De GF & J 217; *Southey* v *Sherwood* 35 ER 1006; (1817) 2 Mer 435; *Clark* v *Freeman* 35 ER 1006; (1817) 2 Mer 435.

or property[233] or in cases where there was a breach of faith and of contract.[234] Consequently, plaintiffs who complained of an invasion of privacy would succeed in obtaining an injunction if they could show that there was a pre-existing relationship, either in confidence or by contract,[235] or if there was defamation.[236] But injunctions remained unavailable in cases concerning mere publication of image or description.[237]

Some privacy interests thus found legal protection at the turn of the twentieth century. But as the century progressed and technology developed, the press became every more powerful and new forms of invasion of privacy emerged such as the unauthorised taking and publication of photographs. An increasingly active press took an interest in the private lives of celebrities. At the same time, celebrities sought to court publicity, in many cases using their name and image in merchandising agreements. Though, on its own, libel proved inadequate to remedy misuse of private information and misappropriation of personality, in many cases courts found alternative solutions.

Tolley v *Fry* (1931) is a neat illustration of these developments.[238] In this case, the defendants published an advertisement in two national newspapers. The advertisement featured a caricature of the plaintiff who was a well-known amateur golfer. The plaintiff brought an action for libel on learning that he had been depicted in the advertisement playing golf, with a bar of the respondents' chocolate in his pocket. While counsel for the plaintiff agreed that the caricature itself was not libellous, they argued that it had created the impression that he had agreed to the advertisement for monetary reward; in other words, he had 'prostituted his reputation as an

[233] See *Hermann Loog* v *Bean* (1884) LR 26 Ch D 306; *Saxby* v *Easterbrook and Hannaford* (1877-78) LR 3 CPD 339; *Thorley's Cattle Food Company* v *Massam* (No 1) (1877) LR 6 Ch D 582.

[234] *Morison* v *Moat* 68 ER 492; (1851) 9 Hare 241.

[235] In *Pollard* v *Photographic Company* (1889), on the plaintiff's instructions, the defendant photographer had taken photographs of the plaintiff for her own personal use. The plaintiff and her husband subsequently discovered that the defendant had retained one of the negatives and reprinted the plaintiff's image on a Christmas card, which he exhibited in his shop. The plaintiff's solicitor instructed his clerk to purchase the card. Counsel for the defendant argued that a 'person has no property in his own features: short of doing what is libellous or otherwise illegal there is no restriction on the photographer to use his negative.' See *Pollard* v *Photographic Company* (1889) LR 40 Ch D 345, at 346. The Court awarded an injunction on the basis of breach of contract.

[236] See *Monson* v *Tussauds Ltd* [1894] 1 QB 671, where the defendant had displayed a wax likeness of the plaintiff in his museum. The plaintiff had stood trial for murder in Scotland but the jury had awarded a verdict of not proven. The wax figure was placed in a room with figures of individuals convicted of murder. The Court of Appeal regarded this as defamatory innuendo and awarded an injunction.

[237] See *Dockrell* v *Dougall* (1899) 80 LT 556 where a doctor's name was used without his consent to advertise medicine. The jury held that the matter was not libellous. Similarly, in *Corelli* v *Wall* (1906) 22 TLR 532, photographs of the plaintiff were reproduced on postcards but these were not considered libellous.

[238] *Tolley* v *Fry* [1931] AC 333.

amateur golf player for advertising purposes… and… had been guilty of conduct unworthy of his status as an amateur golfer.'[239] At first instance, the jury found for the plaintiff and awarded him damages. On appeal, the Court of Appeal held that the award of £1000 in damages was excessive and that the trial judge should have ruled that there was no case to go before the jury.[240] But the House of Lords reversed the Court of Appeal decision. A majority regarded the advertisement as a 'most offensive' imputation.[241] The Lords upheld the award of damages because a '[s]ubstantial wrong had been done to the plaintiff and not one which is technical and insignificant.'[242] While the main issue in this case concerned the interpretation of the innuendo,[243] the case demonstrates that courts were willing to protect against misappropriation of personality in limited circumstances and allowed existing causes of action to act as remedies. We should note, however, that there was no suggestion here that the plaintiff intended to protect commercial interests rather than dignitary interests (whether we can distinguish the two interests in practice will be considered later).

In English law, then, in the 150 years between the *Prince Albert* decision and the introduction of the Human Rights Act 1998, the sporadic use of common law torts, equitable and statutory actions in individual cases has been the characteristic feature of the law on privacy. In cases where confidential commercial information was at stake, courts readily granted injunctions under the equitable doctrine of breach of confidence.[244] However, throughout the twentieth century, courts remained hesitant to award remedies for the misuse of personal information. Unlike Germany and other continental European legal systems at the outset of the twentieth century, English courts rejected the notion of a right to one's own image. In *Sports and General Press Agency* v *'Our Dogs' Publishing Company* (1916),[245] Horridge J summed up the standing of English law by stating that:

> no one possesses a right of preventing another person photographing him any more than he has a right of preventing another person giving a description of him, provided the description is not libellous or otherwise wrongful. Those rights do not exist.[246]

---

[239] *Ibid* at 337.

[240] [1930] 1 KB 467.

[241] [1931] AC 333 at 341 (per Viscount Hailsham).

[242] *Ibid* at 346 (per Lord Buckmaster).

[243] For a discussion on this point see Beverley-Smith, *The Commercial Appropriation of Personality* (2002) pp 253–254.

[244] See, for example, *Morison* v *Moat* (1851) 9 Hare 241; *Gartside* v *Outram* (1857) 26 LJCh (NS) 113; *Pollard* v *Photographic Company* (1888) 40 Ch D 345; *Merryweather* v *Moore* [1892] 2 Ch 518; *Lamb* v *Evans* [1893] 1 Ch 218; *Herbert Morris Ltd* v *Saxelby* [1916] AC 688; *Reid and Sigrist Ltd* v *Moss and Mechanism Ltd.* (1932) 49 RPC 461; *Saltman Engineering Co. Ltd* v *Campbell Engineering Co. Ltd* (1948) 65 RPC 203; *Printers & Finishers Ltd* v *Holloway* [1965] RPC 239; *Coco* v *AN Clark (Engineers) Ltd.* [1969] RPC 41. See further Toulson & Phipps, *Confidentiality* (2006) pp 3–21.

[245] *Sports and General Press Agency* v *'Our Dogs' Publishing Company* [1916] 2 KB 880.

[246] *Ibid* at 884.

Despite occasional references to the contrary,[247] the English position, then, was that there was no right of privacy in English law.[248] Instead, courts have repeatedly reminded claimants that English law seeks to cater for privacy interests in its own way. In *Wainwright* v *Home Office*, Lord Hoffmann described the patchwork of actions available to potential claimants in English law, stating:

> There are a number of common law and statutory remedies of which it may be said that one at least of the underlying values they protect is a right of privacy... Common law torts include trespass, nuisance, defamation and malicious falsehood; there is the equitable action for breach of confidence and statutory remedies under the Protection from Harassment Act 1997 and the Data Protection Act 1998. There are also extra-legal remedies under Codes of Practice applicable to broadcasters and newspapers. But there are gaps; cases in which the courts have considered that an invasion of privacy deserves a remedy which the existing law does not offer. Sometimes the perceived gap can be filled by judicious development of an existing principle.[249]

During the twentieth century, however, the privacy lacuna in English tort law meant that courts were sometimes faced with distinctly awkward claims, in which they recognised significant privacy interests but admitted that there was little that they could do to provide relief.[250] We will consider one of these cases, *Kaye* v *Robertson*, in greater detail in the next chapter. But for now we should note that when justifying these decisions, the courts would normally express concerns about

---

[247] In *British Steel Corporation* v *Grenada Television Ltd* [1980] WL 264756, Denning MR confidently declared that '[t]he courts will always be ready to grant an injunction to restrain a publication which is an infringement of privacy.'

[248] Lord Hoffmann in *Wainwright* makes the distinction between 'identifying privacy as a value which underlies the existence of a rule of law (and may point the direction in which the law should develop) and privacy as a principle of law in itself. The English common law is familiar with the notion of underlying values—principles only in the broadest sense—which direct its development.' He cites the example of *Derbyshire County Council* v *Times Newspapers Ltd* [1993] AC 534. According to Lord Hoffmann, in this case, 'freedom of speech was the underlying value which supported the decision to lay down the specific rule that a local authority could not sue for libel. But no one has suggested that freedom of speech is in itself a legal principle which is capable of sufficient definition to enable one to deduce specific rules to be applied in concrete cases. That is not the way the common law works.' See *Wainwright* v *Home Office* [2004] 2 AC 406 at 422 (per Lord Hoffmann).

[249] *Ibid* at 419.

[250] Alongside *Wainright* consider, for example, *Malone* v *Metropolitan Police Commissioner* [1979] Ch 344 and *Kaye* v *Robertson* [1991] FSR 62.

the dangers of a super tort of invasion of privacy[251] or concerns about judicial law-making.[252]

What is most striking about cases of this sort is the fixity of the rights of action and ensuing potential for judicial paralysis. In these cases, courts recognised that there were significant privacy interests at stake and that the claimants had been wronged as a result of the defendant's actions. But English law, as it stood, could not offer protection in the form of a privacy tort. Instead, claimants had to make use of various common law, equitable and statutory causes of action. However, many of these actions were not designed to cater for privacy interests in the first place and, understood in these terms, their use was not always satisfactory. Significant gaps in the law remained. These gaps were highlighted by the ECtHR in *Earl Spencer* v *United Kingdom*,[253] *Peck* v *United Kingdom*[254] and *Wainwright* v *United Kingdom*.[255] But whatever way we look at this problem, the unhappy conclusion is that for a very long time significant privacy interests did not find protection in English tort law. This would be bad enough on its own but we must remember to consider such developments against the backdrop of a rapidly growing population, more intrusive media and state agencies and private corporations with designs on collecting, storing and monitoring more personal data than ever before.

---

[251] In *Malone*, on the question of a right of privacy for telephone conversations, the Court warned: 'One of the factors that must be relevant in such a case is the degree of particularity in the right that is claimed. The wider and more indefinite the right claimed, the greater the undesirability of holding that such a right exists. Wide and indefinite rights, while conferring an advantage on those who have them, may well gravely impair the position of those who are subject to the rights. To create a right for one person, you have to impose a corresponding duty on another.' See *Malone* v *Metropolitan Police Commissioner* [1979] Ch 344 at 373. We should note, however, that in *Malone* v *United Kingdom* (1984) 7 EHRR 14, the ECtHR subsequently held that the actions in this case were an infringement by a public authority of Art 8 ECHR and Parliament eventually introduced the Interception of Communications Act (1985), which provides a remedy for wrongs of this sort.

[252] In *Kaye*, speaking *obiter*, Glidewell LJ stated that the case was 'a graphic illustration of the desirability of Parliament considering whether and in what circumstances statutory provision can be made to protect the privacy of individuals.' See *Kaye* v *Robertson* [1991] FSR 62 at 66 (per Glidewell LJ).

[253] *Earl Spencer* v *United Kingdom* (1998) 25 EHRR CD 105.

[254] (2003) 36 EHRR 719.

[255] *Wainwright* v *United Kingdom* [2006] ECHR 807. But as Lord Hoffmann argues convincingly in *Wainwright*, the ECtHR, in *Spencer* and *Peck*, did not suggest that the English courts should introduce a general privacy tort, rather the Court was concerned with whether there was an adequate remedy for the particular infringements of Article 8 in the specific cases before it. See *Wainwright* v *Home Office* [2004] 2 AC 406 at 423 (per Lord Hoffmann).

3.7.1.2 German Law

We can find broadly similar social and political trends in *Germany* but, significantly, the German legislature and courts sought to deal with appropriation and misuse of images in a very different way. During the late nineteenth and early twentieth centuries, the *Reichsgericht* and most commentators, apart from von Gierke, strictly followed the wording of the BGB.[256] In hard cases, where there were obvious gaps in protection, the *Reichsgericht* sought other ways to protect personality interests.

In the famous *Nietzsche letter* case,[257] for example, the sister of the deceased philosopher, Friedrich Nietzsche, sued for an injunction against a third party who attempted to publish personal letters that had belonged to the deceased. The claimant attempted to rely on a general personality right as elaborated in the commentaries, but the *Reichsgericht* held that a general subjective personality right was alien to the civil order ('*allgemeines subjektives Persönlichkeitsrecht im geltenden bürglichen Rechte fremd*').[258] Instead, as in *Prince Albert* v *Strange*, the Court granted the injunction by holding that the letters stemmed from 'individual intellectual creation' ('*individuelle Geistesschöpfung*') under the meaning of the *Literaturhebergesetz* (LUG) of 1901.[259] The *Reichsgericht* also made use of the narrowly constructed § 826 BGB in instances when there had been a particularly malicious intention causing economic loss.[260]

The German approach to the use and publication of images is of particular interest because the *Reichsgericht* routinely interpreted the *Kunsturhebergesetz* (KUG)[261] of 1907 broadly and applied it to legal wrongs we might more conveniently label infringements of privacy rather than misuse of image.[262] As we will later see, this tendency to over-rely on the KUG continues to this day.[263] The Act itself was, in many ways, an accident of history. In 1898, following Bismarck's

---

[256] Even though it had a section on fundamental rights, the Weimar constitution of 1919 had very little influence on the development of private law. On this point, see Brüggemeier, 'Constitutionalisation of Private Law' (2006) p 61.

[257] RGZ 69, 401 (*Nietzsche-Briefe*).

[258] RGZ 69, 401, 403.

[259] RGZ 69, 401, 404.

[260] See for example the so-called *Auskunftei* case, in which a credit agency had made the twenty-year-old police records of the claimant publicly available. The Court held that the agency had infringed a 'moral norm' ('*eine sittliche Norm*'). A person should not have to bear the burden of earlier mistakes for a lifetime. RGZ 115, 416, 417. See also RGZ 72, 175 and RGZ 162, 7. See further Halfmeier, *Die Veröffentlichung privater Tatsachen als unerlaubte Handlung* (2000) pp 51–52.

[261] *Gesetz über das Urheberrecht an Werken der bildenden Künste und der Photographie.*

[262] See for example, KG JW 1928, 363 (*Piscator*).

[263] Götting, 'Geschichte des Persönlichkeitsrechts' (2008) p 34.

death, two photographers unlawfully entered his family home in Friedrichsruh and took a photograph of the corpse of the deceased Chancellor.[264] They later attempted to sell the picture and one enterprising publisher planned to make postcards from it. On discovering these plans, Bismarck's children claimed an injunction against the publisher. The lower court, the *Landgericht Hamburg*, found that there was an injury to the rights of personality of the surviving dependents. The *Reichsgericht*, however, rejected the notion that the personality rights of the children were somehow relevant.[265] The Court could not find anything in German legislation prohibiting the unauthorised taking of photographs and the decision had to be made on the basis of the unlawful entering of the house and the *actio ob iniustam causam* of the *Gemeines Recht* (i.e. the *usus modernus*) in order to allow for restitution of the negatives. Following this decision, the legislator sought to address the perceived gap in the law and eventually enacted the KUG. This Act created a distinction between absolute persons of contemporary history (*absolute Personen der Zeitgeschichte*) and relative persons of contemporary history (*relative Personen der Zeitgeschichte*), which exists to this day. The Act and its considerable impact on German law will be examined in the next chapter.

3.7.2 Totalitarianism and Its Aftermath

Totalitarianism was the other great challenge of late modernity that was to have a profound impact on *German* privacy law. In a totalitarian regime, 'all barriers between private life and public life seem to be broken down.'[266] Private life must continue but people are forced to 'extreme situations.'[267] For this reason, as Vincent argues, '[p]aradoxical as it may seem, it may be that private life, understood in the very narrow sense of a secret existence, reaches its highest pinnacle of development under totalitarian regimes.'[268] This is because 'every citizen lives a double life',[269] leading Sartre to provocatively declare: 'we were never so free as under the German occupation.'[270]

How did the Nazis understand privacy? Larenz's infamous definition of legal capacity sums up the 'legal reasoning' of the Nazi period:

---

[264] Brüggemeier, *Haftungsrecht* (2006) p 297 *et seq.*

[265] RG, 28.12.1899, RGZ 45, 170 (*Bismarck*).

[266] Vincent, 'The Secrets of History and the Riddle of Identity' (1991) p 147.

[267] *Ibid* at 147.

[268] *Ibid* at 147–148.

[269] *Ibid* at 148.

[270] *Ibid.*

'Rechtsgenosse ist nur, wer Volksgenosse ist; Volksgenosse ist, wer deutschen Blutes ist. . . . Wer außerhalb der Volksgemeinschaft steht, steht auch nicht im Recht, ist nicht Rechtgenosse'.[271]

'Everyone who is a *Volksgenosse* is a legally privileged person: A *Volksgenosse* is a person who has German blood. . . Whoever is outside the *Volksgemeinschaft* does not have standing in law and is not a legally privileged person.'

The Nazis rejected the notion of a universal natural law but also departed from the subjective economic rights of the BGB, attempting to replace it with a People's Code (*Volksgesetzbuch*).[272] The drafters of this code proposed that those of 'German lineage' (*Volksgenossen*) should be entitled to a legally protected 'private life':

'Wird das berechtigte Interesse eines Volksgenossen am Schutz seiner private Lebensführung dadurch verletzt, dass ein Unberufener Tatsachen seines Privatlebens an die Öffentlichkeit bringt, so kann der Betroffene auf Unterlassung und bei Verschulden auf Schadensersatz klagen (s 22 (1)(1), Buch 1 'Der Volksgenosse')'

'If a *Volksgenosse*'s legitimate interests in the protection of his private life are infringed in such a way that the offending party puts private facts into the public domain, the affected party can sue for an injunction or, in the case of fault, damages.'

Of course, it is absurd to talk of a meaningful right of privacy in a totalitarian state—one wonders how this was supposed to be reconciled with the *Blockleiter* system[273]—but this provision is significant in that it is the first mention of privacy in a German code, albeit a draft code. At the same time, the *Volksgesetzbuch* draft proposed that:

'Jeder Rechtsgenosse genießt Schutz gegen Verletzungen seiner Rechtsstellung. Er wird geschützt gegen Angriffe auf Ehre, Freiheit und Arbeitskraft, auf Leben und Gesundheit, auf sein Eigentum und seine Stellung im Wirtschaftsleben.'[274]

'Every *Rechtsgenosse* enjoys protection against injuries to his legal status. He is protected against infringements of his honour, freedom and his ability to work, his life and health, his property and his position in business life.'

Whitman argues that there is an 'uncomfortable paradox' here.[275] There are of course, he claims, 'prominent aspects' of our modern law of dignity, which can be understood as a reaction to the horrors of the fascist-era, but the 'unpalatable truth' is that other aspects rest on practices during the Nazi period.[276] He contends that the Nazis contributed to a 'leveling up' of honour in the sense that everyone of German blood was 'equal in honour', no matter what their position in society.[277] As we have

---

[271] Larenz, *Grundfragen der neuen Rechtswissenschaft* (1935) p 241.

[272] Brüggemeier, *Haftungsrecht* (2006) p 267.

[273] These were community informants, usually low-ranking Nazi officials. See Bajohr, 'The "Folk Community" and the Persecution of the Jews' (2006).

[274] *Volksgesetzbuch*, § 4, First Book.

[275] Whitman, 'The Two Western Cultures of Privacy' (2004) at 1166.

[276] Whitman, 'On Nazi "Honour" and the New European "Dignity"' (2003) p 244.

[277] Whitman, 'The Two Western Cultures of Privacy' (2004) at 1187.

seen, throughout the eighteenth and early nineteenth centuries, only aristocrats and other prominent members of society could bring a legal action on the basis of injury to personality interests. But Frevert shows that the 'levelling up' was already underway in the late nineteenth century—the practice of duelling, once confined to the aristocracy, became commonplace amongst the bourgeoisie.[278] Whitman contends that this long process of German social change culminated with the 'Nazi notion that everyone was "satisfaktionsfähig," was honourable enough to engage in a duel.'[279] In this way, he argues, Nazi law 'directly prefigured' the law of post-war Germany.[280]

Whitman's insights are profoundly important, for if he is correct, the process of levelling-up that began in England and France centuries earlier, occurred much later in Germany. It is against this background that we must consider the relatively rapid development of a general personality right in the post-war period, which was, at the same time, a reaction to the sheer despair and hopelessness of the 1940s. Brüggemeier aptly writes that the 'new democratic beginning of 1949 was every bit as clear, decisive and dramatic as the end of the (...) Third Reich.'[281] The *Grundgesetz* (GG) contained a catalogue of fundamental rights (Articles 1–19). For our purposes, Article 1(1) and 2(1) are the most significant as they are understood to constitute the basis for the general personality right. Article 1(1) states:

'Die Würde des Menschen ist unantastbar. Sie zu achten und zu schützen ist Verpflichtung aller staatlichen Gewalt.'	'Human dignity is inviolable. All state authorities are under a duty to respect and protect it.'

Article 2(1) refers to the free development of personality:

'Jeder hat das Recht auf die freie Entfaltung seiner Persönlichkeit, soweit er nicht die Rechte anderer verletzt und nicht gegen die verfassungsmäßige Ordnung oder das Sittengesetz verstößt.'	'Everyone has the right to free development of his personality, insofar as he does not infringe the rights of others or offends against the constitutional order or moral law (*Sittengesetz*).'

Common law readers might be surprised to learn that the courts rather than the legislature ensured the necessary legal conditions for a general personality right in tort law.[282] The turning point was the momentous *Schacht/Leserbrief* decision of the Federal Court of Justice in 1954.[283] Dr Hjalmar Schacht was the president of the *Reichsbank* until 1939 and acted as a minister for the economy under Adolf Hitler.

[278] Frevert, *Ehrenmänner* (1991) pp 256–263 cited by Whitman, 'On Nazi "Honour" and the New European "Dignity"' (2003) p 247.

[279] Whitman, 'On Nazi "Honour" and the New European "Dignity"' (2003) p 247.

[280] Whitman, 'The Two Western Cultures of Privacy' (2004) p 1188.

[281] Brüggemeier, 'Constitutionalisation of Private Law' (2006) p 62.

[282] Brüggemeier, *Haftungsrecht* (2006) pp 268–270.

[283] BGHZ 13, 334 = NJW 1954, 1404 (*Schacht – Leserbrief*).

In 1952, a newspaper published an article entitled '*Dr. H.S. & Co: Politische Betrachtung anläßlich der Gründung des neuen Bankhauses*', a critical account of Dr Schacht's new business dealings. Dr Schacht asked his lawyer, the claimant, to write a letter of complaint to the newspaper to rectify what he saw as glaring inaccuracies in the article. The newspaper failed to reply to the lawyer but published his letter as a *Leserbrief* (letter to the editor) alongside other letters from readers expressing opinions about the article in question. The lawyer sued the newspaper demanding that they correct the facts in their next edition. He argued that there was no doubt about the nature of this letter: that it was not an expression of personal opinion but a complaint on behalf of his client. The publication of the letter gave the false impression that the lawyer was a political sympathiser of Mr Schacht.

The Federal Court of Justice found that the Court of Appeal (*Hanseatisches Oberlandesgericht*) erred in failing to examine whether the plaintiff's claim could be justified on the basis of an infringement of his personality rights.[284] The Court accepted that the *Reichsgericht* had not extended the protection of personality (independent of copyright) to correspondence because the German legal order of the time did not have any positive statutory provisions encompassing a general personality right. The key paragraph of the judgment follows:

'Nachdem nunmehr das Grundgesetz das Recht des Menschen auf Achtung seiner Würde (Article 1 GrundG) und das Recht auf freie Entfaltung seiner Persönlichkeit auch als privates, von jedermann zu achtendes Recht anerkennt, soweit dieses Recht nicht die Rechte anderer verletzt oder gegen die verfassungsmäßige Ordnung oder das Sittengesetz verstößt (Article 2 GrundG), muß das allgemeine Persönlichkeitsrecht als ein verfassungsmäßig gewährleistetes Grundrecht angesehen werden.'[285]	'Now that the Grundgesetz recognises the right of an individual to have his dignity respected (Article 1 GG) and his right to free development of his personality to be regarded as a private, universally respected right as long as this right does not infringe the rights of others or the constitutional or moral order (Article 2 GG), the general personality right must be regarded as a constitutionally guaranteed fundamental right.'

Brüggemeier argues that this was a 'revolutionary statement' as, apart from referring to von Gierke and Kohler, the Court did not explain why a constitutionally guaranteed fundamental right should have effect in private law.[286] He goes on to suggest that the Court was 'not bothered by methodological questions; but they knew exactly what they were doing in substance, and moreover what they wanted to do.'[287] On his account, technical questions about whether this decision was an example of direct or indirect horizontal effect of fundamental rights were left to legal scholars. The decision is extremely significant in that not only did it signify

[284] BGHZ 13, 334, 341.

[285] BGHZ 13, 334, 338.

[286] Brüggemeier, 'Constitutionalisation of Private Law' (2006) p 64.

[287] *Ibid* p 66.

the birth of *Drittwirkung* in German law, it also introduced a general personality right, along the same lines as von Gierke's model.[288] In 1957, the Federal Court of Justice provided a dogmatic framework deciding that the general personality right was to be regarded as 'another right' ('*sonstiges Recht*') within the meaning of § 823 I BGB.[289]

The Federal Court took another controversial step a few years later in the so-called *Herrenreiter* case.[290] As noted earlier, according to §§ 823 I, 847 and 253 BGB, claimants were only entitled to sue for pecuniary loss. An injury to personality rights, however, will invariably cause non-pecuniary harm (the issue did not arise in the *Schacht/Leserbrief* case as the claimant did not seek damages). This problem came to the fore in *Herrenreiter* where the claimant, a brewery owner and 'gentleman show-jumper' sued the defendant company for using his image without his permission. The company was a manufacturer of sexual potency drugs and had used a picture of the claimant, while show-jumping, on a poster advertising its products. In a somewhat muddled judgment, the Appeal Court (*Oberlandesgericht Köln*) held that there was no pecuniary loss but simultaneously attempted to award damages on the basis of a fictitious licence fee. Deciding for the claimant, the Federal Court of Justice stated that he found himself humiliated and ridiculed by the poster and in such a situation it would be 'absurd' ('*sinnwidrig*') to award damages on the basis of a fictitious licence fee. The Court went on to say:

'In Wahrheit verlangt er nicht Ersatz eines gar nicht vorhandenen Vermögensschadens, sondern begehrt eine fühlbare Genugtuung für einen widerrechtlichen Eingriff in seine durch § 22 KunstUrhG, Article 1 und 2 Grundgesetz geschützte Persönlichkeitssphäre.'[291]	'In reality, he does not claim compensation for a non-existent economic loss, but a tangible satisfaction for an unlawful infringement of his personality, as protected by § 22 KunstUrhG and Article 1 and 2 of the Grundgesetz.'

Referring to *Schacht/Leserbrief*, the Court went on to reiterate the central importance of human dignity and the right to freely develop one's personality in the *Grundgesetz*. The unauthorised publication of a portrait affects the individual's personality in that he is deprived of the freedom to dispose of this interest in a way he chooses. The Court then had to ascertain how non-pecuniary harm for injury to personality interests could be compensated under § 847 BGB. That provision allows equitable compensation in money for non-pecuniary harm where there is pain and suffering or a 'deprivation of liberty' ('*Freiheitsentziehung*'). Even though this provision clearly refers to freedom of bodily movement, the Court stated that it saw no reason why the provision should not encompass 'intellectual liberty'. In a key passage, the Court reasoned:

---

[288] On *Drittwirkung*, see generally Beckmann *et al*, 'Germany' (2010).

[289] BGHZ 24, 72 (*Persönlichkeitsrecht*).

[290] BGHZ 26, 349 = NJW 1959, 479 (*Herrenreiter*).

[291] BGHZ 26, 349, 353.

'. . . so ist kein sachlicher Grund ersichtlich, der es hindern könnte, die in § 847 BGB getroffene Regelung im Wege der Analogie auch auf solche Eingriffe zu erstrecken, die das Recht der freien Willensbetätigung verletzen, zumal auch bei dieser Freiheitsberaubung "im Geistigen" in gleicher Weise wie bei der körperlichen Freiheitsberaubung in der Regel eine Naturalherstellung ausgeschlossen ist.'[292]

'. . .there is no objective reason as to why § 847 BGB should not be extended by analogy to such infringements that injure the right to free exercise of the will, especially where a natural restitution in respect of the deprivation of "intellectual" freedom is impossible, just as it would be with deprivation of bodily freedom.'

Brüggemeier emphasises that the Court was at pains to use the 'verbal crutch of a "deprivation of intellectual liberty" in order to underline the analogy with an infringement of the freedom of bodily movement.'[293] The obvious implication was that this was judicial law making *contra legum*. But despite the protests of some commentators, such as Larenz,[294] following *Herrenreiter*, it has become the norm for courts to award damages for non-pecuniary harm to personality rights where the harm is objectively serious. A couple of years after the decision in *Herrenreiter*, the Federal Court of Justice held that injunctive relief under § 1004 BGB was possible in cases where personality rights were at stake.[295] Eventually, in 1973, the Constitutional Court confirmed that this line of case law was constitutional in the so-called *Soraya* case,[296] insisting that the Constitution does not limit judges to a literal interpretation of statutes but rather judges can 'discover' the law emanating from the constitutional order where the interests of justice require them to do so.[297] However, the precise methodological approach for awarding damages for non-pecuniary harm to personality rights remained unsettled until 1994, when the Federal Court of Justice affirmed that compensation for infringements to the general right of personality is not a matter of compensation for pain and suffering under § 847 BGB, but is a remedy directly based on Articles 1(1) and 2(1) GG.[298]

[292] BGHZ 26, 349, 356 (*Herrenreiter*).

[293] Brüggemeier, 'Constitutionalisation of Private Law' (2006) p 67.

[294] See Larenz's critical note on the decision NJW 1958, 571.

[295] BGHZ 30, 7 = NJW 1959, 1269 (*C Valente*).

[296] BVerfGE 34, 269 = NJW 1973, 1221 (*Soraya*).

[297] BVerfGE 34, 269, 287.

[298] BGHZ, 128, 1 = NJW 1995, 861 = JZ 1995, 360 m Anm Schlechtriem (*Caroline von Monaco I*). On this point, see Brüggemeier, 'Constitutionalisation of Private Law' (2006) pp 67–68.

The *allgemeine Persönlichkeitsrecht* thus became an established part of German law.[299]

The experiences of Second World War were also to influence *English* law, albeit indirectly in the form of the ECHR. The ECHR was ratified by the UK in 1951 and the individual right of petition was recognised in 1966. The UK has a dualist system and as such the ECHR did not have any legal effect in the domestic setting until it was incorporated by an Act of Parliament.[300] The HRA came into force in 2000 and courts accepted that the Act fundamentally changed the legal relationship between the citizen and the state.[301] Given this context, just before the introduction of the Human Rights Act, Lord Irvine confidently declared that the judiciary was 'pen-poised' to develop a right of privacy in the common law.[302] We will discover in the next chapter whether he was right.

3.8 Conclusions

I have sought in this chapter to show that the history of privacy is one of a relatively steep inclining curve. As civilisation advanced, the 'split' between public and private spheres, between public and private behaviour became more apparent. Elias explains that this 'split is taken so much for granted, becomes so compulsive a habit, that it is hardly perceived in consciousness.'[303] Understood in this way, the expectation of having an individual private sphere becomes imprinted in the minds of children and so, with each generation, the privacy curve steepens. This is a

[299] The general personality right is a *Kombinationsgrundrecht* (Höfling, 'Die Unantastbarkeit der Menschenwürde' (1995) 857, 862) based on the protective remit of Art 2(1) and Art 1(1) GG. On this point, see Vesting 'Einführung' (2008) at 101–120. We must distinguish, however, between the constitutional and private law right. As a constitutional right it is considered an '*unbenanntes Freiheitsrecht*' (BVerfGE 54, 148, 153 (*Eppler*)). Brüggemeier argues that the private law term 'general personality right' is misleading. Use of the term in tort law can be explained by the property right terminology of § 823 I BGB (*sonstiges Recht*) but also the constitutional term 'fundamental rights'. However, the general personality right is not a classical *subjektives Ausschließlichkeitsrecht* but an *Autonomierecht*. Brüggemeier describes it as an expression for the *Achtungsanspruch der Person*, representing a range of legally protected interests. See Brüggemeier, *Haftungsrecht* (2006) p 270.

[300] However, we must note that even before the HRA came into force the ECHR indirectly influenced English law in cases where the ECtHR held that the UK was in violation of the Convention. It was also open to counsel to use the ECHR before an English court but open to the court, at the same time, to reject such arguments. The most prominent example of the impact of the ECHR was the defamation case of *Sunday Times* v *United Kingdom (No 1)* (1980) 2 EHRR 245, which led to the reform of the law of contempt by the Contempt of Court Act 1981.

[301] *Thoburn* v *Sunderland City Council* (2003) QB 151 . See also *R* v *Ofen* [2001] 2 All ER 154; *McCartan Turkington Breen* v *Times Newspapers Ltd* [2001] 2 AC 1805. For further discussion, see Bamforth, 'Parliamentary Sovereignty and the Human Rights Act 1998' [1998].

[302] HL Deb 24 November 1997, vol 583, col 784.

[303] *Ibid* p 160.

process of 'sociogenetic' change. In this way, according to Elias, there is a 'continuous correspondence between the social structure and the structure of the personality, of the individual self'.[304]

Contemporary understandings of privacy, then, are the product of a gradual and on-going process of socio-genetic change that has manifested itself over millennia. This is our shared experience of privacy. Among other things, this chapter provides support for my argument that the three conjectures about privacy outlined in Chap. 2 go some way towards elaborating its content.

The idea of privacy being an essential constituent of *personality* has its roots in late scholastic thinking on the conceptual relationship between personal dignity and the Roman action of *iniuria*. But the social and political change of the seventeenth and eighteenth centuries inspired the natural lawyers to write about legal duties to respect individual dignity and these writings were eventually to inform the drafting of the major European civil codes. Throughout this chapter, we have encountered references to an understanding of privacy as *property*. We find examples in the early Germanic laws of the privacy of private property but even as late in the nineteenth century both English and German courts remained hesitant to award damages for 'injured feelings' and sought instead to base their decisions on 'interference with property' analogies. The relationship between the individual and the *community* is another recurring theme in the privacy curve. In ancient Rome, whether one possessed *dignitas* or not was entirely dependent on one's participation in the *bios politicos*. Much later still, during the Middle Ages, we find that individuals used their wider community of peers (represented by the *homme d'honneur*) as a reference point in assessing the appropriateness of their own behaviour. This way of thinking has had a profound influence on our shared experience of privacy. As we shall see in the next chapter, in invasion of privacy cases, courts continue to use community mores (in the personage of the reasonable person) as a standard in assessing the admissibility of privacy claims.

I have conjectured that there are six inclining gradients in this curve but there may be many more; indeed, these gradients can perhaps be expressed in different ways. But common to all gradients in the privacy curve, howsoever expressed, is the trend of individualisation.

Given this conclusion, some readers might (not unreasonably) question why I imparted the history of privacy interests in this way? Why employ an elaborate privacy curve? Would I not have reached a similar conclusion about individualism had I simply traced the concept of privacy and adopted a standard historical narrative about the influence of Enlightenment thinkers?

I would respond to this criticism with a further reference to geometry. In theoretical physics, an invariant is a 'reality that does not change in going from one representation to the other'.[305] As Vignale explains, a square always remains a

---

[304] *Ibid* p 160. This chimes with the Hegelian idea, explored in the last chapter, of the agent's simultaneous independence and dependence on society; in other words, the 'I' that is 'We' and the 'We' that is 'I'.

[305] Vignale, *The Beautiful Invisible* (2011) p 108.

square regardless of where it is put or how it is turned.' It may well be that distances and angles seem different, however spatial relations 'between different parts of the object' are still perceived by us as constant.'[306] In geometry and physics, then, 'different representations are equivalent'. Understood in this way, the historical *fact* of individualisation will emerge from any serious historical study; it is so obvious that it cannot possibly be overlooked.

I chose not to adopt a standard historical narrative because my study is based on a method of refinement rather than passive observation. In physics, while different representations are equivalent in theory (once we accept the existence of invariants), they are 'not all equivalent when it comes to their practical or psychological value.' Vignale explains that:

> [f]acts that are hard to see in one representation may become manifest in another. Complex calculations often simplify dramatically when approached from the right angle. And, most importantly, different representations stimulate our imagination in different ways, producing vastly different results.[307]

Our privacy curve has provided us with insights that we would have overlooked, I think, had we adopted a standard historical narrative of individualisation. In particular, what has emerged from this chapter is that one's social rank was profoundly important in pre-modern societies and determined the extent to which one possessed legal interests in personality—consider, for example, the *scandalum magnatum*. In many ways, the history of privacy is a history of levelling-up of rank. Understood in this way, a commitment to egalitarianism (the idea that every person is of equal rank by virtue of their humanity) forms an important part of our shared experience of privacy. We shall revisit this argument in the final chapter. But for now we must carefully consider the contemporary legal context.

---

[306] *Ibid* p 109.

[307] *Ibid* p 113.

Chapter 4
Comparing Hard Cases

Nothing indeed could be less trustworthy for acquiring knowledge and approaching truth than passive observation or mere contemplation. In order to be certain one [has] to make sure, and in order to know one [has] to do.
- Hannah Arendt

4.1 Introduction

We have come to value privacy through a process of socio-genetic change. Privacy is an essential constituent of the human personality, property and the community. Normative agency and all that we know and cherish is not possible without it. Respect for privacy is therefore crucial in a liberal democracy and it follows that privacy warrants legal protection.

The aim of this chapter is to test the methods of legal protection. In Chap. 1 I argued that we create sufficiently stringent tests (in Popper's terms) by selecting 'special cases'. My objective here is to select hard cases from English law and hypothesise how these cases might be decided by German courts.[1] By 'hard cases', I simply mean cases for which there are no easy answers or, as Dworkin puts it, 'when no settled rule dictates a decision either way'.[2] Privacy law is full of such cases. This is because interests in privacy often clash with interests in freedom of expression, resulting in 'tragic choices' for courts.[3] In each of the hard cases that follow, the claimant is a celebrity or a 'public person'. This was not a deliberate choice on my part; almost without exception, the claimants in English privacy cases

[1] For a similar approach to comparative study, see Markesinis et al, *Tortious Liability of Statutory Bodies* (1999).

[2] Dworkin, 'Hard Cases' (1975) at 1060.

[3] Alder, 'Dissents in Courts of Last Resort' (2000) at 224.

DOI 10.1007/978-3-642-31884-9_4, © Springer-Verlag Berlin Heidelberg 2013

are public figures. I will argue in the next chapter that this is a consequence of English lawyer's narrow understanding of privacy.

In testing these hard cases, we will gain instructive insights about both English and German law and we will be better placed to identify gaps in protection. This analysis will also provide grounds for arguing that the German civil law on invasion of privacy is more principled and adheres to the regulative ideals of justice and the rule of law. But before we test our hard cases, we must first briefly consider the current standing of English law.

4.2 Privacy in English Tort Law

Privacy interests can and often do find protection in other branches of English law. So, for example, aggrieved individuals can sometimes rely on statutes such as the Data Protection Act (1998) and the Protection from Harassment Act (1997) where they have certain privacy-related grievances.[4] Importantly, since the introduction of the Human Rights Act, it is possible to take an action against the State or a public authority for invasion of privacy. As we have seen, what is lacking, however, is a general privacy action in tort law.

Courts have responded in some part to this problem and have afforded indirect horizontal effect to Article 8 ECHR in a limited range of circumstances.[5] Giving effect in private law to an international human rights treaty is not uncontroversial, but courts have accepted the need to do so because: 'the values enshrined in Articles 8 and 10... are as much applicable in disputes between individuals or between an individual and a non-governmental body such as a newspaper as they are in disputes

[4] The Data Protection Act allows the individual to 'control' the personal data stored in databases though is generally not used as a cause of action for invasion of privacy claims in tort. *Campbell* v *MGN Ltd* [2004] 2 AC 457 is an exception but the data protection claim was not explored by the House of Lords. The Protection from Harassment Act provides for a civil remedy of an injunction in cases of criminal harassment. Scott details some successful actions for injunctions under the Act. In each case, the claimant was a public figure who had been harassed by 'persistent pursuit'. See Scott, 'Harassment' (2010) p 791.

[5] While Article 8 ECHR, as originally conceived, enjoys *vertical* effect, courts and commentators have agreed that states also have a positive obligation to take measures to ensure that the right of an individual under Article 8 is not infringed by another *private* party. See *X and Y* v *Netherlands* (1985) 8 EHRR 235; *A* v *United Kingdom* (1998) 27 EHRR 611, *MC* v *Bulgaria* (2005) 40 EHRR 20, *Pla and Puncernau* v *Andorra* (2006) 42 ECHR 25, *von Hannover* v *Germany* (2005) 40 EHRR 1. See also Clapham, *Human Rights Obligations of Non-State Actors* (2006) pp 349–352. Indirect horizontal effect in this context means the use of existing causes of action or equitable doctrines in order to give effect to ECHR rights. English courts have found it easier to defend this sort of incremental development. On their account, they 'will not invent a new cause of action to cover types of activity which were not previously covered.' See *Campbell* v *MGN Ltd* [2004] 2 AC 457 at 495 (per Baroness Hale).

between individuals and a public authority.'[6] On this basis, English courts have cautiously expanded the equitable doctrine of breach of confidence to cater for one particular type of invasion of privacy: misuse of private information.[7] These developments, described by one commentator as a 'pantomime',[8] have been well-documented elsewhere.[9] Breach of confidence, as relied upon in unauthorised disclosure of personal information claims, has evolved from the *Coco* v *Clark*[10] doctrine and can now be described as a tort of invasion of informational privacy or a tort of misuse of private information.[11]

If we are to test this method of legal protection, it is worth paying close attention to the new tort's decision procedure. The first step is to establish whether there is a reasonable expectation of privacy. This finds its origins in Baroness Hale's speech in *Campbell* where she stated, 'the exercise of balancing Article 8 and Article 10 may begin when the person publishing the information knows or ought to know that there is a reasonable expectation that the information in question will be kept confidential.'[12] Of course, the claimant will generally have a (subjective) expectation of privacy (hence the reason for the claim) but reasonableness acts as an 'objective check'.[13] Understood in this way, the first step acts as a 'gateway test'[14] and it does not take into account those 'considerations which should more properly be considered at the later stage of proportionality.'[15]

In *Campbell* and subsequent cases, once the *prima facie* invasion of privacy was established, courts proceeded to define the scope of privacy interests. In other words, the courts attempted to establish whether there were any 'limiting principles'. A close inspection of recent authorities reveals that the courts have identified at least four such principles. We should emphasise that these are *limiting* principles—the presence of one or all does not automatically *exclude* a claim. Much will depend, of course, on the individual facts but the presence of these limiting

---

[6] *Campbell* v *MGN Ltd* [2004] 2 AC 457 at 465 (per Lord Nicholls).

[7] The *Coco* v *Clark* doctrine continues to apply to photographs with commercial value: see *OBG Ltd* v *Allan* [2008] 1 AC 1.

[8] Morgan, 'Hello! Again' (2005) at 550.

[9] See, for example, Morgan, 'Privacy, Confidence and Horizontal Effect' (2003); Phillipson, 'Transforming Breach of Confidence?' (2003); Moreham, 'Privacy in the Common Law' (2005); Sims, 'A Shift in the Centre of Gravity' [2005]; Mulheron, 'A Potential Framework for Privacy?' (2006); Aplin, 'The Development of the Action for Breach of Confidence in the Post-HRA Era' [2007]; Witzleb, 'Monetary Remedies for Breach of Confidence in Privacy Cases' (2007).

[10] *Coco* v *Clark* [1969] RPC 41.

[11] Lord Nicholls refers to the equitable doctrine as a tort in *Campbell*: 'The essence of the tort is better encapsulated now as misuse of private information'. See *Campbell* v *MGN Ltd* [2004] 2 AC 457 at 465 (per Lord Nicholls).

[12] *Ibid* at 495 (per Baroness Hale).

[13] *Ibid.*

[14] Scott, 'Introduction' (2010) at 18.21.

[15] *Campbell* v *MGN Ltd* [2004] 2 AC 457 at 466 (per Lord Nicholls).

principles will (generally) make it more difficult for the claimant to sustain an action.

The first limitation concerns information that is already in the public domain. As a matter of principle, how can we label information 'private' if it is already 'generally accessible'?[16] Lord Goff in *Spycatcher* indicated that 'as a general rule, the principle of confidentiality can have no application to [such information]'.[17] We arrive at the second limiting principle through a similar process of reasoning. If an individual consents to an invasion of privacy, how do we justify a subsequent claim on the basis of that same infringement?[18] I suspect that this reflects the popular view on privacy and personal responsibility but it also gives expression to a principle that is 'deeply embedded in the history of tort law'.[19] Zimmerman reminds us that the existence of consent has 'traditionally negated the existence of a whole range of intentional torts.'[20] On her account, the 'idea that one cannot both consent (or appear to do so) and then complain about the consequences reflects traditional, deeply-held notions both of personal responsibility and of respect for individual autonomy.'[21] The third limiting principle is what we might call a *de minimus* threshold. What is clear from *A-G* v *Guardian Newspapers Ltd (No 2)* is that a duty of confidence does not apply to 'useless information' or 'trivia'.[22] Finally and perhaps most significantly, we encounter a limiting principle concerning the public interest (as opposed to what the public finds interesting). As we will see, in such cases, courts are required to engage in what is now known as the 'ultimate balancing exercise'. In other words, once a reasonable expectation of privacy has been established, the court will move on to employ the 'new methodology' in deciding the case before it. This has been summarised by Lord Steyn in *In re S (A Child)*[23]:

i) First, neither article [Article 8 nor Article 10] has *as such* precedence over the other.
ii) Secondly, where the values under the two articles are in conflict, an intense focus on the comparative importance of the specific rights being claimed in the individual case is necessary.

---

[16] *Attorney General* v *Observer Ltd* [1990] 1 AC 109 at 282B-F.

[17] *Ibid.*

[18] On consent see *A* v *B and C* (2 March 2001, unreported). On the question of capacity, see *T* v *BBC* [2008] 1 FLR 281 in which a documentary was made about intimate details of a vulnerable adult's life. The Court found that the individual did not have capacity to give consent to her participation in the documentary. See Scott, 'Misuse of Private Information' (2010) at 19.74.

[19] Zimmerman, 'The "New" Privacy and the "Old"' (2012) at 125.

[20] *Ibid.*

[21] *Ibid.*

[22] *Attorney General* v *Observer Ltd* [1990] 1 AC 109 at 148 (per Lord Goff). Though, as Eady J held in *McKennitt*: 'the mere fact that information concerning an individual is "anodyne" or "trivial" will not necessarily mean that Article 8 is not engaged.' On his account, it depends on the circumstances of the case in question. See *McKennitt* v *Ash* [2006] EMLR 10 at para 58 (per Eady J).

[23] *In re S (A Child)* [2005] 1 AC 593 at 603 (per Lord Steyn).

iii) Thirdly, the justifications for interfering with, or restricting, each right must be taken into account.
iv) Finally, the proportionality test must be applied to each.

As to the third aspect of the methodology, one can only interfere with or restrict these rights when three conditions are fulfilled. Baroness Hale's dictum in *Campbell* has been widely cited and is as follows[24]:

i) The interference or restriction must be "in accordance with the law"; it must have a basis in national law which conforms to the Convention standards of legality.
ii) It must pursue one of the legitimate aims set out in each article. Article 8 (2) provides for the "protection of the rights and freedoms of others". Article 10 (2) provides for the 'protection of the reputation or rights of others' and for "preventing the disclosure of information received in confidence". The rights referred to may either be rights protected under the national law or other Convention rights.
iii) Above all, the interference or restriction must be "necessary in a democratic society"; it must meet a "pressing social need" and be no greater than is proportionate to the legitimate aim pursued; the reasons given for it must be both "relevant" and "sufficient" for this purpose.

What has emerged from recent balancing exercises is that when courts have regard to freedom of expression they must evaluate how the defendant has used or intends to use her right to freedom of expression.[25] According to Baroness Hale in *Campbell*, we must pay close attention to the 'nature' of the freedom of expression at stake. She went on:

> There are undoubtedly different types of speech, just as there are different types of private information, some of which are more deserving of protection in a democratic society than others. Top of the list is political speech. The free exchange of information and ideas on matters relevant to the organisation of the economic, social and political life of the country is crucial to any democracy. Without this, it can scarcely be called a democracy at all. This includes revealing information about public figures, especially those in elective office, which would otherwise be private but is relevant to their participation in public life. Intellectual and educational speech and expression are also important in a democracy, not least because they enable the development of individuals' potential to play a full part in society and in our democratic life. Artistic speech and expression is important for similar reasons, in fostering both individual originality and creativity and the free-thinking and dynamic society we so much value. No doubt there are other kinds of speech and expression for which similar claims can be made.[26]

Understood in these terms, 'political speech' may have a higher value than mere 'tittle tattle'.[27] But this does not mean that lower-order speech is valueless or, to put it differently, there is 'nothing to justify interfering with it'.[28]

[24] *Campbell* v *MGN Ltd* [2004] 2 AC 457 at 497.

[25] *Mosley* v *News Group Newspapers Ltd* [2008] EMLR 20 at 689.

[26] *Campbell* v *MGN Ltd* [2004] 2 AC 457 at 499 (per Baroness Hale).

[27] *Jameel* v *Wall Street Journal Europe SRPL (No 3)* [2007] 1 AC 359 at 408 (per Baroness Hale).

[28] *Campbell* v *MGN Ltd* [2004] 2 AC 457 at 501 (per Baroness Hale). For an interesting comparison, see also the New Zealand case of *Hosking* v *Runting* [2003] 3 NZLR 385.

We find in English law, then, a relatively clear decision procedure for misuse of private information claims. While this procedure is shaped by common law thinking (hence the references to standards of reasonableness), the direct references to the provisions of the ECHR and proportionality demonstrate the Strasbourg influences. While the decision procedure appears neat and concise, in what follows, I argue that that it is based on unsound doctrinal foundations.

4.2.1 The Unsound Doctrinal Foundations of the 'Privacy Tort'

What is particularly striking about English misuse of private information cases is the increasing frequency of references to the ECHR and the decisions of the ECtHR in the balancing process. Given this context, it is important to consider the scope of Article 8 ECHR.

Some argue that Article 8 calls for a narrow interpretation and refers only to privacy interests and respect for the home. Robertson and Nicol make this point in reference to the original debates and drafting of Article 8 in 1951, when the drafters decided to omit the right to honour and reputation from the scope of the Convention because honour was 'too amorphous (and Napoleonic) a concept'.[29] At the same time, the drafters did not view reputation as a free-standing right rather a 'subsidiary right' found in Article 10 (2), where a restriction may be necessary 'for the protection of the reputation or rights of others.' However, in recent years, the ECtHR has interpreted Article 8 broadly. One example is *von Hannover* v *Germany (No 1)*,[30] in which photographs taken of Princess Caroline of Monaco in public places and in 'scenes from her daily life' were published in the German press. As we will see later in this chapter, Princess Caroline brought a series of actions before the German courts. She was unsuccessful in some of these actions and contended that the decisions of the German courts infringed her Article 8 right to respect for her private and family life. The ECtHR agreed and stated that one of the most important factors when assessing the public interest in such private information was whether the person in question exercised an 'official function'. If so, taking into account the 'watchdog function of the press', there may be a public interest in private information which is of direct relevance to this particular function and, thus, an appropriate contribution to a 'debate of general interest.' In describing private life,[31] the Court stated:

> [P]rivate life, in the Court's view, includes a person's physical and psychological integrity; the guarantee afforded by Article 8 of the Convention is primarily intended to ensure the

[29] Robertson & Nicol, *Media Law* (2007) p 67.

[30] *von Hannover* v *Germany (No 1)* (2005) 40 EHRR 1.

[31] I again use the verb 'to define' very cautiously here given that the ECtHR has, in the past, stated that it 'does not consider it possible or necessary to attempt an exhaustive definition of the notion of "private life".' See *Niemetz* v *Germany* (1992) 16 EHRR 97, at para 29.

> development, without outside interference, of the personality of each individual in his relations with other human beings ... There is therefore a zone of interaction of a person with others, even in a public context, which may fall within the scope of private life.[32]

The Court, here, takes a very broad view of what falls under Article 8 and seems to equate private life with personality generally. Article 8, we are told, is primarily concerned with the free development of personality. Robertson and Nicol have criticised the Court for its 'unprincipled and unprecedented frolics' in including free development of personality under Article 8.[33] Kay points out that there are only a handful of 'grievances' that would not fall under a 'claim of interference' with personality.[34] He further states that if this were to apply in private law, then 'we could, effectively have a situation where the Convention obliges every person to respect every other person's "physical and psychological integrity" – except when, all things considered, it is better not to do so.'[35]

Since *von Hannover (No 1)*, we have seen a marked increase in 'Strasbourg speak' in English decisions. In *Douglas (No 3)*, for instance, the Court of Appeal indicated that the decision in *von Hannover (No 1)* signifies that states are required to provide a privacy remedy against private actors.[36] For this reason, the Court admitted that its earlier decision of November 2000 to lift the injunction against Hello magazine was wrong. This is because it:

> did not have the benefit of the reasoning in the House of Lords in *Campbell* v *MGN* or, even more significantly for present purposes, the reasoning of the ECtHR in *von Hannover (No. 1)* v *Germany*. Had the court had the opportunity to consider those two decisions, we believe it would have reached the conclusion that the Douglases appeared to have a virtually unanswerable case for contending that publication of the unauthorised photographs would infringe their privacy.[37]

The reasoning of the Court of Appeal is a clear signal that the decision of the ECtHR in *von Hannover (No 1)* has had and will continue to have implications for the development of privacy law in England. This is evident in more recent privacy cases including *McKennitt*, *HRH The Prince of Wales*[38] and *Mosley*. In these cases, the High Court emphasised the importance for UK courts of taking the decision in *von Hannover (No 1)* into account, particularly the considerations that a public figure is entitled to a private life and that the protection of private life '...extends

---

[32] *Ibid*, para 50.

[33] Robertson & Nicol, *Media Law* (2007) p 70.

[34] Kay, 'The European Convention on Human Rights and the Control of Private Law' (2005) at 477.

[35] *Ibid* at 477.

[36] According to Lord Phillips: 'the ECtHR has recognised an obligation on member states to protect one individual from an unjustified invasion of private life by another individual and an obligation on the courts of a member state to interpret legislation in a way which will achieve that result.' *Douglas* v *Hello (No 3)* [2006] QB 125 at 149 (per Lord Phillips MR).

[37] *Ibid* at 201.

[38] *HRH Prince of Wales* v *Associated Newspapers Ltd* [2008] Ch 57.

beyond the private family circle and also includes a social dimension.'[39] Two points about the influence of *von Hannover (No 1)* are of particular note. First, it appears that English courts consider the publication of private images to be particularly intrusive. In *Douglas*, the Court of Appeal explained that '[s]pecial considerations attach to photographs in the field of privacy'. This is because:

> [t]hey are not merely a method of conveying information that is an alternative to verbal description. They enable the person viewing the photograph to act as a spectator, in some circumstances voyeur would be the more appropriate noun, of whatever it is that the photograph depicts. As a means of invading privacy, a photograph is particularly intrusive. This is quite apart from the fact that the camera, and the telephoto lens, can give access to the viewer of the photograph to scenes where those photographed could reasonably expect that their appearances or actions would not be brought to the notice of the public.[40]

This is particularly the case when the photographs depict information of an intimate nature[41] or when the images are obtained improperly.[42] The second way in which *von Hannover (No 1)* has influenced English judges is illustrated by remarks in *McKennitt*. In the Court of Appeal, Buxton LJ rejected the arguments that *von Hannover (No 1)* must be applied in cases of media intrusion only.[43] According to him, 'it is not possible to say that the general statements of principle [from *von Hannover (No. 1)*] are so limited'.[44] If we pay close attention to Buxton LJ's remarks at least two interpretations emerge. First, on a more modest level, it may well be that the he has only misuse of private information claims in mind. Understood in this way, the *von Hannover (No 1)* principles also apply to private actors other than the media in cases of invasion of informational privacy. But a second interpretation of the Court's obiter in *McKennitt* is more concerning. This is because the implication is that the *von Hannover (No 1)* principles have a potentially broader remit—that they can be applied to privacy cases generally, including

---

[39] *McKennitt* v *Ash* [2006] EMLR 10 at para 57.

[40] *Douglas* v *Hello* [2006] QB 125 at 157.

[41] See, for example, *Theakston* v *MGN Ltd* [2002] EMLR 398 in which the claimant was pictured outside a brothel. Ouseley J held that he could not prevent the verbal description of the claimant's activities being published but he could enjoin the publication of the photographs. He considered at 401 'that even though the fact that the claimant went to the brothel and the details as to what he did there were not to be restrained from publication, the publication of photographs taken there without his consent could still constitute an intrusion into his private and personal life and would do so in a peculiarly humiliating and damaging way. It did not seem to be remotely inherent in going to a brothel that what was done inside would be photographed, let alone that any photographs would be published.'

[42] In *D* v *L*, Waller LJ explains: 'A court may restrain the publication of an improperly obtained photograph even if the taker is free to describe the information which the photographer provides or even if the information revealed by the photograph is in the public domain. It is no answer to the claim to restrain the publication of an improperly obtained photograph that the information portrayed by the photograph is already available in the public domain.' See *D* v *L* [2004] EMLR 1 at 10 (per Waller LJ).

[43] *McKennitt* v *Ash* [2008] QB 73 at 90.

[44] *Ibid.*

intrusion upon a person's seclusion. If this interpretation is correct, then it indicates that Buxton LJ is not too concerned about the broadly phrased nature of the ECtHR's understanding of privacy.

I imagine most would agree with the ECtHR that there is merit in respecting everyone else's integrity but statements of this sort provide little guidance to judges bearing the 'burden of judgment' in hard cases. Following the decision in *von Hannover (No 1)*, the Strasbourg Court has continued to say similarly vague things about privacy.[45] In *Storck* v *Germany*, for instance, the Court held that 'even a minor interference with the physical integrity of an individual must be regarded as an interference with the right to respect for private life under Article 8 if it is carried out against the individual's will'.[46] Descriptions of privacy of this sort have crept into domestic jurisprudence. In *R (Countryside Alliance)* v *Attorney General*, Baroness Hale spoke of 'the personal and psychological space within which each individual develops his own sense of self and relationships with other people'.[47] In *R (Purdy)* v *DPP*,[48] the Divisional Court opined that the *Countryside Alliance* case 'gave general support for broadening the scope of Article 8 (1) to cover personal autonomy' though we should note that the House of Lords refused to take this step on appeal.[49]

Developments of this sort must be considered against the backdrop of the Strasbourg Court interpreting the remit of Article 8 in an ever-broader manner. The Court has seemingly extended the understanding of private life under Article 8 to include reputation.[50] Scott calls this a 'surprising innovation'[51] but it becomes less surprising, perhaps even understandable, if we recall the history of the action of *iniuria*, a concept with which judges trained in civil law legal systems are most familiar. Understood in this way, this also explains why the ECtHR has become

[45] It must be noted, however, that in *von Hannover (No 2)*, perhaps mindful of such criticisms, the ECtHR has made an effort to set out a number of 'criteria relevant for the balancing exercise' of Arts 8 and 10. Drawing on previous decisions, the Court identifies the following considerations: 'contribution to a debate of general interest', 'how well known is the person concerned and what is the subject of the report?', 'prior conduct of the person concerned', 'content, form and consequences of the publication' and 'circumstances in which the photographs were taken'. See *von Hannover* v *Germany (No 2)* (Judgment of February 2012) (Applications nos 40660/08 and 60641/08) at paras 108–113.

[46] *Storck* v *Germany* (2006) 43 EHRR 96, para 143.

[47] *R (Countryside Alliance)* v *Attorney General* [2008] 1 AC 719 at 774 (per Baroness Hale).

[48] *R (Purdy)* v *DPP* [2008] EWHC 2565 (Admin) para 54.

[49] *R (Purdy)* v *DPP* [2010] 1 AC 345.

[50] See also the more recent case of *Axel Springer* v *Germany* (Judgment of February 2012) (Application no 39954/08), in which the ECtHR at para 83 confirms that Art 8 ECHR extends to the protection of reputation. The Court notes, however that '[i]n order for Article 8 to come into play... an attack on a person's reputation must attain a certain level of seriousness and in a manner causing prejudice to personal enjoyment of the right to respect for private life.'

[51] Scott, 'Introduction: Privacy and Publication' (2010) p 579.

increasingly willing of late to apply Article 8 in protection of image cases.[52] One interpretation of these developments is that the ECtHR is treating Article 8 as a general personality right. But we face a difficulty here. Again, I must emphasise that the remit of Article 8, as defined by the ECtHR, is so broadly construed that it can only offer limited guidance to civil courts. In what follows, I identify three hard cases from English private law in order to illustrate that many complex cases cannot be decided on the basis of Strasbourg principles alone. At the same time, I consider how these cases might be decided in Germany. The German experience offers some instructive insights. Not only do German doctrines give effect to the purposes of privacy, they also conform to our regulative ideas of justice, legal certainty and the rule of law. I will argue that English courts must develop their own set of privacy principles that are *at once* suited to the complexities of private law *and* informed by the ECHR and Strasbourg jurisprudence.

4.3 Misuse of Private Information

Our first hard case is *Mosley* v *News Group Newspapers Ltd.*[53] This is a highly significant case as (for the first time) the High Court adopts an almost identical approach to the ECtHR on important questions of limiting principles and balancing of interests. We must therefore pay close attention to the facts of the case and the Court's reasoning.

4.3.1 The Hard Case: Mosley v News Group Newspapers

Max Mosley was the President and trustee of the charitable arm of the FIA, the governing body for Formula 1 Racing. He is also the son of Sir Oswald Mosley, leader of a British wartime fascist organisation, the Blackshirts, and prominent Nazi sympathiser during the 1930s. On 30 March 2008, the *News of the World*, a British tabloid newspaper, published an article with the heading 'F1 Boss has Sick Nazi Orgy with 5 Hookers: Son of Hitler-loving fascist in sex-shame.' The newspaper included a 'lurid and graphic account' of a BDSM sex party involving Mr Mosley.[54] In addition, it published the same information, along with images of the party on its website. The newspaper alleged that the party had a 'Nazi theme' and the following week published another article entitled 'Exclusive: Mosley Hooker Tells All: My Nazi Orgy with F1 Boss'. This article included what was claimed to be an interview

[52] See, for example, *Reklos* v *Greece* [2009] EMLR 290; *Sciacca* v *Italy* [2006] 43 EHRR 20.

[53] *Mosley* v *News Group Newspapers Ltd* [2008] EMLR 20.

[54] *Ibid* at 679.

with one of the alleged female participants who had secretly filmed the party with a concealed camera.

Mr Mosley claimed that the information published was inherently private and there was a pre-existing relationship of confidentiality between the participants. The female participant who secretly filmed the party had breached that trust and the journalist who published the information ought to have known of the relationship of confidentiality. Mr Mosley further denied that the party had a 'Nazi theme'. In response, the defendants argued that the claimant had no reasonable expectation of privacy in relation to the information or images. However, if he did have such an expectation, then his right under Article 8 was outweighed by a greater public interest in disclosure under Article 10. According to the defendants, the public had a right to know about the alleged Nazi or concentration camp-themed sex party.

Eady J found for the claimant. He began by emphasising that in cases of this sort there was no longer any need to base the claim on the equitable doctrine of breach of confidence. The law now protects information over which there is a reasonable expectation of privacy and a pre-existing legal relationship in confidence does not need to be shown. Citing *Campbell*, Eady J stated that the values protected by Articles 8 and 10 ECHR also apply in disputes between individuals to the extent that they apply in the relationship between an individual and a public authority.[55] Eady J explained that these developments were not the consequence 'of "unaccountable" judges running amok' rather that the law 'is concerned to prevent the violation of a citizen's autonomy, dignity and self-esteem.'[56] He was keen to demonstrate that the influence of Articles 8 and 10 and the jurisprudence of the ECtHR means that this new action is a very different creature to the breach of confidence doctrine used in privacy cases some years earlier. He added that:

> This modern approach of applying an "intense focus" is thus obviously incompatible with making broad generalisations of the kind to which the media often resorted in the past such as, for example, "Public figures must expect to have less privacy" or "People in positions of responsibility must be seen as "role models" and set us all an example of how to live upstanding lives". Sometimes factors of this kind may have a legitimate role to play when the "ultimate balancing exercise" comes to be carried out, but generalisations can never be determinative. In every case "it all depends" (i.e. upon what is revealed by the intense focus on the individual circumstances).[57]

The circumstances of this particular case concerned the disclosure of intimate details relating to the sexual activity of the claimant. For these reasons, Eady J considered that a reasonable expectation of privacy also extended to a 'paid' sexual relationship, as long as this was between consenting adults.[58]

Once Eady J had established a reasonable expectation of privacy, he moved on to consider any potential limiting principles. In particular, he paid close attention to

---

[55] *Ibid* at 687.

[56] *Ibid* at 686.

[57] *Ibid* at 688.

[58] *Ibid* at 708.

the question of whether there was a public interest to justify interference with the right. On the allegation of a Nazi-theme and mockery of Holocaust victims, Eady J confirmed that information of this sort, if it could be shown to be true, would be in the public interest since it would call into question the claimant's suitability in his role as President and trustee of the FIA. However, no such evidence was provided to the Court and thus the secret filming and publication could not be justified on the basis of a public interest.[59] The defendant further argued that the immorality, depravity and adultery in this particular case meant that the information in question was in the public interest. In response to these arguments, Eady J referred to the 'strict criteria [he is] required to apply, in the modern climate'.[60] By this he meant the new 'rights-based environment introduced by the Human Rights Act.'[61] Referring to the decision in *CC* v *AB*, detailed below, he acknowledged criticisms of 'moral relativism' but argued that the approach he was required to employ meant that judges could not be 'swayed by personal distaste'.[62] In other words, the fact that the activities in question were adulterous or unconventional does not mean that a reasonable expectation of privacy cannot exist; in such cases the media does not have a carte blanche.[63]

For these reasons, Eady J held that no limiting principle was present. The claimant had suffered an invasion of privacy and the defendants were liable. On the question of remedies, he explained that although some analogies can be drawn, there is a distinction between compensation for libel and breach of privacy. In privacy cases, the law protects 'dignity, autonomy and integrity.'[64] Understood in this way, damages for this type of infringement reflect the 'distress, hurt feelings and loss of dignity.'[65] Damages might also serve the purpose of vindicating the right.[66] But in privacy cases, the individual cannot be restored to his original position before the invasion of privacy in the same way that the symbolism of a financial award in defamation can re-establish the esteem of the individual whose reputation had been slurred. The most appropriate remedy in cases of this sort is an injunction. While dismissing the plea for exemplary damages on the basis of their 'chilling effects', Eady J concluded that a financial award must be made available in order to acknowledge 'the fact that an unlawful intrusion has taken place while affording some degree of *solatium* to the injured party.' This is the only option available to a judge when 'the traditional object of *restitutio* is not available.'[67]

---

[59] *Ibid* at 713.
[60] *Ibid* at 716.
[61] *Ibid* at 715.
[62] *Ibid.*
[63] *Ibid* at 714.
[64] *Ibid* at 732.
[65] *Ibid.*
[66] See also *Ashley* v *Chief Constable of Sussex* [2008] 2 WLR 975; *Chester* v *Afshar* [2005] 1 AC 134.
[67] *Mosley* v *News Group Newspapers Ltd* [2008] EMLR 20 at 736.

Eady J's decisive finding of an invasion of privacy is highly significant not least because a finding of this sort would have been unlikely pre-*von Hannover (No 1)*. Eady J attempted to sound the retreat from what he clearly regarded as a restrictive approach to informational privacy disputes in English law. In a very real sense, he attempted to reconcile *von Hannover (No 1)* with the decision of the House of Lords in *Campbell*. But there are weaknesses in Eady J's line of argument. Recall that he criticised the press for making 'broad generalisations' about public figures in the past. These include the suggestions that public figures are entitled to less privacy because of their celebrity status or that public figures should act as role models. He stressed that generalisations can never be determinative. What is clear from this part of Eady J's judgment is that his interpretation of the law was influenced by the approach of the Strasbourg Court—the starting point is that public and non-public figures enjoy an equal claim to the right of privacy. We need only apply a multi-factorial balancing exercise following an 'intense focus' on the facts of the case and then assess the results. The status of the claimant and the quality of the information may be relevant some of the time but not all of the time. In reaching this conclusion, Eady J roundly condemned the 'generalisations' made by media outlets in the past. But, in doing so, he failed to highlight that the courts, including the House of Lords, have made broad and consistently determinative generalisations about the public status of claimants in misuse of private information cases. English courts have frequently highlighted the role model function of public figures.[68] Moreover, in *Campbell*, their Lordships agreed that there was a public interest in the disclosure of information concerning the appellant's use of drugs as she had, in the past, publicly denied having ever taken drugs. As a celebrity, whose 'trade' was publicity, the press had a right under Article 10 of the Convention to correct this information.

This has long been a troublesome area of law. But Eady J's attempt in *Mosley* to reconcile *von Hannover (No 1)* with *Campbell* generates more questions than answers. It is a measure, I suggest, of how difficult it is to rely on vague ECtHR pronouncements as a set of guidelines in private law cases. Indeed, rarely has a single decision attracted such criticism from the press. Following the decision, Paul Dacre, editor of the *Daily Mail*, stated: 'The freedom of the press, I would argue, is far too important to be left to the somewhat desiccated values of a single judge who clearly has an animus against the popular press and the right of people to freedom of expression.'[69]

Of course it would be ludicrous to suggest that Eady J was wrong because his decision perturbed the editor of a tabloid newspaper. Be that as it may, Eady J's eagerness to adopt the Strasbourg approach raises broader questions about potential chilling effects on freedom of expression. It is at this point that we must turn to consider the German approach to cases of this sort. As we will see, the German law on civil liability for misuse of private information is more developed and more

---

[68] *Theakston* v *MGN Ltd* [2002] EMLR 22; *A* v *B plc* [2003] QB 195.

[69] Quoted in Bennett, 'Corrective Justice and Horizontal Privacy' (2010) at 552.

principled. Yet, at the same time, German courts have traditionally applied a categorisation of claimants test, under which there is a presumption of lawfulness when private information is disclosed about a public person. The reason for this is rooted in concerns about chilling effects on freedom of expression. To this extent, at least, the German experience is highly instructive.

4.3.2 How Might a German Court Decide Mosley?

In what follows, I consider how a German court might decide *Mosley*. In effect, the discussion is divided into two parts. First, I consider the traditional German approach to informational privacy and the doctrines that have been developed by the courts since the 1950s. Second, I consider the influence of the ECtHR decision in *von Hannover (No 1)* on German law. The full extent of the impact of *von Hannover* remains to be seen but already in Germany there is some evidence of courts moving away from the traditional doctrines. I consider the implications of these developments later in this chapter.

How, then, might German courts decide *Mosley*, applying the traditional private law doctrines? In cases such as these, the starting point in German legal discourse is that everyone has the right to determine for himself whether and how he makes information available to the general public.[70] While we must also consider potential limiting principles in German law, the principle of self-determination remains core to the legal reasoning. Götting terms the right of self-determination the '*übergreifended dogmatisches Fundament*' ('underlying dogmatic basis') of the general personality right.[71] This right has its roots in the Constitutional Court decision in *Lebach*, which established the '*Verfüngungsrecht über die Darstellung der Person*' ('right of disposal over the representation of the person').[72] As a result of the *Eppler*[73] and *Volkszählungs*[74] decisions, the Constitutional Court gradually developed this principle into a right of informational self-determination.[75] This does not mean, however, that an individual can always insist on being represented by others only 'in the way in which he sees himself or would like to be seen'.[76] This would amount to an undue interference with freedom of expression. Thus, in many disclosure cases, courts face a conflict between the personality right under Articles 1 (1) and 2 (1) GG (and Article 8 (1) ECHR) and freedom of the press under Article

---

[70] BVerfGE 65, 1 = NJW 1984, 419 (*Volkszählung*).

[71] Götting, 'Inhalt, Zweck und Rechtsnatur des Persönlichkeitsrecht' (2008) p 11.

[72] BVerfGE 35, 202 = NJW 1973, 1226 (*Lebach I*).

[73] BVerfGE 54, 148 = NJW 1980, 2070 (*Eppler*).

[74] BVerfGE 65, 1 = NJW 1984, 419 (*Volkszählung*).

[75] Wanckel, 'Der Schutz vor Indiskretion' (2008) p 332.

[76] *Ibid*, citing BVerfG NJW 2000, 1021, 1022 (*Caroline von Monaco*).

5 (1) GG (and Article 10 (1) ECHR).[77] As we will see, civil courts try to achieve a *praktische konkordanz* (practical concordance) where the restriction of one right is legitimate if both rights are still able to 'unfold in their own content and effect'.[78] Before we move on to consider these points in greater detail, it is worth reflecting on whether the invasion of privacy in *Mosley* would be actionable under German law as this provides us with several instructive insights.

4.3.2.1 Would Mosley be Actionable Under German Law?

The disclosure of true but embarrassing or sensitive information may be actionable under the tortious liability clause of § 823(1) BGB. Persons who are in the public eye (*absolute und relative Personen der Zeitgeschichte*), and those who are not, are entitled to this protection, but traditionally to different degrees, as we will see below. In principle, an individual is understood to have a right to anonymity (*Recht auf Anonymität*).[79] This proposition is generally uncontroversial in cases involving non-public persons, particularly when intimate details are reported upon such as the health or sexual orientation of the individual.[80] The issue becomes more difficult when a public figure is the subject of the information disclosed. In some cases, the lawfulness of the disclosure is obvious. This is the case, for instance, when disclosed information sheds light on corruption by public officials—this presumption of lawfulness arises from the importance afforded by the Constitutional Court to freedom of expression in enabling public debate in a democratic society.[81] The difficulties emerge in borderline cases involving celebrities or other well-known public personalities when the information in question does not appear to be attached to their official function in any way. Traditionally, here, courts have been reluctant to impose liability on media outlets because of fears of chilling effects on freedom of expression. As we will see, these concerns are reflected in the structure of German doctrine—publication is presumed lawful unless the claimant can show that a 'legitimate interest' has been infringed. More difficult still are cases involving the privacy interests of criminals. Are such individuals to be considered non-public persons? Or does the fact that they have committed a crime mean that they take the mantel of a public person? The answer, it seems, depends on the degree of gravity of the crime.[82] The more serious the crime, the more likely it is that information can be made available, particularly their name and image.[83]

---

[77] Brüggemeier, *Haftungsrecht* (2006) p 286.

[78] See Hesse, *Grundzüge des Verfassungsrechts der Bundesrepublik Deutschland* (1993) paras 72, 317 *et seq.*

[79] Brüggemeier, *Haftungsrecht* (2006) pp 289–291.

[80] *Ibid* p 290.

[81] See BVerfGE 7, 198, 208 (*Lüth*).

[82] BVerfGE 35, 202 = NJW 1973, 1226 (*Lebach I*).

[83] See also OLG Nürnberg, NJW-RR 2007, 1267 (*Anforderungen an Unterlassungsantrag wegen Verletzung des Persönlichkeitsrechts*).

The traditional approach to the privacy claims of public figures and criminals reveals that German courts have proceeded very carefully to avoid interfering with interests in freedom of expression. This observation is amply borne out by the so-called *Verzichtstheorie* (waiver theory) in disclosure of private information cases.[84] The underlying idea is that if a celebrity (or anyone else in the public eye) has courted publicity in the past or provided details about her private life to the media, then that individual has waived her right of privacy. The Constitutional Court has suggested an approach of this sort in the past[85] but this has been heavily criticised by scholars[86] and, as we will see, it is questionable whether the Court would adopt this approach in the post-*von Hannover (No 1)* setting. We will return to this point later in the chapter.

What all of this means, in effect, is that it is probable that Mr Mosley's claim would be actionable under German law. Most likely, given his former position as head of the FIA, Mr Mosley would not be considered a non-public person but a public person (as we will see below, he would probably be considered an absolute person of contemporary history). In principle, he would enjoy a right to self-determination under German law but the press would undoubtedly claim that there is a public interest under Article 5 (1) GG and Article 10 ECHR in reporting the story and in publishing the images and footage.

4.3.2.2 The Images in Question

Before we move on to consider how a German court might balance these rights, we must first pay close attention to the fact that the defendant newspaper also published images and video footage of the claimant. We learned in Chap. 3 that the right of image falls under the umbrella of the general personality right in German law. It has a double function as a dignitary and publicity right. Here we examine the dignitary aspect of the right of image—in other words, cases where the taking and/or publication of photographs lead(s) to an invasion of privacy.

The Dissemination/Publication of Images

As noted in Chap. 3, partly for historical reasons, photographs/images form a special category in the German law on personality interests. The right to one's own image is expressly provided by statute under the KUG of 1907, enacted following public disquiet concerning an attempt to publish photographs taken of

[84] On this point, see Götting, 'Allgemeine Fragen' (2008) p 8.

[85] BVerfGE 101, 361, 389ff = NJW 2000, 1021, 1023 (*Caroline von Monaco*).

[86] See Götting, 'Allgemeine Fragen' (2008) pp 8–9.

Bismarck on his deathbed.[87] Under the Act, both public and non-public persons are entitled, in principle, to compensation for economic and non-economic loss if photographs of them are published without their consent.[88] §§ 23 and 24 KUG set out limitations to this general rule—in other words instances when photographs can be published without consent, most notably where the photographs depict 'situations of contemporary history' ('*aus dem Bereiche der Zeitgeschichte*'). German legal discourse has divided public figures into two categories—absolute persons of contemporary history (*absolute Personen der Zeitgeschichte*) and relative persons of contemporary history (*relative Personen der Zeitgeschichte*).[89]

The first category includes prominent politicians, royalty, celebrity actors and musicians, who through noteworthy activities or achievements in the arts, politics, sport or science have become part of the 'cultural history' of the country.[90] Examples in case law range from former chancellors such as Gerhard Schröder[91] and Willy Brandt[92] to performers such as the Backstreet Boys.[93] Photographs of such figures may be published without their consent where there is 'a legitimate informational interest on the part of the public' ('*ein berechtigtes Informationsinteresse der Öffentlichkeit*').

The second category, relative persons of contemporary history, consists of individuals who are only in the public eye for a limited period of time and thereafter return to the status of non-public person. Photographs of these persons can be published without their consent when the information is in the public interest and relates to the particular event or circumstance that made them famous in the first place. Examples include soap stars, television talent show participants and individuals affected by 'spectacular criminal trials or civil suits'.[94] Relatives or friends of prominent persons may also be considered relative persons of contemporary history, especially if they are photographed accompanying an absolute person of contemporary history to a public event.[95] The children of celebrities are singled

[87] Brüggemeier, *Haftungsrecht* (2006) p 297.

[88] §§ 22 and 23 KUG. The person, however, must be 'sufficiently recognisable' in the photograph according to BGH, NJW 1979, 2205 = GRUR 1979, 732 (*Fußballtorwart*). Nude photographs are an exception to this general rule. Even if the person depicted is unrecognisable from the photograph and even if the person has consented to the *taking* of the photograph, *publication* can still be declared unlawful due to the fact that nude photographs constitute a particularly serious injury to personality. See BGH, NJW 1974, 1947 (*Nacktfotos*).

[89] Neumann-Deusberg, 'Bildberichterstattung über absolute und relative Personen der Zeitgeschichte' 114.

[90] See Schertz, 'Das Recht am eigenen Bild' (2008) at 227.

[91] LG Berlin AfP 2003, 176 (*Gerüchte über die Kanzler Ehe*).

[92] BGH AfP 1996, 66 (*Abschiedsmedaille/Gedenkmedaille*).

[93] OLG Hamburg AfP 1999, 486 (*Backstreet Boys*).

[94] BVerfGE 35, 202 = NJW 1973, 1226 (*Lebach I*).

[95] But if they are merely accompanying the absolute person in an *Alltagssituation*, then it is unlikely that they will be considered a person of contemporary history. See, for example, BGH, NJW 2007, 3440 (*Lebensgefährtin H Grönemeyers*); BGH, NJW 2008, 3138 (*Einkaufsbummel im Urlaub*).

out as particularly vulnerable and courts highlight the need to ensure that they have the opportunity to 'fully develop their personality' in private.[96] As such, they are not automatically considered relative persons of contemporary history unless a legitimate public interest in the publication of their photograph can be demonstrated.[97]

The categorisation of claimants as absolute or relative persons of contemporary history attempts to delineate an area of press freedom in respect of public figures and, as argued by the German government in *von Hannover (No 1)*, endeavours to strike a fair balance between competing equally-weighted interests. The German courts have repeatedly acknowledged that even public figures are entitled to enjoy the protection of the right of privacy.[98] The categorisation does not deprive the celebrity claimant of access to justice in the individual case; it merely acts as a presumption of lawfulness and places the onus on the claimant to show that there has been an infringement of her privacy. Once a person of contemporary history claims a legitimate interest has been infringed, courts proceed to undertake a balancing exercise, drawing on a non-exhaustive list of relevant considerations, some of which we will examine below. So, while the ECtHR in *von Hannover (No 1)* criticised the German categorisation of public figures, the judges were in fact objecting to the German courts' interpretation of a legitimate informational interest, the scope of which they considered too broad.[99]

The *von Hannover (No 1)* decision was enthusiastically received by several prominent commentators in Germany who claimed that the categorisation of public figures was an outdated approach to privacy and image disputes.[100] The highest courts have followed suit in recent decisions, ostensibly distancing themselves from the categorisation of public figures and interpreting *zeitgeschichtliches Ereignis* in a far more restrictive manner.[101] Nonetheless, as we will see later, in all of the decisions following *von Hannover (No 1)*, and despite indications to the contrary, a categorisation of public figures is still implicit in the reasoning of the courts, with the Federal Court of Justice stressing that the press is free to decide, within legal limits, what is in the public interest.[102] This immediately begs the question whether

---

[96] BVerfG AfP 2000, 75 (*Caroline von Monaco*).

[97] See, for example, BVerfG, NJW 2000, 2191 (*Pierre Casiraghi*); BVerfG NJW 2005, 1857 (*Charlotte Casiraghi*).

[98] See, for example, BGH, NJW 2004, 762 (*Sabine Christiansen*); BGH, NJW 2007, 1981 (*Caroline und Ernst August von Hannover (No 1)*); BGH, NJW 2008, 749 (*Oliver Kahn*).

[99] See, for instance, BGH NJW 1996, 1128, 1129 (*Caroline von Monaco IV*).

[100] Forkel, 'Das "Caroline-Urteil" aus Straßburg' (2005); Teichmann, 'Abschied von der absoluten Person der Zeitgeschichte' [2007]; Herrmann, 'Anmerkung zum Urteil des EGMR vom 24.6.2004' (2004).

[101] See, for example, BGH, NJW 2007, 1977 (*Caroline im Urlaub*) where the photographs of the claimant on holiday were not considered to be a *zeitgeschichtliches Ereignis*.

[102] BGH, NJW 2007, 1977, 1978.

the courts have made anything more than cosmetic changes to German doctrine following *von Hannover (No 1)*. We shall revisit this argument later.

The Production/Taking of Images

It is important to note here that the KUG only protects an individual against the *dissemination/publication* of images. The *production/taking* of an image, however, may also be deemed unlawful.[103] While this is not provided in statute, a long line of case law has made this explicit.[104] The 'making of an image' encompasses all visual representations of a person, including everything from film and photograph to satirical cartoons.[105] An image that depicts a public or a non-public person in a private setting may be deemed an unlawful infringement of the general personality right under § 823 (1) BGB.

In cases involving the *production/taking* of an image, difficulties arise within the context of the *öffentlich-privaten Bild* (a 'public/private image'), as Brüggemeier puts it.[106] What are the relevant considerations, for example, when a non-public person claims against the taking of a photograph of him in a public setting or in his workplace? Non-public individuals generally retain a right to prevent photographs being taken of them, even in a public setting. An exception is found within § 23 (1) KUG. If the photograph focuses on the public setting or an event and does not single out the individual in question, then the taking of the photograph is considered lawful. A workplace might be considered quasi-public and whether it is lawful to take a photograph in this context depends on the facts of the case.[107]

The assessment of the public/private setting when persons of contemporary history are involved is more difficult still. As noted earlier, traditionally in Germany, celebrities could not prevent photographs being taken of them outside the walls of their own homes. This orthodoxy has been challenged in a line of cases initiated by Caroline von Hannover (formerly Caroline von Monaco) in the 1990s. We will return to this authority below.

In relation to the images and video footage in *Mosley*, then, it is possible to envisage a claim based on the unlawful taking *and* the unlawful publication of the material. This is because the images did not depict a public scene nor were they *öffentlich-privat*—they quite clearly depicted a scene in a private house. There is

---

[103] See Brüggemeier, *Haftungsrecht* (2006) pp 301–310.

[104] BGHZ 24, 200 = NJW 1957, 1315 (*Spätheimkehrer*); BGH, NJW 1966, 2353 (*Vor unserer eigenen Tür*); BGHZ 20, 345 = NJW 56, 1554 (*Paul Dahlke*).

[105] Brüggemeier, *Haftungsrecht* (2006) p 301.

[106] *Ibid* p 302.

[107] OLG München ZUM 1997, 388, 390 (*Abbildung einer Person in einem Lichtbildwerk*). Employers are allowed to secretly film their employees, if a crime is suspected and all other means of establishing this have been exhausted. See BAGE 105, 356 = NJW 2003, 3436 (*Videoüberwachte Kassiererin*).

then a *prima facie* infringement of the claimant's right of image. However, this information alone is not enough to justify judgment in Mr Mosley's favour—the German court would have to consider potential limiting principles. But before we move on to consider these limiting principles in greater detail, we must first pay close attention to the sphere of privacy that has been invaded.

4.3.2.3 The Sphere Test

The so-called sphere test was first mooted by Hubmann[108] and was adopted by the Constitutional Court in *Eppler*.[109] This test is based on a 'dialectic between private and public' ('*Dialektik zwischen Privatheit and Öffentlichkeit*')[110] and seeks to 'incrementally grade the tension' between the right of the individual to be 'let alone' and the public interest.[111] As a doctrinal device it aids the court in assessing the nature of the information disclosed.

The first sphere is the *intimate sphere*, which incorporates *inter alia* nude photographs and information relating to sexual relationships and illnesses. This sphere is seen as a 'taboo zone' where the self-determination rights of the individual are absolute.[112] However, courts interpret this sphere narrowly, especially where absolute persons of contemporary history are involved, and often information that might ordinarily be considered intimate falls under a second sphere, the *private sphere*.[113] This sphere consists of information relating to family and home life, including births, marriages and divorces.[114] Here, a balancing exercise will take place, but the publication of such information will only be permitted when there is an 'overriding public interest' in disclosure.

The third sphere is the *public* or *social sphere*, which includes so-called *Alltagssituationen* (activities from daily life carried out in public), for example, shopping, working, attending social events, walks in the park etc. There may still be a right of privacy in such a situation, especially where non-public persons or relative persons of contemporary history are concerned. But this will probably be of a lower order than the first two spheres and should be balanced accordingly. Traditionally, as we have already learned, public figures were unlikely to succeed unless the photographs depicted the claimants within the 'four walls' of their

---

108 Hubmann, *Das Persönlichkeitsrecht* (1967).

109 BVerfGE 54, 148, 154 = NJW 1980, 2070 (*Eppler*).

110 Baston-Vogt, *Der sachliche Schutzbereich des zivilrechtlichen allgemeinen Persönlichkeitsrechts* (1997) p 186.

111 Götting, 'Allgemeine Fragen' (2008) p 5.

112 Wanckel, 'Der Schutz vor Indiskretion' (2008) p 349.

113 See, for example, BGH NJW 1999, 2893 (*Ehebruch*). Confirmed in BVerfG NJW 2000, 2189 (*Scheidungsgrund*).

114 BGH NJW 2005, 2844, 2848 (*Esra*).

home.[115] In recent decisions, however, courts have rejected the notion that such spatial considerations should be determinative and held that a person has an expectation of privacy when he has taken steps to seclude himself from the general public and this is objectively recognisable to third persons.[116]

The question we face here is whether a German court would consider the information about Mr Mosley's sex life part of the intimate sphere or private sphere? This is significant because if the information falls to be considered under the intimate sphere, Mr Mosley's right to self-determination would be absolute and an invasion of privacy on public interests grounds could not be justified. However, perhaps mindful of the potential chilling effect of this test, courts interpret this sphere very narrowly. If the information in question falls under the private sphere, this increases the likelihood of disclosure being allowed if an overriding public interest can be shown.

How, then, would a German court proceed? In a number of high-profile cases,[117] the courts have held that information relating to lawful sexual activities forms part of the intimate sphere.[118] This general principle also applies to persons of contemporary history though here it will depend on the amount of detail provided in the information disclosed. General information, for instance, about sexual activities that led to a marital separation of a prominent couple was considered by the Federal Court of Justice and Constitutional Court to fall under the private sphere and was therefore subjected to a balancing exercise.[119] However, it is likely that information will fall under the intimate sphere when photographs or video footage are present.[120]

At first glance, then, it appears that the information (particularly the images and video footage of Mr Mosley's sexual activities) would form part of the intimate sphere within the meaning of German law. However, we must note here the allegations made by the newspaper that Mr Mosley's sex party had a Nazi-theme and for this reason, according to the newspaper, there was a public interest in disclosure. In Germany, the public use of Nazi symbols or greetings is prohibited under § 86 of the Penal Code (*Strafgesetzbuch*—StGB). But two important points must be mentioned here. First, in *Mosley*, Eady J found no evidence that the sex-party had a Nazi or Holocaust camp theme. Second, even if evidence of this theme had been found, in our hypothetical case, the German court would then have to

[115] Wenzel, *Das Recht der Wort- und Bildberichterstattung* (1994).

[116] BGHZ 131, 332, 339 (*Caroline von Monaco*); BVerfG NJW 2000, 1021, 1022 (*Caroline von Monaco*). See Dannemann, 'Of Princesses and Politicians' (2005).

[117] See, for example, BGH NJW 1988, 1984, 1985 (*Telefonsex*); LG München I ZUM 2005, 922 (*Nichte Veraces*).

[118] On this point, see Wanckel, 'Der Schutz vor Indiskretion' (2008) pp 349–354.

[119] BGH NJW 1999, 2893 (*Ehebruch*), confirmed by the Constitutional Court in BVerfG NJW 2000, 2189 (*Scheidungsgrund*).

[120] See, for example, LG München I NJW 2004, 617, 618 (*FKK-Gelände*); BGH NJW 1985, 1617, 1618 (*Sexualkundelehrbuch*); OLG Stuttgart NJW-RR 2004, 619, 623 (*Sexvideo*).

consider whether the party would be considered 'public' under the meaning of the StGB. This finding would be unlikely given that the party took place in a private house. However, given the historical and political context in Germany, the mere presence of allegations of this sort (especially concerning an absolute person of contemporary history) may result in a German court treating this as 'private sphere' information in order to induce a balancing exercise. If this were the case, then a balancing of competing rights would become necessary. We now turn to consider how this might take shape.

4.3.2.4 Relevant Considerations in the Balancing Exercise

Central to the approach of the German courts is taking all of the circumstances of the case into account and applying a balancing of interests, where each interest influences and counter-influences the other.[121] Courts stress that this is a 'delicate process' and, if there are any doubts, freedom of expression must have priority.[122] The factors that a court will take into account depend on the individual case but there are certain common themes evident in the case law. They include[123]:

(a) Does the information in question contributes to public debate?
The defendant in *Mosley* claimed that disclosure of the information in question was in the public interest. A core consideration in the balancing exercise undertaken by German courts is whether the information contributes to public debate.[124] Clearly, in our hard case this conclusion hinges on the allegations made and whether or not they can be shown to be true. Again, Eady J found no evidence of a Nazi-theme so under these circumstances and considering the German case law on the privacy of sexual activities, it is unlikely that the information would be understood as contributing to public debate.
(b) The type of speech involved and the motives of the defendant
This is a similar approach to that outlined by Baroness Hale in *Campbell* when she considered the differences between higher-order speech, such as political speech, and mere gossip. In Germany, a presumption of freedom of expression attaches itself to higher-order speech in Baroness Hale's sense, but speech aimed at insulting or humiliating an individual will tend towards an injury to personality.[125] At the same time, German courts take the motives of the wrongdoer into account. Did the wrongdoer invade privacy for financial gain? In our case, the newspaper was clearly motivated by financial gain (but then most media outlets, like any other private enterprises, need to make an

[121] This is known as the *Wechselwirkungstheorie*.
[122] BVerfGE 34, 269 = NJW 1973, 1221 (*Soraya*).
[123] See further Wagner, 'The Protection of Personality Rights' (2005).
[124] BVerfGE 7, 198 = NJW 1958, 257 = JZ 1958, 119 (*Lüth*).
[125] BGH, NJW 1994, 124 (*Alle reden vom Klima*).

operating profit), however, it is likely that the newspaper would claim that it was acting in the public interest.

(c) The claimant's behaviour
Just as the motives of the wrongdoer will be taken into account, German courts also consider the behaviour of the injured party when balancing the interests. In the *Terroristentochter* case, for example, the claimant, who happened to be the daughter of Ulrike Meinhof, the RAF terrorist, sought an injunction against a newspaper that had called her a 'daughter of a terrorist'.[126] The newspaper claimed freedom of expression under Article 5 (1) GG and this was upheld by the Federal Court of Justice, but the decision was partly based on the claimant's own behaviour. In the past, she had publicly described herself as the daughter of a terrorist. Under such circumstances she was not entitled to recourse to the general personality right under § 823 (1) BGB. A similar line of argument can be found in other case law.[127] In this context, then, it is likely that the German courts would have approached *Campbell* in the same way as the House of Lords. The information detailing the claimant's medical treatment would be considered to form part of her intimate sphere, under which she has an absolute right of self-determination, but it is probable that disclosure of information about her use of drugs would be permitted given her public denial of drug-taking in the past. It is instructive to note the similarities between the most authoritative English decision on informational privacy and the German approach. Understood in this way and given the case law in this area, it is at least possible that the German courts would treat Mr Mosley's risk-taking as a factor in the balancing exercise (we should note that in *Mosley* Eady J considered personal responsibility and the risk of blackmail when discussing the question of causation, rather than the balancing exercise itself).[128]

(d) The way in which the information was obtained
The way in which the information was obtained by the defendant is a consideration in the balancing exercise. If the information was obtained by illegal means, the scales will tip towards an injury to personality but this is by no means a strict rule. In some cases, the disclosure of information obtained illegally may be in the public interest.[129] Likewise, similar considerations apply where the information was obtained surreptitiously—for instance the use of a telephoto lens may act as a presumption of invasion of privacy.[130] In our case, the fact that the information was obtained surreptitiously would form a part of the balancing exercise. In *Mosley* (as in *Douglas*), the Court made note of the

[126] BGH NJW 2007, 686 (*Terroristentochter*).

[127] See, for example, BGH, NJW 2005, 594 (*Uschi Glas*).

[128] *Mosley* v *News Group Newspapers Ltd* [2008] EMLR 20 at 735.

[129] BVerfGE 66, 116 = BVerfGE 66, 116 (*Springer/Wallraff*).

[130] BGHZ 131, 332 = NJW 1996, 1128 (*Caroline von Monaco*).

surreptitious recording of the event but it does not appear that this was a consideration in Eady J's balancing exercise.

(e) Location

Traditionally, as we have seen, public figures could not prevent photographs being taken of them outside the walls of their own homes.[131] This remained the case until the Federal Court of Justice extended the spatial dimension to areas outside the home.[132] Two conditions were attached to this extension.[133] Firstly, the location where the person was photographed had to be secluded to a certain degree from the general public, and secondly the photograph must have depicted a 'typically private' situation. This must also have been 'objectively recognisable' to third persons and the taking of the photograph must have had a surreptitious quality.[134] In *Mosley*, both of these conditions are satisfied and it is likely that the location would be considered a private place within the meaning of German law.

(f) The Audience/Readership

Another relevant consideration is the make-up of the audience or readership. German courts take the number of people to whom the information has been disclosed into account. The larger the audience/readership, the more the scales will tip towards an injury to personality. This was the case, for instance, in *Lebach* where the fact that the documentary had been broadcasted on television meant that this special consideration came into play.[135] In *Mosley*, the information was disclosed not just to the readership of the defendant newspaper but to the world at large on the defendant's website.

(g) Truth/Falsity

An important consideration for the German courts is that of the truth or falsity of the information disclosed. Has the media outlet fabricated the story such as was apparent in the *Caroline von Monaco* cases in which a media outlet had invented an 'exclusive interview'? If so, this will indicate a more 'intense' injury to an individual's personality right.[136] In English law, if the information reported is false and harms the reputation of the claimant in the eyes of right-thinking members of society, there is, potentially, a claim in defamation. The new tort of misuse of private information concerns the disclosure of true facts only. However, if the disclosure is accompanied by defamatory material, would an English court also regard the invasion of privacy as more intense? In our case, there is nothing to suggest in Eady J's judgment that the falsity (recall that

---

[131] See Wenzel, *Das Recht der Wort- und Bildberichterstattung* (1994).

[132] BGHZ 131, 332 = NJW 1996, 1128 (*Caroline von Monaco*).

[133] See Dannemann, 'Of Princesses and Politicians' (2005) p 36.

[134] BGHZ 131, 332, 339 (*Caroline von Monaco*).

[135] BVerfGE 35, 202, 226 f. = NJW 1973, 1226 (*Lebach I*).

[136] BGHZ 128, 1, 16 = NJW 1995, 861 = JZ 1995, 360 (*Caroline von Monaco*). See also BVerfGE 34, 269, 283 ff. = NJW 1973, 1221 (*Soraya*).

he found the allegations to be untrue)[137] of the Nazi-theme allegations influenced the balancing exercise. This can be explained, at least in part, by the leeway granted by English courts to editorial judgement. In the seminal case in this area, *Jameel* v *Wall Street Journal*, Lord Bingham stressed that the 'due allowance' extended to editorial judgement also applies to editorial decisions 'made at the time [of publication], without the knowledge of falsity which is a benefit of hindsight'.[138] Understood in these terms, in the context of media disclosure, it is unlikely that an English court would consider an invasion of privacy to be more serious on the basis that some of the information disclosed was untrue—the risk of a 'chilling effect' on press freedom is too great.

(h) Information already in the Public Domain
Whether and to what extent the information disclosed has already been in the public domain is another consideration in the balancing exercise in Germany. This is illustrated by a case involving a well-known television journalist and presenter who sought an injunction preventing the publication of aerial photographs of her holiday home and directions on how to find it.[139] The Federal Court of Justice held that although the unauthorised publication of photographs of a property injures the general personality right, the claimant could not demand an injunction in this particular case as she had previously published pictures of her home in two books and three magazines. The Court made it clear that a person who opens up his or her private sphere to the public could not simultaneously rely on that private sphere being protected from the public. This is context specific, so in this sense is not so much a waiver, as discussed above, rather a recognition of the difficulties in attaching a label of 'private' to information that has been previously made public. In our hard case, we do not have any evidence that the private information in question had already been in the public domain.

4.3.2.5 Summing Up the Traditional Approach

None of the considerations outlined are seen as determinative and the weight attached to them will depend on the circumstances of the case. We should also note that underlying the balancing exercise is the principle of proportionality. The personality right or the right of freedom of expression can only be limited in so far as it is necessary in order to ensure the unfolding of both rights 'in their own content and effect'.[140] Understood in this way, if a German court found there was a public interest in publication of information about Mr Mosley, it is likely that the

---

[137] *Mosley* v *News Group Newspapers Ltd* [2008] EMLR 20 at 717.

[138] *Jameel* v *Wall Street Journal Europe SRPL (No 3)* [2007] 1 AC 359 at 377 (per Lord Bingham).

[139] BGH, NJW 2004, 762 (*Sabine Christiansen*).

[140] See Hesse, *Grundzüge des Verfassungsrechts der Bundesrepublik Deutschland* (1993) paras 72, 317 *et seq.*

publication of the images and video footage would still be prohibited. This is because the public interest requirement would be satisfied in the reporting of the information alone; in the likely view of a German court, publication of the images and video footage would not be necessary in order to ensure that freedom of expression fully unfolds in its own content and effect.

What do we learn, then, about the German approach to disclosure of private information cases? It is likely that Mr Mosley's claim for an injunction would have been successful in the first instance, though much depends on whether the court would regard the information as falling under the intimate or private sphere. As we have seen, this decision would most likely depend on how the court treats the allegations of a 'Nazi theme'. If the information falls under the intimate sphere, then Mr Mosley would have an absolute right to informational self-determination and the court would enjoin publication of all information relating to the event. This would be the case notwithstanding Mr Mosley's status as an absolute person of contemporary history. Should it fall under the private sphere, then a balancing exercise becomes necessary. Here, again, the case hinges on the truth or falsity of the allegations, but given that the information was found to be false, it is likely that the claimant's general personality right would be given more weight by a German court. This is because the information, which included falsities, does not contribute to public debate, was obtained surreptitiously, and was published to the world at large. Moreover, the location was private and the information had not already been in the public domain.

4.3.2.6 The Impact of *von Hannover (No 1)* on German Law

This is, at least, how a German court might have decided *Mosley* before the ECtHR's decision in *von Hannover (No 1)*. As noted earlier, the Strasbourg decision has impacted both English and German law in this area. For this reason, we must consider *von Hannover (No 1)* in the context of German law.

Caroline von Hannover is a princess of the principality of Monaco and is married to Prince Ernst August of Hannover. For many years, her private life has been a popular subject for tabloid and gossip magazines, particularly in continental Europe. Given her royal status, in Germany, Princess Caroline was considered an absolute person of contemporary history. For our purposes, the most significant German court decisions result from the first series of cases taken by the Princess.[141] In these cases, she sought remedies against two magazines that had published photographs of her with a French actor at a holiday resort in South Africa. The photographs showed her eating in a restaurant, shopping at a market, paddling a canoe with her daughter and riding a horse. One photograph, taken by a camera with telephoto lens, showed Caroline's male companion kissing her hand in a dimly lit

[141] OLG Hamburg, NJW-RR 1995, 790 (*Caroline von Monaco*); BGHZ 131, 332 = NJW 1996, 1128 (*Caroline von Monaco*); BVerfGE 101, 361 = NJW 2000, 1021 (*Caroline von Monaco*).

restaurant. Given the claimant's status as an absolute person of contemporary history, the Federal Court of Justice held that the publication of the majority of photographs was lawful.[142] But this case is significant because the Court departed, for the first time, from the strict rules relating to spatial privacy. It emphasised that an individual's private sphere was not limited to his home; rather there are places outside of the home (even if these places are freely accessible to the public) that can be considered private.[143] The publication of the photograph of the scene in the dimly-lit restaurant was therefore deemed unlawful.

Following this decision, Princess Caroline filed a constitutional complaint with the Constitutional Court, claiming that her general personality right had been infringed.[144] The Court confirmed that the Princess, as an absolute person of contemporary history, had to tolerate such actions on the part of the media unless there was an overriding legitimate interest in privacy on her part. The Court also confirmed the constitutionality of the Federal Court of Justice's approach to spatial privacy, arguing that free development of personality would not be possible unless allowance was made for some places outside the four walls of the home to be considered private. On the Court's account, this private sphere is to be determined on the facts of the individual case, but it must be 'objectively recognisable' that the individual in question has 'retreated from the public glare'.[145]

Taking into account Princess Caroline's position as an absolute person of contemporary history, the Court held that the freedom of the press had priority over the claimant's personality rights. It referred to the important function of the press in contributing to the public debate in a democratic society. But this function does not just encompass political issues, it also extends to entertainment. On the Court's account:

'Aber auch der bloßen Unterhaltung kann der Bezug zur Meinungsbildung nicht von vornherein abgesprochen werden. Es wäre einseitig anzunehmen, Unterhaltung befriedige lediglich Wünsche nach Zerstreuung und Entspannung, nach Wirklichkeitsflucht und Ablenkung. Sie kann auch Realitätsbilder vermitteln und stellt Gesprächsgegenstände zur Verfügung, an die sich Diskussionsprozesse und Integrationsvorgänge anschließen können, die sich auf Lebenseinstellungen, Werthaltungen und Verhaltensmuster beziehen, und erfüllt insofern wichtige gesellschaftliche Funktionen. Unterhaltung in der Presse ist aus diesem Grund, gemessen an dem Schutzziel der Pressefreiheit, nicht

'Nor can mere entertainment be denied any role in the formation of opinions. That would amount to unilaterally presuming that entertainment merely satisfies a desire for amusement, relaxation, escapism or diversion. Entertainment can also convey images of reality and propose subjects for debate that spark a process of discussion and assimilation relating to philosophies of life, values and behaviour models. In that respect it fulfils important social functions. When measured against the aim of protecting press freedom, entertainment in the press is neither negligible nor entirely worthless and therefore falls within the scope of application of fundamental rights. The same is true of information about people.

142 BGHZ 131, 332 = NJW 1996, 1128.

143 BGHZ 131, 332, 339.

144 BVerfGE 101, 361 = NJW 2000, 1021 (*Caroline von Monaco*).

145 BVerfGE 101, 361 = NJW 2000, 1021, 1023.

unbeachtlich oder gar wertlos und deswegen ebenfalls in den Grundrechtsschutz einbezogen.
Das gilt auch für die Berichterstattung über Personen. Personalisierung bildet ein wichtiges publizistisches Mittel zur Erregung von Aufmerksamkeit. Sie weckt vielfach erst das Interesse an Problemen und begründet den Wunsch nach Sachinformationen. Auch Anteilnahme an Ereignissen und Zuständen wird meist durch Personalisierung vermittelt. Prominente Personen stehen überdies für bestimmte Wertvorstellungen und Lebenshaltungen. Vielen bieten sie deshalb Orientierung bei eigenen Lebensentwürfen. Sie werden zu Kristallisationspunkten für Zustimmung oder Ablehnung und erfüllen Leitbild- oder Kontrastfunktionen. Darin hat das öffentliche Interesse an den verschiedensten Lebensbezügen solcher Personen seinen Grund.'[146]

Personalization is an important journalistic means of attracting attention. Very often it is this which first arouses interest in a problem and stimulates a desire for factual information. Similarly, interest in a particular event or situation is usually stimulated by personalised accounts. Additionally, celebrities embody certain moral values and lifestyles. Many people base their choice of lifestyle on their example. They become points of crystallisation for adoption or rejection and act as examples or counter-examples. This is what explains the public interest in the various ups and downs occurring in their lives.'[147]

In many cases, the public has a legitimate interest in knowing what absolute persons of contemporary history do outside of their official functions. In respect of any 'official function' test the court stated:

'Es kennzeichnet häufig gerade das öffentliche Interesse, welches solche Personen beanspruchen, daß es nicht nur der Funktionsausübung im engeren Sinn gilt. Vielmehr kann es sich wegen der herausgehobenen Funktion und der damit verbundenen Wirkung auch auf Informationen darüber erstrecken, wie sich diese Personen generell, also außerhalb ihrer jeweiligen Funktion, in der Öffentlichkeit bewegen. Diese hat ein berechtigtes Interesse daran zu erfahren, ob solche Personen, die oft als Idol oder Vorbild gelten, funktionales und persönliches Verhalten überzeugend in Übereinstimmung bringen.'[148]

'Very often the public interest aroused by such figures does not relate exclusively to the exercise of their function in the strict sense. It can, on the contrary, by virtue of the particular function and its impact, extend to information about the way in which these figures behave generally – that is, also outside their function – in public. The public has a legitimate interest in being allowed to judge whether the personal behaviour of the individuals in question, who are often regarded as idols or role models, convincingly tallies with their behaviour on their official engagements.'[149]

Here, the Court highlighted the risks in restricting the publication of photographs of public persons to reports about their official functions. It stated that this would deprive the public of certain necessary possibilities of forming judgements about

[146] BVerfGE 101, 361 = NJW 2000, 1021, 1024.

[147] Reproduced from the ECtHR decision in *von Hannover (No 1)* (2005) 40 EHRR 1.

[148] BVerfG, NJW 2000, 1021, 1025 (*Caroline von Monaco*).

[149] Reproduced from the ECtHR decision in *von Hannover (No 1)* (2005) 40 EHRR 1.

such persons (especially when they exercise a 'role model' function). On the other hand, the press is not allowed to do whatever it pleases with pictures of public persons, but the provisions of the KUG adequately deal with situations where the legitimate interests of a public person are infringed.

On this basis, the Court held that the Federal Court of Justice was right when it decided that the publication of the majority of photographs was lawful and that it had properly followed the provisions of the KUG in line with the *Grundgesetz*. Incidentally, the other two groups of cases, initiated by Princess Caroline, also failed on similar grounds.[150] The Constitutional Court considered, however, that the publication of photographs of Princess Caroline with her children was unlawful. This is because the press had to satisfy a more restrictive standard when photographing children in order to protect the wellbeing of the child. According to the Court, constant media presence was a hazard to the personal development of the children.[151] The personality right protection arising from Articles 1(1) and 2(1) GG for the parent-child relationship is given further force through Article 6(1) and (2) GG which obliges the State to secure the proper living conditions of the child, as well as proper parental care. This was considered by the Court to be an infringement of Princess Caroline's general personality right.[152]

We see here an incremental gnawing away of the traditional doctrines governing media access to absolute persons of contemporary history in these cases. In the Federal Court of Justice decision, the Court extended the sphere of privacy to encompass cases, in which, to borrow the English legal terminology, a reasonable expectation of privacy existed. In the Constitutional Court decision, the Court held that the publication of photographs of the children was unlawful. The claimant, however, remained unsatisfied with these developments and applied to the European Court of Human Rights on the basis that the German state had violated her rights under Article 8 ECHR.[153] As we have seen, Princess Caroline was successful. I have discussed the main principles arising from this decision early in this chapter but we should note the differences between the German and Strasbourg approaches here. The ECtHR rejected the German classification of public figures and stressed that reports about the private lives of celebrities have no bearing on the public debate in a democratic society. The basic consideration, reminiscent of the French approach,[154] is that all persons, whether public or private, have a right to respect for their private lives, unless they have otherwise consented to an infringement.

---

[150] The second group of cases concerned photographs of Princess Caroline with her husband Prince Ernst August *von Hannover (No 1)*: OLG Hamburg, 10.3.1998 (7 U 206/97); BVerfG, NJW 2000, 2194. The third group concerned the 'Beach Club' Monte Carlo photo: OLG Hamburg, 13.10.1998 (7 U 63/98); BVerfG, NJW 2000, 2192.

[151] BVerfG, NJW 2000, 1021, 1023 (*Caroline von Monaco*).

[152] BVerfG, NJW 2000, 1021, 1026.

[153] *von Hannover (No 1)* v *Germany* (2005) 40 EHRR 1.

[154] See, for example, Cass Civ, 8.7.1981, D 1982, 65, note Lindon.

This decision caused much unrest in German legal circles. The German government convened to discuss its consequences but decided not to appeal the decision to the Grand Chamber, preferring instead to allow the decision to 'stimulate debate' among German judges.[155] The extent to which the decision has indeed stimulated debate in the German courts is evidenced by more recent decisions concerning the publication of private information relating to absolute persons of contemporary history. These cases include two separate actions brought by Princess Caroline[156] and her husband[157] concerning the same articles and photographs. The claim, in each case, was for an injunction against re-publication of the pictures and articles. The photographs depicted Princess Caroline and her husband on holiday in St. Moritz, including standing in the street, surrounded by members of the public, and on a ski-lift; they accompanied various articles about their holiday and the illness of Prince Rainier of Monaco.

At first instance, the *Landgericht* awarded the injunctions, but on appeal the *Oberlandesgericht* lifted them and dismissed the claim. On the Appeal Court's account, while Article 8(1) ECHR ought to be considered in such cases, the *Grundgesetz* had priority. Understood in this way, under § 23 (1) (1) KUG, the claimant, as an absolute person of contemporary history, must tolerate photographs being published of her without her consent. The exception under § 23 (2) KUG was not applicable as the photograph in question could not possibly be considered private, depicting, as it did, a street scene with many members of the public present.

On appeal, the Federal Court overturned the decision of the Appeal Court, criticising the judges for not properly taking into account the decisions of the Federal Court of Justice and the Constitutional Court following the ECtHR decision in *von Hannover (No 1)*.[158] The Court reasoned that the pictures in question could constitute an infringement of the claimant's legitimate interests under § 23 (2) KUG. This question must be decided on a case-by-case basis considering all of the circumstances of the case.[159] At the same time, it is for the press to decide, within 'legal limits', what is in the public interest.[160] For this reason, there has to be a balancing of the informational interests of the public on one side, and the protection of the claimant's private sphere on the other. The greater the informational value for the public, the more the personality rights of the injured party must give way.[161] Conversely, the more severe the injury to personality interests, the less the information is of value to the general public. The interest of the reader in mere

[155] Wagner, 'The Protection of Personality Rights Against Invasions By Mass Media in Germany' (2005) p 154.

[156] BGH, NJW 2007, 1977 (*Caroline im Urlaub*).

[157] BGH, NJW 2007, 1981 (*Caroline und Ernst August von Hannover (No 1)*).

[158] BGH, NJW 2007, 1977, 1978 (*Caroline im Urlaub*).

[159] *Ibid* citing BVerfG, NJW 2006, 3406, 3407 f (*Uschi Glas*).

[160] *Ibid* citing BVerfG, NJW 2000, 1026 but also citing *von Hannover (No 1)* v *Germany* (2005) 40 EHRR 1.

[161] BGH, NJW 2007, 1977, 1979 (*Caroline im Urlaub*).

entertainment generally has less weight than the protection of personality, but entertainment can sometimes contribute to a public debate, depending on the facts of the case.[162]

In deciding in this manner, the Federal Court was following the Constitutional Court, which had only just confirmed that courts do not need to take into account the individual's degree of fame in assessing the circumstances of the case.[163] The Court referred to this category as the '*bisher so genannten Personen der Zeitgeschichte*' ('the up until now so-called persons of contemporary history'). According to the Federal Court, this does not mean that the degree of fame of the individual is never relevant in assessing the public interest. It may well be that the degree is relevant in some cases but this will depend on the individual facts of the case. In this particular case, the Federal Court of Justice held that the photographs did not contribute to a debate of general interest and did not provide information about a *zeitgeschichtliches Ereignis*. The pictures showed the claimant on holiday, a fundamental part of the private sphere, according to the Court. In the balancing of interests, information that is considered mere entertainment *and* has no 'societal relevance' has less weight than the claimant's right of personality. For these reasons, the Court reinstated the injunction against the publication of all of the photographs but held that those articles which related to the illness of Prince Rainier could be published given their capacity to contribute to a debate of general interest in a democratic society.[164] At the same time, the Court refused to examine the content of the written accounts stating that freedom of press had priority in this particular situation.[165] The method used in this new approach is called the '*abgestuftes Schutzkonzept*' (the concept of variable protection').[166] We should note that the constitutionality of this method has recently been confirmed by the Constitutional Court, reemphasising that entertainment continues to fall under the remit of the right to freedom of expression.[167]

Subsequent cases involving the partner of the singer Herbert Grönemeyer,[168] the footballer Oliver Kahn[169] and another set of cases involving Princess Caroline and her husband[170] have been decided under precisely the same methodological framework. A recent case involving the talk show host Sabine Christiansen again confirms this 'new' approach towards public figures, but also highlights some

---

[162] *Ibid* citing BVerfGE 34, 269, 283 = NJW 1973, 1221 (*Soraya*); BGHZ 131, 332, 334 = NJW 1996, 1128 (*Caroline von Monaco*).

[163] BVerfG, NJW 2006, 3406, 3407 (*Uschi Glas*).

[164] BGH, NJW 2007, 1977, 1980 (*Caroline im Urlaub*).

[165] *Ibid.*

[166] BGH GRUR 2007, 523 (*Abgestuftes Schutzkonzept*). See further Coors, 'Headwind from Europe' (2010).

[167] BVerfG, NJW 2008, 1793 (*Caroline von Monaco*).

[168] BGH, NJW 2007, 3440 (*Lebensgefährtin H Grönemeyers*).

[169] BGH, NJW 2008, 749 (*Oliver Kahn*).

[170] BGH, NJW 2009, 754 (*Caroline von Monaco und Prinz Ernst August von Hannover*).

other interesting points.[171] Similar to the other cases, the claimant was on holiday in Mallorca and was photographed shopping with her cleaner. The Court held that the article alone may have been justified but the picture was an unwarranted infringement of the claimant's personality. Moreover, the fact that the claimant had opened her private life to the press in the past was not relevant to the finding of infringement of personality on the facts of this particular case.

What emerges from this glance at recent developments is that following *von Hannover (No 1)*, in cases involving high-profile celebrities, formerly known as absolute persons of contemporary history, the courts have, for all intents and purposes, abandoned the categorisation stemming from the KUG. This has also been argued in the literature.[172] In reaching this conclusion, the courts have not held that the individual's degree of fame is irrelevant, rather this will depend on the facts of the case. But it is certainly clear that German courts no longer place the same emphasis on categorising public figures. Yet, the courts must (as they have acknowledged) follow the express will of the legislator under the KUG. What all of this means, in effect, is that public figures must still tolerate photographs being taken of them when they depict a *zeitgeschichtliches Ereignis* but it appears that courts are much more willing to find the infringement of a legitimate interest under § 23 (2) KUG and thus a balancing exercise becomes necessary. Being on holidays, even if surrounded by members of the public, is considered part of a celebrity's private sphere. In theory, then, the courts have edged German law closer to the approach of the ECtHR and the general position in French law; in other words, everyone, whether in the public eye or not, has a right to respect for their private life, unless the information in question contributes to a debate of general interest. The courts insist that a *zeitgeschichtliches Ereignis* is to be interpreted broadly and can include mere entertainment, but this will depend on the facts of the case.

We should also note that in *Von Hannover (No 2)*,[173] the ECtHR has had opportunity to consider the *abgestuftes Schutzkonzept* albeit not *in abstracto* but in the context of whether it was applied in such a way that infringed the applicant's Article 8 rights.[174] The ECtHR found that both German courts 'carefully balanced' the rights of freedom of expression and respect for private life.[175] As part of this exercise, the national courts considered whether the information in question contributed to a debate of general interest.[176] For these reasons, the ECtHR was satisfied that the German courts took adequate account of von *Hannover (No 1)* and

[171] BGH, NJW 2008, 3138 (*Einkaufsbummel im Urlaub*).

[172] See Teichmann, 'Abschied von der absoluten Person der Zeitgeschichte' [2007].

[173] *von Hannover* v *Germany (No 2)* (Judgment of 7 February 2012) (Applications nos 40660/08 and 60641/08).

[174] *Ibid* at para 121.

[175] *Ibid* at para 124.

[176] *Ibid*.

that they had not 'failed to comply with their positive obligations under Article 8 of the Convention.'[177]

What are the implications of these developments for our task? How might a German court decide *Mosley* in the post-*von Hannover (No 1)* setting? While there may be some differences in the terminology used by the court, I fail to see how the reasoning would change in substance. Despite the intense excitement generated by the initial *von Hannover* decision, one has to question whether the abandonment of the categorisation of public figures doctrine in favour of the *abgestuftes Schutzkonzept* changes anything in practice. Indeed, this was one of the applicant's arguments in *von Hannover (No 2)*. On this account, the German courts have continued to apply a categorisation test, albeit not expressed in those terms; rather, the German courts now refer to 'prominent persons' or 'high profile persons' in its place.[178] But how can it be otherwise? It is obvious that celebrities will attract more public attention than ordinary individuals who are not normally in the public eye. Clearly it would be wrong to say that the private lives of public figures are fair game for the media[179] but it would be equally wrong to take no account of the public profile of the claimant in an action. After all, this public profile explains the media interest and it is more likely that disclosure will contribute to a debate of general interest than would be the case where the information relates to a non-public person. The central question, therefore, is not how we categorise claimants but *whether there is a public interest in disclosure*. In other words, in the context of our hard case, I suspect that we would reach the same conclusion applying the *abgestuftes Schutzkonzept* as we did when we applied the categorisation of persons test. Under German law, in the absence of an overriding public interest, Mr Mosley would be likely to have obtained an injunction to prevent publication of both the images *and* the written account of the private party. If a public interest had been established, then, taking the principle of proportionality into account, it is probable that the publication of the images would have been enjoined but the written account permitted.

4.3.3 Discussion

I will argue in the next chapter that the various doctrinal tests we have just considered help promote clarity and transparency while at the same time give

[177] *Ibid* at para 126.

[178] *Ibid* at para 84.

[179] We should note that the old German categorisation did not suggest anything of this sort—it merely created a presumption in law that the publication of private information about absolute persons of contemporary history was in the public interest (and therefore lawful) unless the absolute person could demonstrate that one of his legitimate interests (such as privacy) was at stake.

expression to clear ideals of justice and core constitutional and private law principles. The upshot is a clearer sense of purpose in German law, especially when compared to English law.

Nonetheless, it is possible to identify some similarities between the English and German approaches, particularly in claims for misuse of private information. When English courts employ the reasonable expectation test, for instance, they have identified clear principles and, incidentally, points of intersection with German law, for example the notion that the publication of photographs is more invasive than mere words, and the need to provide a higher level of protection for children.[180] Moreover, parallels can be drawn between the reasonable expectation test and the German categorisation of public figures. Moreham views the reasonable expectation test as going 'some way towards striking an appropriate balance between objective and subjective measures.[181] The test is assessed from the perspective of the claimant and this is subjectively sensitive. Did the individual in question have an expectation that the information would be kept private? However, the use of the term 'reasonable' can be regarded as an 'objective check'.[182] Moreham maintains that the test enables 'a court to distinguish between X, an outspoken, "out" campaigner for gay rights, and Z, who has never discussed his homosexuality, and between Y, who voluntarily appeared on a 24-hour surveillance "reality TV" show, and Z, who has never sought publicity.'[183] A categorisation of claimants is thus implicit within the reasonable expectation test.

There are also similarities between the reasonable expectation test and German doctrine on spheres of privacy. Consider *Campbell.* In this case there are two different types of information at stake: firstly that the appellant had been taking drugs, a charge which she vehemently denied in the past. This arguably falls under the *public sphere* and all five judges considered that the press had the right to correct this information. The second type of information, the photographs of the appellant taken outside a Narcotics Anonymous meeting, pertained to her medical treatment and could therefore be regarded as falling under the *intimate sphere*. The majority of their Lordships held that Ms Campbell was entitled to damages for the publication of these photographs, recognising that even a celebrity who actively seeks publicity has the right to keep certain intimate information private. Another indication that the graded sphere test is compatible with English law stems from Baroness Hale's speech in *Campbell* where, in effect, she sets out at a similar graded analysis of free speech, with degrees ranging from political to artistic speech.[184]

---

[180] *Cf*, for instance, *Murray* v *Big Pictures Ltd* [2008] 3 WLR 1360 and BVerfG AfP 2000, 75 (*Caroline von Monaco*).

[181] Moreham, 'Privacy in the Common Law' (2005) at 645.

[182] *Ibid.*

[183] *Ibid.*

[184] *Campbell* v *MGN Ltd* [2004] 2 AC 457 at 499 (per Baroness Hale).

Despite these similarities, what is clear from our overview is that the lack of purpose in English law leads to confusion and creates an impression of arbitrary decision-making. This problem is neatly illustrated by the English courts' treatment of information about sexual activities. While the courts have been forced to concede that 'to most people the details of their sexual lives are high on their list of those matters which they regard as confidential',[185] there does not appear to be agreement in the case law on whether all types of sexual activity automatically attract a reasonable expectation of privacy. In *A* v *B plc*, Jack J asserted that 'the law should afford the protection of confidentiality to facts concerning sexual relations within marriage (which is surely straightforward) and, in the context of modern sexual relations, it should be no different with relationships outside marriage'.[186] However, in the Court of Appeal, Lord Woolf criticised this approach saying that it makes no allowance for 'the very different nature of the [relationships in that particular case] from that which would exist within marriage.' On his account, 'there is a significant difference. . .between the confidentiality which attaches to what is intended to be a permanent relationship and that which attaches to [other more transient relationships such as short-term affairs]'.[187] Similarly, in *Theakston* v *MGN Ltd*, Ouseley J considered it:

> impossible however to invest with the protection of confidentiality all acts of physical intimacy regardless of circumstances. I consider it artificial to draw a line at full sexual intercourse in the context of confidentiality, such that anything short of that is not confidential. Whilst the degree of intimacy is a very relevant factor, it cannot be taken in isolation from the relationship within which the physical intimacy occurs and from the other circumstances particularly the location. . . .Sexual relations within marriage at home would be at one end of the range or matrix of circumstances to be protected from most forms of disclosure; a one night stand with a recent acquaintance in a hotel bedroom might very well be protected from press publicity. A transitory engagement in a brothel is yet further away.[188]

In these cases, the nature of the sexual relationship in question was pivotal and courts would not prevent publication of information about 'non-permanent' relationships. But the prominence given to a relationship's duration in these analyses is unfortunate. It creates the impression that the lawfulness of any particular disclosure depends on what the judge understands as constituting a permanent as opposed to a 'transient' relationship. Scott argues that '[i]n general terms, this view is no longer considered to be an accurate statement of the approach of the law'.[189] But in support of this proposition, he merely cites Eady J's warning in *CC* v *AB*:

> Judges need to be wary about giving the impression that they are ventilating, while affording or refusing legal redress, some personal moral or social views, and especially

[185] *Stephens* v *Avery* [1988] Ch 449 at 454 (per Sir Browne-Wilkinson VC).

[186] *A* v *B plc* [2001] 1 WLR 2341 at 2353.

[187] *A* v *B plc* [2003] QB 195 at 216.

[188] *Theakston* v *MGN Ltd* [2002] EMLR 22 at 418.

[189] Scott, 'Misuse of Private Information' (2010) p 598.

> at a time when society is far less homogeneous than in the past. . . .A judge, like any one else, is obviously entitled to hold personal moral views about the issues of the day, but it is important not to let them intrude when interpreting and applying the law. Such issues are best avoided—at least without some statutory sanction. No doubt many people, especially those with a strong religious faith, will disapprove of adultery. Many others, on the other hand, will not give it a second thought, while moving easily through a series of medium or short-term relationships as they feel it appropriate. With such a wide range of differing views in society, perhaps more than for many generations, one must guard against allowing legal judgments to be coloured by personal attitudes. Even among judges, there is no doubt a wide range of opinion. It is all the more important, therefore, that the outcome of a particular case should not be determined by the judge's personal views or, as it used to be said, by "the length of Chancellor's foot".[190]

According to Eady J, judges must opt instead for the 'new methodology' and apply an 'intense focus' to the facts of the case 'in order to avoid the appearance of cases being decided on the basis of arbitrary personal differences between the judges.' This is 'plainly undesirable because it would undermine faith in the rule of law'.[191] Eady J is right to highlight the concerns about arbitrary decision-making but his view that the 'new methodology' is the solution to our problem is curious. Can we be so sure that applying an 'intense focus' to the facts of the case relieves the anxiety about arbitrary decision-making? We shall revisit this question in the next chapter.

In this overview, we find that the German approach to misuse of private information cases is more principled and coherent. We now turn to consider a type of invasion of privacy for which legal protection is lacking: intrusion into a person's seclusion.

4.4 Intrusion into a Person's Seclusion

Our next hard case is *Kaye* v *Robertson*. This case involves both a disclosure of private information *and* at the same time an intrusion into a person's seclusion. However, it is only this latter privacy interest that we consider here. This form of invasion of privacy is becoming all the more common as technology advances and takes the form of 'prying, spying, telephone-tapping, bugging, interception of correspondence, searches, and other physical intrusions.'[192] But English tort law, as it stands, lacks a general cause of action or a combination of actions that cater for this specific type of invasion of privacy.

---

[190] *CC v AB* [2007] EMLR 11 at 319.

[191] *Ibid.*

[192] See Hong Kong Law Reform Commission, *Consultation Paper on Civil Liability for Invasion of Privacy* (1999) p 70.

4.4.1 Hard Case: *Kaye* v *Robertson*

Kaye v *Robertson* is a remarkable case for it encapsulates the awkwardness resulting from a lack of an effective remedy in English law. The plaintiff in this case was Mr Gordon Kaye, a well-known television actor. In early 1990, Mr Kaye was involved in a traffic accident and suffered 'severe injuries to his head and brain.'[193] He was transported to hospital and was placed on a life-support machine for three days before being moved to a private room. Given Mr Kaye's fame, there was intense media interest in the accident and his condition. As a result, the hospital authorities decided to place notices on the premises requiring visitors to first report to a member of staff. A list of persons authorised to visit Mr Kaye was placed outside his room. The defendants in this case were the editor and publisher of the *Sunday Sport*, a weekly tabloid newspaper, described by Potter J at first instance as having a 'lurid and sensational style'.[194] On 13 February 1990, a *Sunday Sport* journalist and photographer gained access to the ward in which Mr Kaye was being treated. They ignored the notices and entered the actor's room and alleged that the plaintiff agreed to provide an interview. They then proceeded to take photographs of the plaintiff and his surroundings. When the hospital staff discovered what was happening, the journalists were ejected from the building.

In the course of the trial, medical evidence was provided to the court that showed that Mr Kaye was not in a 'fit condition' to provide consent for the interview. At first instance, Potter J granted interlocutory relief criticising the actions of the newspaper.[195] The defendants appealed the decision arguing that they had achieved a 'great old-fashioned scoop', adding that the plaintiff 'only had to refuse'.[196] The Court of Appeal was very critical of the reporters and indicated that the claimant's interest in being left alone, particularly while ill in hospital, was deserving of protection. But English law, as it stood, could not offer any real protection and the Court confirmed that there was no right of privacy in English law. Bingham LJ spoke for the Court when he recorded:

> If ever a person has a right to be let alone by strangers with no public interest to pursue, it must surely be when he lies in hospital recovering from brain surgery and in no more than partial command of his faculties. It is this invasion of his privacy which underlies the plaintiff's complaint. Yet it alone, however gross, does not entitle him to relief in English law.[197]

Glidewell LJ presented the problem facing the court in the following way: '[I]n the absence of such a right the plaintiff's advisers have sought to base their claim to

---

[193] *Kaye* v *Robertson* [1991] FSR 62 at 63.

[194] *Ibid* at 64.

[195] *Ibid* (per Glidewell LJ) citing Potter J at first instance.

[196] *Ibid*.

[197] *Ibid* at 70 (per Bingham LJ).

injunctions upon other well-established rights of action.'[198] The Lord Justice intimated that where a plaintiff cannot depend on the 'right' in question, he must attempt to rely on other procedural 'rights of action' that may or may not protect his interests. In this particular case, these rights of action included libel, malicious falsehood, trespass to the person and passing-off. Whether consciously, or not, Glidewell LJ highlighted the remedial focus of English law, *ubi remedium ibi jus*.[199] The Lord Justice indicated that the article itself could be considered libellous on the authority of *Tolley* v *Fry* but emphasised that the jurisdiction to award interim injunctions in libel actions should be 'exercised only sparingly' and he could not say for sure whether a jury would find libel.[200] On trespass, the Lord Justice was unwilling to treat a flash of a camera light as battery and the requirements for passing-off were not met as the plaintiff could not be regarded as a 'trader' within the meaning of the action.[201] Glidewell LJ reasoned, however, that the tort of malicious falsehood could provide relief in this case. The words contained in the article were false and, given Mr Kaye's condition in hospital, publication of the article would be malicious. The particular difficulty with this cause of action was that special damage had to be shown as a consequence of the malicious falsehood. But here Glidewell LJ argued that Mr Kaye had 'a potentially valuable right to sell the story of his accident and his recovery'. If the defendants were allowed to publish the article in the way they proposed, the 'value of this right would... be seriously lessened, and Mr Kaye's story thereafter would be worth much less to him.'[202] In this way, at a stretch, the Court was able to justify an interlocutory injunction. Bingham LJ warned that had the plaintiff 'failed to establish any cause of action, [and] we should of course have been powerless to act, however great our sympathy for the plaintiff and however strong our distaste for the defendant's conduct.'[203]

4.4.2 How Might a German Court Decide Kaye?

In the general personality right jurisprudence of the German civil courts, the protection of the physical private sphere is of paramount importance, so much so that a spatial understanding of privacy constituted the original approach of the

[198] *Ibid* at 66 (per Glidewell LJ).

[199] See also Markesinis, 'The Calcutt Report must not be forgotten' (1992).

[200] *Kaye* v *Robertson* [1991] FSR 62 at 67. Glidewell LJ stated that the judgment of the Master of the Rolls in *Coulson* v *Coulson* [1887] 3 TLR 46 is 'still the rule in actions for defamation, despite the decision of the House of Lords in *American Cyanamid Co* v *Ethicon Ltd* [1975] AC 396 in relation to interim injunctions generally.'

[201] *Kaye* v *Robertson* [1991] FSR 62 at 68–69.

[202] *Ibid* at 68.

[203] *Ibid* at 70.

German courts. The home, in particular, is considered the 'core of the physical private sphere' ('*Kern der räumlichen Privatsphäre*').[204] As early as 1957, the Federal Court of Justice understood this core as extending to private places outside the home, such as a business office.[205] For its part, the Constitutional Court treats a private space as any place where an individual is or should be free from public surveillance.[206] The German courts have held that the '*Kern*' of the physical private sphere extends to places where the individual temporarily resides.[207] This applies to hotel rooms and holiday homes,[208] for example, and presumably would also apply to a private hospital room, as in *Kaye*. Visitors to a family home (and, by analogy, to a hospital room) are not permitted to disseminate publicly what they have seen and heard, even in cases where the visitor has been told or shown the private information in person.[209] While there are also potential criminal provisions that are relevant here,[210] it is likely that a German court would consider the actions of the journalists in *Kaye* an injury to the general personality right and therefore the claimant would be entitled to both an injunction (if applicable) and damages under § 823 (1) BGB.

4.4.3 Discussion

The brevity of this account of German law is in itself revealing for it highlights that the outcome of cases such as these is generally clear and uncontroversial in Germany. An individual, who intrudes upon the seclusion of another person, commits a legal wrong. If we contrast this position with the conclusion the Court of Appeal reached in *Kaye*, the deficiencies in English law become apparent and we have to question the veracity of Denning's confident declaration in *British Steel Corp* v *Grenada Television Ltd* (1980) that '[t]he courts will always be ready to grant an injunction' where there is an invasion of privacy.[211] However, it is even more remarkable that despite the Human Rights Act and all of the fanfare surrounding the development of a new privacy tort, we still find no formal protection for these sorts of interests in English tort law. It is difficult to see how the tort of

---

[204] Wanckel, 'Der Schutz vor Indiskretion' (2008) p 337.

[205] BGH NJW 1957, 1315, 1316 (*Spätheimkehrer*).

[206] BVerfG NJW 2000, 1021, 1022 (*Caroline von Monaco*).

[207] On this point, see Wanckel, 'Der Schutz vor Indiskretion' (2008) p 337.

[208] BGH GRUR 2004, 438, 439 (*Feriendomizil I*).

[209] Wanckel, 'Der Schutz vor Indiskretion' (2008) p 338 citing BGH NJW 1981, 1366, 1367 (*Aufmacher II*).

[210] Consider, for example, *Hausfriedensbruchs* (breach of the peace of the home) under § 123 StGB and the various provisions on breach of confidentiality under §§ 201–203 StGB. On this point, see Heuchemer, 'Die Verletzung des persönlichen Lebens- und Geheimbereichs' (2008) pp 459–465.

[211] *British Steel Corp* v *Grenada Television Ltd* [1980] WL 264756.

misuse of private information (especially when we consider trappings such as the ultimate balancing test) could be used as a cause of action by a claimant such as Mr Kaye. While we should note that some judges have made reference (*obiter*) to the absurdity of this situation,[212] it remains the case that there is no suitable cause of action for intrusion cases in English tort law. We will revisit these points in the next chapter but for now we turn to consider a branch of privacy law where the protection is not so much lacking rather the approach is in itself confused.

4.5 Misappropriation of Personality

I have conjectured that property and privacy are interdependent. In this section, we will consider the hard case of misappropriation of personality and the interaction between commercial and dignitary interests. Appropriation of personality overlaps considerably in practice with the other types of invasion of privacy but the distinguishing feature here is that it will generally be at stake when a person's name or likeness already has commercial value. Understood in these terms, the claimants in these cases are generally public figures. As noted earlier, this issue became more pertinent as the twentieth century progressed. Globalised merchandising supported by an increasing emphasis on celebrity culture means that the use of celebrity personas has become a multi-million dollar industry. This chimes with those who argue that any loss of control of personality should be understood as an interference with a property or 'publicity' right.[213] Others argue that while the interests in question appear to be proprietary, the appropriation of personality is in actuality an affront to human dignity. Bloustein has written that:

> No man wants to be "used" by another against his will, and it is for this reason that commercial use of a personal photograph is obnoxious. Use of a photograph for trade purposes turns a man into a commodity and makes him serve the economic needs and interest of others. In a community at all sensitive to the commercialization of human values, it is degrading to thus make a man a part of commerce against his will.[214]

As we will see below, this dichotomy is also evident in the case law—we find some examples of commercial appropriation that (according to the court) humiliate, embarrass and injure human feelings and we also find examples that supposedly involve economic interests only. These cases neatly demonstrate what Brüggemeier refers to as the *Doppelfunktion* of the right of image.[215]

---

[212] Lord Walker in *Douglas (No 3)*, speaking obiter, contrasted the Douglases' claim of invasion of privacy and the claimant's predicament in *Kaye*. See *Douglas* v *Hello (No 3)* [2008] 1 AC 1 at 81 (per Lord Walker).

[213] See, for example, Wacks, *Personal Information, Privacy and the Law* (1993) p 38.

[214] Bloustein 'Privacy as an Aspect of Human Dignity' (1964) at 988.

[215] Brüggemeier, *Haftungsrecht* (2006) p 300.

While the English law in this area remains underdeveloped, English courts have variously spoken of the publicity attributes of celebrities. In *Campbell*, for example, Lord Hoffmann stated that:

> Naomi Campbell is a famous fashion model who lives by publicity. What she has to sell is herself: her personal appearance and her personality. She employs public relations agents to present her personal life to the media in the best possible light just as she employs professionals to advise her on dress and make-up. That is no criticism of her. It is a trade like any other. But it does mean that her relationship with the media is different from that of people who expose less of their private life to the public.[216]

Yet, despite remarks of this sort, English courts have been reluctant to formally recognise a right of publicity. Rather, as is the case with other types of invasion of privacy, courts have sought to remedy wrongdoings in other ways, generally by drawing on intellectual property law and breach of confidence.[217] And so we return to the central issue—the obvious gaps in the English law. Our next hard case, *Douglas* v *Hello*, illustrates another such gap.

[216] *Campbell v MGN Ltd* [2004] 2 AC 457, at 470.

[217] Perhaps the most common action in publicity-type cases is passing-off. But this cause of action too provides only limited protection in cases where an individual is subjected to the commercial appropriation of her personality. This is because a successful action in passing-off requires the following elements to be present: '(1) A misrepresentation, (2) made by a trader in the course of trade, (3) to prospective customers of his or ultimate consumers of goods or services supplied by him, (4) which is calculated to injure the business or goodwill of another trader and (5) which causes actual damage to a business or goodwill of the claimant or will probably do so'. See *Erven Warnink Besloten Vennootschap and Another* v *J Townend & Sons (Hull) Ltd* [1979] AC 731 at 742 (per Lord Diplock). What proves most problematic for claimants is demonstrating that they have 'trading goodwill' within the meaning of the action. Taken on its own, this is a significant obstacle, but in *McCulloch* v *May*, Wynn-Parry J introduced the further requirement that there has to be a common field of activity between the claimant and defendant. See *McCulloch* v *Lewis A May (Produce Distributors Ltd)* [1947] 2 All ER 845. Despite the existence of such procedural hurdles, the courts have been willing to allow claims in passing-off in a limited range of circumstances. In *Irvine* v *Talksport*, Laddie J held that the modern law of passing-off should apply to cases where there is a false claim or implication that the claimant has endorsed a product. According to him, the claimant has to prove that he had significant reputation or goodwill at the time of the infringement. Moreover, he has to show that the actions of the defendant gave rise to a false message which would be understood by 'a not insignificant section of his market' that the product had been endorsed by the claimant. See *Irvine* v *Talksport Ltd* [2002] FSR 60, at 959. Yet, despite decisions of this sort, on the whole, courts have remained unmoved by arguments to extend the passing-off doctrine to cater for publicity interests generally. Pure character merchandising, for instance, is not actionable under the tort of passing-off. See, for example, *Elvis Presley Trademarks* [1999] RPC 567 at 597–8 (per Brown LJ).

4.5.1 Hard Case: Douglas v Hello

Douglas v *Hello* is in fact a series of cases with 'a complex factual and procedural history'.[218] In what follows, I detail the Court of Appeal decision and House of Lords appeal in *Douglas* v *Hello (No 3)*.[219] This is because questions about the boundaries of privacy and commercial interests were considered by the Lords.

The first named claimants, Michael Douglas and Catherine Zeta Jones announced in 2000 that they intended to marry. From the very moment of the announcement, there was what one of the claimants called a 'media frenzy' and 'intense interest' on the part of certain publishers.[220] The publishers of Hello! and OK! magazines approached the couple with proposals to publish photographs of the wedding in return for a fee. Both magazines sought an exclusive right of publication. The couple decided to grant the right of publication to one publisher only because, according to Mr Douglas, this was 'the best way to control the media and to protect our privacy.'[221] The couple chose OK! magazine and entered into a contract under which they were to receive £500,000 each in return for the exclusive right to publish photographs of and information about the wedding for a period of 9 months. Of particular note is clause 6 of the contract, which stipulated that the couple were to 'use their best efforts to ensure that no other media… shall be permitted access to the wedding, and that no guests or anyone present at the wedding… shall be allowed to take photographs.'[222] Moreover, the magazine agreed that it would only publish photographs that had been approved by the Douglases. Despite the couple taking what they regarded as adequate precautions, a paparazzo, Mr Rupert Thorpe, managed to gain access to the wedding reception and surreptitiously photographed proceedings. Through an intermediary, these photographs were eventually sold to Hello! magazine. On learning that Hello! intended to publish these unauthorised photographs, the Douglases and OK! sought and obtained an interlocutory injunction restraining publication. Hello! appealed and the Court of Appeal lifted the injunction.[223] As a result, both OK! and Hello! magazines published the authorised and unauthorised photographs simultaneously in their next issues. Following the discharge of the injunction, the claimants then sought damages.

In the High Court, Lindsay J found for the claimants.[224] On his account, there was an obvious breach of confidence in the context of a private event. He awarded the Douglases damages, though these were of a nominal nature reflecting the

---

[218] *Douglas* v *Hello (No 3)* [2006] QB 125 at 140 (per Phillips MR).

[219] *Douglas* v *Hello (No 3)* [2006] QB 125; *Douglas* v *Hello (No 3)* [2008] 1 AC 1.

[220] *Douglas* v *Hello (No 3)* [2006] QB 125 at 140.

[221] *Ibid.*

[222] *Ibid* at 141.

[223] *Douglas v Hello! Ltd* [2001] QB 967.

[224] *Douglas v Hello* [2003] 3 All ER 996.

distress caused by the publication of unapproved photographs, and rejected the argument that damages ought to be estimated on the basis of a notional licence fee. He awarded OK! over one million pounds reflecting the loss of profit arising from the unauthorised publication. According to Lindsay J, the breach of confidence suffered was akin to a trade secret. This is because the law of confidence protects 'those who seek to manage their publicity as part of their trade or profession and whose private life is a valuable commodity.'[225] In this sense he treated the information as property, the benefit of which could be 'shared between and... enforceable by co-owners or by a successor in title.'[226] In effect, then, the trial judge drew a distinction between privacy and commercial confidence. The Douglases suffered an invasion of privacy when unauthorised photographs over which they had no control were published. At the same time, there was a commercial wrong and this was recognised in the damages awarded for the labour and expense of editing the photographs for OK! magazine at short notice (once Hello!'s intention to publish had been discovered).

The Court of Appeal dismissed Hello!'s appeal against those aspects of Lindsay J's judgment dealing with the Douglases' privacy and commercial confidence.[227] The Court accepted that there had been an invasion of privacy. On its account, it could not be the case that the contract entered into with OK! magazine meant that the Douglases were precluded from treating their wedding as a private event.[228] The publication of the unauthorised photographs was simply a case where information that 'the claimant could reasonably expect would remain private has been made public'[229] and the claimants retained a 'residual right of privacy' in these details.[230] Referring to the commercial interests, the Court stated that 'this head of damage had nothing to do with interference with private life. It was based on an assertion that the Douglases had a commercial interest in making public information about their wedding, which they were entitled to protect.'[231] The Court went on:

> Recognition of the right of a celebrity to make money out of publicising private information about himself, including his photographs on a private occasion, breaks new ground. It has echoes of the *droit à l'image* in Article 9 of the French Code Civil and the German cause of action that Professor Markesinis describes as the 'tort of publicity claim'. . . .We can see no reason in principle why equity should not protect the opportunity to profit from confidential information about oneself in the same circumstances that it protects the opportunity to profit from confidential information in the nature of a trade secret.[232]

[225] *Ibid* at 1053.

[226] *Ibid.*

[227] *Douglas* v *Hello (No 3)* [2006] QB 125.

[228] *Ibid* at 163.

[229] *Ibid* at 162.

[230] *Ibid* at 169.

[231] *Ibid* at 163.

[232] *Ibid* at 164.

The Court described its recognition of this protection as breaking new ground.[233] However the Lord Justices disagreed with Lindsay J who maintained that the information in question could be treated as property and therefore could be owned and transferred. The Court reached this conclusion after carefully examining the contract provisions agreed between the Douglases and OK! magazine. It was clear that the contract 'did not purport to transfer to or share with OK! the right to use, or even know of, any photographic information about the wedding other than the approved photographs released to OK! by the Douglases for publication…'.[234] In this sense OK!'s right to use the photographs was no more than an licence, albeit an exclusive licence, to commercially exploit those photographs for a certain time period. The licence did not carry with it any assignment rights. The Court referred to the case of *Allen & Hanbury Ltd* v *Generics Ltd*,[235] in which Lord Diplock stated that a licence passes no proprietary interest in anything; it only makes an action lawful which would otherwise have been unlawful. In the absence of statutory provisions such as copyright law, which gives an exclusive licensee of intellectual property the right to sue an infringer, a mere licence to use approved photographs of an event does not carry with it the right to sue a third party for infringement. That right rests with the licensor. The publication of unauthorised photographs invaded the Douglases' privacy and it was they, not OK!, who had the right to protect this area of privacy. Therefore, the Court allowed Hello!'s appeal against Lindsay J's award of £1 million reflecting loss of profit.

Understood in these terms, the Court of Appeal drew a distinction between dignitarian privacy interests and interests in commercial confidence. For this reason, it questioned why the Douglases contended that they were entitled to a notional licence fee on the basis of the fee they would have charged to Hello! magazine for publication of the photographs. The Court emphasised that the:

> whole basis of [the Douglases'] (as opposed to OK!'s) complaint about Hello!'s publication of the unauthorised photographs is upset and affront at invasion of privacy, not loss of the opportunity to earn money. Indeed, they have already claimed and been paid, damages assessed on that former basis.[236]

---

[233] The Court cited a number of English cases including *Saltman Engineering Co Ltd* v *Campbell Engineering Co Ltd* (1948) 65 RPC 203; *Mustad & Son* v *Dosen (Note)* [1964] 1 WLR 109; *Shelley Films Ltd* v *Rex Features Ltd* [1994] EMLR 134; *Creation Records Ltd* v *News Group Newspapers Ltd* [1997] EMLR 444. From these cases, the Court extracted the following general principle: 'Where an individual ("the owner") has at his disposal information which he has created or which is private or personal and to which he can properly deny access to third parties, and he reasonably intends to profit commercially by using or publishing that information, then a third party who is, or ought to be, aware of these matters and who has knowingly obtained the information without authority, will be in breach of duty if he uses or publishes the information to the detriment of the owner.' *Ibid* at 165.

[234] *Ibid* at 168.

[235] *Allen & Hanbury Ltd* v *Generics Ltd* [1986] RPC 203.

[236] *Douglas* v *Hello (No 3)* [2006] QB 125 at 200.

In reflecting *obiter* on this distinction between privacy and commercial interests, the Court maintained that damages could not be an adequate remedy in cases of invasion of privacy causing distress. On its account, 'only by the grant of an interlocutory injunction could the Douglases' rights have been satisfactorily protected.'[237] While *Cream Holdings Ltd* v *Banjerjee* ensures that claimants must satisfy a high threshold test in seeking an interlocutory injunction,[238] the court suggested that 'with the benefit of the reasoning' in Campbell and *von Hannover (No 1)*, the Cream Holdings test would have been satisfied in this particular case.

The House of Lords granted leave of appeal to OK! magazine on the question of the damages for loss of profit. A majority allowed the appeal and reinstated Lindsay J's original award on the basis of breach of confidence.[239] The photographic images were capable of being protected by the traditional doctrine of breach of confidence in that they were of commercial value and the Douglases had sufficient control to enable them to impose an obligation of confidence. There was no public policy reason why the doctrine of breach of confidence should not protect such information. Lord Hoffmann insisted that this was merely using the doctrine of breach of confidence in a way that made business sense and the decision does not create an image right or 'any other unorthodox form of intellectual property.'[240] Lords Nicholls and Walker dissented on the grounds that breach of confidence had been stretched too far from its original purpose. On their account, it was not possible to establish the existence of a trade secret.[241]

Douglas v *Hello* is revealing for it highlights the complexity of publicity claims, especially the interaction between dignitarian and commercial interests. What emerges from our overview is that the English courts are keen to distinguish the two interests. But, as we will see, German courts have reached an entirely different conclusion.

---

[237] *Ibid* at 202.

[238] *Cream Holdings Ltd* v *Banjerjee* [2005] 1 AC 253.

[239] *Douglas* v *Hello (No 3)* [2008] 1 AC 1.

[240] *Ibid* at 49.

[241] Lord Nicholls argued that the 'secret information cannot lie in the differences between the unapproved photographs and the approved photographs. The secret cannot lie there, because the six unapproved photographs contained nothing not included in the approved photographs. That is common ground. This being so, the inevitable differences, in expression and posture and so on, cannot constitute "confidential" information for the purposes of this equitable principle. The expression of the bride in one wedding photograph compared with her expression in another is insufficiently significant to call for legal protection. It has not been suggested that the unapproved photographs were embarrassing in any way, or that they were detrimental to the Douglases' image. Accordingly, once the approved pictures were published, albeit simultaneously, publication of the unapproved pictures was not a breach of confidence.' *Ibid* at 73.

4.5.2 *How Might a German Court Decide Douglas?*

In *Douglas*, citing Markesinis, the Court of Appeal refers to a German cause of action called a 'tort of publicity claim'.[242] But this is not entirely accurate. While some German scholars have argued for a freestanding right of publicity existing alongside the dignitarian general personality right (a *Dualistischer Ansatz*),[243] most argue for a *Monistischer Ansatz*—in other words, the commercial publicity interest remains an aspect of the general personality right.[244] The idea that personal and commercial (*ideelle und materielle*) interests are inseparable appears to have been accepted by the German courts.[245] This blurs the ostensibly sharp division between dignitarian and commercial interests. In order to explain why this is so, we must first pay close attention to the line of relevant authority in Germany.

The legal recognition of publicity interests has its roots in the KUG but that statute, as originally drafted, was not designed to protect commercial interests attached to an image.[246] Soon enough, the *Reichsgericht* was faced with this problem when a company used the name and portrait of Count Zeppelin as a trademark for its tobacco product.[247] The Court held that nobody has the right to use the name or image of another person as a trademark without that person's knowledge or consent. The right to one's own name and image is not assignable but that does not exclude the possibility of permitting another to use the name or image as a trademark by contract.[248] Brüggemeier argues that the *Reichsgericht* recognised *in effect* the economic aspects of the right of name and image. Earlier authors, such as von Gierke, had argued that some personality rights could also be regarded as property rights but the *Reichsgericht* refused to take this step.[249]

The first significant step taken towards the formal recognition of commercial publicity interests as an aspect of the personality right came in 1956. A photographer had taken (with consent) a picture of the famous actor Paul Dahlke sitting on his scooter, but subsequently sold the photograph to a scooter manufacturer, in breach of the original terms.[250] The photographer told the manufacturer that Dahlke

---

[242] *Douglas* v *Hello (No 3)* [2006] QB 125 at 113.

[243] Heitman, *Der Schutz der materiellen Interessen an der eigenen Persönlichkeitssphäre durch subjektiv-private Rechte zugleich ein Beitrag zur Abgrenzung des allgemeinen Persönlichkeitsrechts* (1963) cited by Götting, 'Ideeller und kommerzieller Persönlichkeitsschutz' (2008) p 198.

[244] On the distinction between a *Dualistischer* and *Monistischer Ansatz*, see Götting, *ibid* pp 197–199.

[245] *Ibid* p 199.

[246] *Ibid* pp 311–316.

[247] *Ibid* p 311 citing RGZ 74, 308 (*Graf Zeppelin*).

[248] RGZ 74, 308, 311–312.

[249] Brüggemeier, *Haftungsrecht* (2006) p 311 citing von Gierke, *Deutsches Privatrecht* (1895) p 706.

[250] BGHZ 20, 345 = NJW 1956, 1554 (*Paul Dahlke*).

had agreed to such use of his photograph and the manufacturer thus published several advertisements containing the image. On learning of these developments, Dahlke sued for compensation. The Federal Court of Justice first held that such images could fall under the KUG but based its decision on the doctrine of unjust enrichment. On this account, celebrities normally command a substantial fee for the use of their photographs in advertisements. The injury here was therefore not a mere injury to personality interests but an injury to economic interests. The claimant was thus entitled to a restitutionary award in the form of a hypothetical licence fee under § 818 (2) BGB.[251] A similar process of reasoning can be found in other decisions. One such case involved Hans Joachim Fuchsberger, a popular game show host in Germany.[252] He had permitted a clothes shop to use a photograph of him opening a clothes shop. A group of opticians bought the photograph from the shop and used it in its advertisements. Fuchsberger sued one of the firms, which had used his image six times in the local press. The Court held that there was an unjust enrichment in the sense of § 812 BGB and the claimant was entitled to a hypothetical licence fee award under § 818 (2) BGB.

Recent case law gestures towards a formal recognition of the *Monistischer Ansatz*. In the *Marlene Dietrich* case, the daughter of the deceased actress sued the defendant for unauthorised use of her mother's name and life story in the production of a musical.[253] The defendant's company had registered the trade mark 'Marlene' and sold the right to other companies to advertise using the mark and an image of Dietrich. The claimant argued that this was an infringement of Dietrich's personality rights. The Court recalled that the general right of personality and its special manifestations, such as image and name, primarily protect non-economic interests, particularly the 'personality's entitlement to value and respect' ('*Wert- und Achtungsanspruchs der Persönlichkeit*').[254] While this protection often manifests itself in defensive actions, sometimes the injured person can claim compensation for economic and non-economic harm, the latter if there is a serious intrusion and the harm cannot be compensated in any other way.[255] Again, we must note that this claim was not based on pain and suffering under § 847 BGB but the protective mandate of Articles 1 (1) and 2 (1) GG.

As well as placing emphasis on the non-economic interests, the Court stressed that the general right of personality also protects those interests of an individual that are of economic worth. The Court explained:

'Der Abbildung, dem Namen sowie sonstigen Merkmalen der Persönlichkeit wie etwa der Stimme kann ein betraechtlicher	A considerable economic value can attach to the image, name and other features of the personality, like for example the voice. This

[251] BGHZ 20, 345, 353.

[252] BGH, NJW 1992, 2084 (*Fuchsberger*).

[253] BGHZ 143, 214 = NJW 2000, 2195 (*Marlene Dietrich*).

[254] BGHZ 143, 214, 218.

[255] *Ibid.*

wirtschaftlicher Wert zukommen, der im allgemeinen auf der Bekanntheit und dem Ansehen der Person in der Öffentlichkeit – meist durch besondere Leistungen etwa auf sportlichem oder künstlerischem Gebiet erworben – beruht. Die bekannte Persönlichkeit kann diese Popularität und ein damit verbundenes Image dadurch wirtschaftlich verwerten, dass sie Dritten gegen Entgelt gestattet, ihr Bildnis oder ihren Namen, aber auch andere Merkmale der Persönlichkeit, die ein Wiedererkennen ermöglichen, in der Werbung für Waren oder Dienstleistungen einzusetzen. Durch eine unerlaubte Verwertung ihrer Persönlichkeitsmerkmale etwa für Werbezwecke werden daher häufig weniger ideelle als kommerzielle Interessen der Betroffenen beeinträchtigt, weil diese sich weniger in ihrer Ehre und ihrem Ansehen verletzt fühlen, als vielmehr finanziell benachteiligt sehen.'[256]

value is generally based on the person's fame and reputation in the public eye – mostly as a result of special achievements in, for example, the areas of sport or the arts. A well-known personality can exploit this popularity and the image connected with it economically by allowing third parties to use his picture or his name and also other features of his personality which facilitate recognition in advertising for goods or services in return for money. Frequently therefore fewer non-material than commercial interests of the person affected are harmed by an unauthorised use of the features of his personality for the purpose for instance of advertising, because he will feel himself harmed less in his honour and his reputation than he will see himself as disadvantaged financially.[257]

A person has the right to freely decide whether and under what conditions his image or name is used by a third party for commercial purposes. If the individual is deceased this right passes to the heirs.[258] This recognition of the inheritability of economic interests connected to the human personality is highly significant. Unlike the personal elements that protect non-economic interests, the Court held that the elements of economic value could be inherited by Dietrich's daughter, her sole heir.[259] While the Federal Court of Justice had not expressly recognised this element of the personality right before, it reasoned that this was implicit in some of its decisions, such as *Mephisto*.[260] The Court argued that this extension was necessary for policy reasons stating that the character of a right can change in the estimation of a legal order.[261] In other words, the decision reflected the realities of the media age. The Court went on:

'Das Bild, der Name und andere kennzeichnende Persönlichkeitsmerkmale können schon seit jeher – als ein Reflex der von der Rechtsordnung gewährten Abwehrrechte gegenüber einer unbefugten Verwendung –

'The picture, name and other characterising features of the personality have always been capable – as a reflection of the defensive rights granted by the legal order against an unauthorised use – of being exploited

[256] BGHZ 143, 214, 219.

[257] Reproduced from the Institute for Transnational Law website, available at: www.utexas.edu/law/academics/centers/transnational/work_new/german/case.php?id=726

[258] BGHZ 143, 214, 220 (*Marlene Dietrich*).

[259] *Ibid.*

[260] BGHZ 50, 133, 137 = NJW 1968, 1773 (*Mephisto*).

[261] BGHZ 143, 214, 222 (*Marlene Dietrich*).

kommerziell verwertet und insbesondere für Werbezwecke eingesetzt werden. Damit war stets auch ein Schutz vermögenswerter Interessen verbunden, der aber nicht notwendig als ein selbständiger Bestandteil des Persönlichkeitsrechts angesehen werden musste. In den vergangenen Jahrzehnten haben sich die technischen, wirtschaftlichen und gesellschaftlichen Verhältnisse jedoch geändert. Persönlichkeitsmerkmale können mit verbesserten technischen Möglichkeiten in Bild und Ton festgehalten, vervielfältigt und verbreitet werden. Sie sind aufgrund der fortschreitenden Entwicklung der Massenmedien in einem zuvor nicht gekannten Ausmass wirtschaftlich nutzbar geworden. In der Werbung spielt der sogenannte Imagetransfer eine grosse Rolle, bei dem es darum geht, positive Assoziationen, die die Verbraucher mit einer bekannten Persönlichkeit verbinden, auf das zu bewerbende Produkt umzuleiten. In dieser Hinsicht tragen bekannte Persönlichkeiten in nicht unerheblichem Umfang zur Wertschöpfung bei. Die Möglichkeit der Vermarktung der Persönlichkeit etwa bekannter Sportler oder Künstler ist – ohne diesen Vorgang zu bewerten – zu einem wichtigen, nicht mehr wegzudenkenden Faktor in der Produktentwicklung geworden.'[262]

commercially and in particular of being used for advertising purposes (reference omitted). Protection of interests of financial value was also always connected with this, but it did not necessarily have to be regarded as an independent element of the right of personality. However in past decades technical, economic and business conditions have changed (reference omitted). Features of the personality can with improved technical opportunities be recorded in sound and vision, and copied and disseminated. They have become economically exploitable to an extent not previously known, because of the continuing development of the mass media. So-called image transfer has a large role to play in advertising. It involves diverting the positive associations, which consumers connect with a well-known personality, to the product to be advertised. In this respect well-known personalities contribute to creation of value to a considerable extent. The possibility of marketing the personality of, for instance, well-known figures in sport or the arts has – without passing judgement on this occurrence – become an important factor in product development which can no longer be imagined as not existing.'[263]

On this account, the recognition of the inheritability of certain economic elements of the general right of personality is absolutely essential in order to protect against commercial exploitation of the personality of a deceased person. Understood in this way, the heir adopts the role of the holder of the personality right and defends those interests in the way the deceased would have done had she been alive.[264]

The decision in *Marlene Dietrich* is a culmination of movements towards the express recognition of the *Monistischer Ansatz* in German law. This publicity right remains an aspect of the dignitarian general personality right.[265] What is significant about *Marlene Dietrich*, however, is that the Court went much further than it had in the past in that it indicated that publicity interests can also be inheritable. This case should be distinguished, however, from cases such as *Mephisto*, in which highly

[262] BGHZ 143, 214, 222–223.

[263] Reproduced from the Institute for Transnational Law website, available at: www.utexas.edu/law/academics/centers/transnational/work_new/german/case.php?id=726

[264] BGHZ 143, 214, 223 (*Marlene Dietrich*).

[265] For an enlightening analysis of these points, see Peifer, *Individualität im Zivilrecht* (2001).

personal claims can continue to exist after death but the next-of-kin are only entitled to defensive claims, such as injunction.[266] The difference in *Marlene Dietrich* is that the heir was entitled to claim for compensation. While the Court held that the question of assignation or transferability of such interests between living persons did not need to be decided in the present case, it is implicit in the judgment that the Court believed that such interests could be transferred during an individual's lifetime.[267] In a very real sense, then, it appears that the basic principles of property law apply to these interests[268] and as such it is almost beyond question that German civil law now protects commercial publicity interests as an aspect of the general personality right. Taken together, these authorities lend support to the proposition that the *Monistischer Ansatz* is formally recognised in German law.

It is therefore fruitful to consider how a German court might decide *Douglas*. First, given the case law in this area, it is likely that a German court would recognise (without difficulty) the commercial interests at stake. Understood in this way, it is possible that the Douglases would succeed in an action against Hello! magazine on the basis of a hypothetical licence fee under § 818 (2) BGB. Second, it is unlikely that a German court would come to the same conclusion as the English Court of Appeal on the relationship between privacy and publicity interests. The Court of Appeal argued that the Douglases' were 'entitled to protect' the 'commercial interest in making public information about their wedding' but argued that this interest had 'nothing to do with interference with private life.'[269] If it is indeed the case that German courts understand publicity interests as forming part of a *Monistischer Ansatz* of a general personality right, a German court would not accept, then, that publicity interests have 'nothing to do' with privacy interests. In that both interests speak to essential informing purposes of the personality, they are ontologically inter-dependent and inseparable. Conceivably, then, under the umbrella of the general personality right, the Douglases could claim for both an invasion of privacy and an injury to their publicity interests.

4.5.3 Discussion

The law of publicity rights is an extraordinarily complex field.[270] For this reason, my purpose here was not to provide a detailed exposition on this area of law, rather it was to sketch its contours and emphasise some of the complexities associated with attempting to establish the conceptual boundaries of privacy. The House of

---

[266] BGHZ 143, 214, 221–222 (*Marlene Dietrich*).

[267] *Ibid.*

[268] Brüggemeier, *Haftungsrecht* (2006) p 313.

[269] *Douglas* v *Hello (No 3)* [2006] QB 125 at 163.

[270] See in particular, Beverley-Smith, *The Commercial Appropriation of Personality* (2002); Black, *Publicity Rights and Image* (2011); McCarthy, *The Rights of Publicity and Privacy: Vols I & II* (2008).

Lords decision in *Douglas (No 3)* sheds some light on the status of publicity interests in English law but does not address all the unanswered questions. A number of points can be gleaned from our analysis. First, it appears reasonably certain that there are two types of breach of confidence actions in English law. One is the altered action, now better known as a tort of disclosure of private facts or tort of invasion of informational privacy. The second is the traditional action of breach of confidence, as set out in *Coco* v *Clark*. This latter action will be relevant in cases concerning commercially sensitive information (including photographs with a commercial value). This proposition is supported by Lord Nicholls' statements in *Douglas (No 3)* in which he confirms that there are now 'two distinct causes of action, protecting two different interests: privacy, and secret ("confidential") information'.[271] In some cases, it may be that information qualifies for protection from both of these causes of action.[272] Thus far, English courts have remained unmoved by arguments that they should formally recognise a publicity right, akin to property.

What is most significant about the English law in this area, then, is that it offers little guidance on how to manage the complex interaction between dignitarian and commercial interests. There are occasional exceptions. The remarks of the Lord Walker in *Douglas (No 3)*, in particular, deserve close attention because he considers in some detail the conceptual difficulties with a simultaneous assertion of invasion of privacy and commercial confidence.[273] For Lord Walker, the Douglases had 'both a personal and a commercial interest in the matter' but these two interests 'sat uneasily together.'[274] In illustrating this point, he made reference to a Council of Europe Resolution from 1998, which had been quoted by Lindsay J at first instance. In it, the Council states that 'people's private lives have become a highly lucrative commodity for certain sectors of the media. The victims are essentially public figures, since details of their private lives serve as a stimulus to sales.'[275] Drawing on this document, Lindsay J stated that he was 'untroubled' by an understanding of breach of confidence that would make a distinction between those whose 'private life is a valuable commodity' and 'those whose is not'.[276] Lord Walker questioned why Lindsay J was not troubled by the idea that celebrities whom the Council of Europe calls 'victims' were at the same time benefitting from their 'valuable trade asset'[277] For Lord Walker, the Douglas litigation concerned interests of a 'specialised commercial character, far removed from the sort of intrusion on the privacy of a seriously ill patient which the Court of Appeal

---

271 *Douglas* v *Hello (No 3)* [2008] 1 AC 1 at 72.

272 *Ibid.*

273 *Ibid* at 75–86.

274 *Ibid* at 84.

275 Council of Europe Res 1165 of 1998, para 6.

276 *Douglas v Hello* [2003] EMLR 31 at 711.

277 *Douglas* v *Hello (No 3)* [2008] 1 AC 1 at 79.

considered (but felt unable to remedy) in *Kaye* v *Robertson*.'[278] In short, this case concerned celebrity control over their image rather than distress following invasion of privacy. Understood in this way, the remarks of Miss Zeta-Jones provided in evidence are particularly revealing:

> Both Michael and I are in the business of "name and likeness." Any photographs of us that are published are important to us, not just personally but professionally as well. People go to see movies specifically because either Michael or I are in them and they have expectations, among other things, of the way we will look. Those expectations are created to a significant degree by the images they see of us in the media. Directors take into account the public's perception of actors and actresses when casting for films. The hard reality of the film industry is that preserving my image, particularly as a woman, is vital to my career.[279]

For Lord Walker, these claims are similar to the 'character right' or rights of image that have been rejected in English law.[280]

While his Lordship is correct to emphasise that the Douglases' claim is a very different one to that of Mr Kaye, I am not convinced that we can neatly delineate the interests at stake. There are two reasons why I reach this conclusion. First, though *Douglas* was about control of image for commercial purposes, it was also a case in which a paparazzo surreptitiously took photographs of an intimate occasion and sold them to a third party who published them to the world at large. The claimants did not have advance warning, nor did they know what the photographs in question depicted. Even if we apply a very restrictive approach, one cannot but reach the conclusion that this was an invasion of privacy. Second, this privacy claim was accompanied by a claim to protect the commercial interests at stake. While Lord Walker opined that these claims 'sat uneasily together', if we recall the discussion in Chap. 2 and if we accept that dignity and autonomy (in the form of control of property) are interdependent, then, in practice, how do we identify the boundaries between the dignitarian and the commercial interests? These observations provide grounds for arguing that the German *Monistischer Ansatz* is not only more coherent but it also gives full expression to the informing purposes of privacy. We shall revisit this argument in the next chapter.

4.6 Conclusions

What emerges from our comparative study is that there are significant gaps in English tort law. Though courts have developed a basic framework for misuse of private information claims, the doctrinal foundations remain unsound. English courts are too reliant on vague pronouncements of the Strasbourg court. Moreover,

[278] *Ibid* at 81.

[279] *Ibid* at 80.

[280] *Ibid*. Consider, for instance, *Elvis Presley Trademarks* [1999] RPC 567.

in paying so much attention to this relatively narrow area of privacy law, courts have failed to take account of other important privacy questions—how do we remedy intrusion upon a person's seclusion and must we delineate dignitarian and commercial interests in publicity cases?

By contrast, the protective remit of German law encompasses a much wider range of privacy interests. We find that the German approach is more principled and coherent, though perhaps highly formalistic at times. The very notion of 'taking all the circumstances of the case into account', for instance, is problematic since circumstances can be described and redescribed endlessly and contexts can be demarcated in so many ways. Courts sometimes allude to judicial discretion when, for example, referring to the balancing exercise as a 'delicate process'. However there is a tendency in the case law to hide discretion behind the veil of doctrine, to minimise the human dimension in the decision-making process. But, as I will argue in the next chapter, for all their failings, the German law doctrines provide two distinct benefits. Firstly, they give expression to our shared experience of privacy and invest the law with a readily intelligible sense of purpose. Secondly, they promote a greater degree of clarity and transparency than the ECtHR/French approach and in this way adhere to the regulative ideals of justice, legal certainty and the rule of law.

Chapter 5
Conclusions

> If we look to the laws, they afford equal justice to all in their private differences; if no social standing, advancement in public life falls to reputation for capacity, class considerations not being allowed to interfere with merit; nor again does poverty bar the way.
>
> - Pericles (431 BC)

5.1 Refining Privacy

In this book, I have sought to advance knowledge in tort law scholarship through a refinement of various theories of privacy and the methods of legal protection. At the outset of the study, I emphasised Arendt's warnings about the dangers of mere 'passive observation' in scholarship. On her account, '[n]othing could be less trustworthy for acquiring knowledge and approaching truth' than this scholarly method. For Arendt, 'in order to know, one [has] to do' and we advance knowledge 'only through more doing' or 'testing' in Popper's sense.

But are these concerns overstated? Would I have come to different conclusions in this study had I adopted a method of passive observation rather than refinement? Is it not likely that I would have identified many of the same similarities and differences between the English and German approaches to civil liability for invasion of privacy? Indeed, on the basis of these observations, would I not have been in a position to make recommendations for the future development of English law? In other words, I could have proposed various 'lessons to be learned' from the German approach. In this narrow sense, it may indeed be possible to claim some degree of advancement of knowledge on the basis of passive observation. But given the number of comparative studies on this topic and the corresponding number of lessons already proposed, it is unlikely that passive observation, on its own, would afford us any new and significant insights.

P. O'Callaghan, *Refining Privacy in Tort Law*,
DOI 10.1007/978-3-642-31884-9_5, © Springer-Verlag Berlin Heidelberg 2013

This is why I sought to adopt the 'institutional perspective' in this study. I began by critically assessing the proposition that privacy warrants legal protection in the first place. Drawing on Wright Mill's idea of a sociological imagination, we imagined a world in which privacy had no value and a world in which privacy had absolute value. It is worth repeating the conjectures that emerged from this exercise:

1. Privacy is an essential constituent of personhood; an absence of privacy undermines basic interests in dignity and therefore normative agency.
2. If we accept this to be the case, it follows that we are required to consider potential proprietary aspects of privacy for, as Kant and Hegel emphasise, private property is vital for autonomy.
3. Personhood (and therefore privacy) is ontologically dependent on the community. Moreover, an absence of privacy also threatens the very existence of our equalitarian community.

This is not a reductionist argument. I do not claim, for instance, that the wrongness of a violation of privacy can be explained by references to dignity and autonomy alone. I do not deny that this may have been the situation in the past—as we learned in Chap. 3, the ancients had a very different understanding of the boundaries between the *res publica* and the *res privata*. But the historical fact of the slow process of individualisation and levelling-up (through socio-genetic change) since the Middle Ages means that the basic premise for our way of life (and I include liberal democracy here) is that each individual has the 'capacity to choose and to pursue [his or her] conception of a worthwhile life' (in other words, normative agency).[1] At the same time, if we recall that a world without privacy is a world in which others might have access to the 'sheer tropical luxuriance of the inner life', as Nagel puts it,[2] we cannot but reach the conclusion that normative agency (as we understand and value it) is not possible without privacy. For this reason, we must also value privacy.

Once we adopt the 'institutional perspective' and pay attention to the value and nature of privacy, the extent to which English law lacks a clear sense of purpose becomes apparent. This was undoubtedly the case before the introduction of the Human Rights Act when a patchwork of torts, equitable doctrines and statutory causes of action were understood as partially protecting a small number of privacy interests. However, the Human Rights Act was the great hope for privacy activists. Lord Irvine, for instance, confidently declared that the judiciary was 'pen-poised' to develop a right of privacy in the common law.[3] Fourteen years later we might question the accuracy of this prediction and whether the Human Rights Act has truly brought privacy rights home. While *Campbell* and subsequent decisions have provided more certainty through the elaboration of a rudimentary framework for a

[1] Griffin, *On Human Rights* (2008) p 45.

[2] Nagel, 'Concealment and Exposure' (1998) at 4.

[3] HL Deb 24 November 1997, vol 583, col 784.

tort of invasion of informational privacy, it can hardly be said that a general right of privacy, encompassing *inter alia* intrusion and misappropriation of personality torts, exists in English law.

The lack of purpose in English privacy law is accentuated by an overdependence on 'Strasbourg-speak.' In 1997, Lord Irvine went on to state that any privacy law developed by the judges will be 'a better law' after the incorporation of the Convention because judges will have to balance Articles 8 and 10.[4] This enthusiastic deference to ECHR provisions and the decisions of the Strasbourg Court has become almost commonplace in judicial and academic circles. Fenwick and Phillipson, for instance, talk about 'resolving the conflict [between privacy and free speech] in domestic courts by importing Strasbourg principles.'[5] These include the principle that Articles 8 and 10 have equal weight and that the outcome of any balancing exercise should be determined by considerations of proportionality. As we have seen, here, English courts refer to the 'ultimate balancing exercise' whereby the outcome of each case is determined through an 'intense focus' on the individual circumstances.

But the so-called 'Strasbourg principles', while indispensable, are not as illuminating as some might contend, and, taken on their own, give rise to a lack of clarity and also induce complacency. Moreover, if we adopt a multi-factorial balancing exercise as the centrepiece of judicial reasoning, without simultaneously affording clear guidance to judges, we risk corroding the rule of law. Declaring that this balancing exercise takes place following an 'intense focus' on the facts of the case does little to reassure—no matter how intensely we concentrate on the facts, hard cases will continue to arise and judges will continue to bear the 'burden of judgment'. Judges encounter these burdens in every case where there is a 'basic question of justice' and, as Rawls puts it, '[m]any hard decisions may seem to have no clear answer.'[6] Those who carry the 'burden of judgment' on their shoulders must continue to make 'tragic choices'.[7] The 'new methodology' will not make these decisions any easier because '[w]e are doomed to choose, and every choice may entail an irreparable loss.'[8]

Rather than look to Strasbourg for inspiration, English courts must draw upon their own rich common law culture and survey the experiences of other legal systems operating with fully developed privacy torts. As noted earlier, the approach of the House of Lords in *Campbell*, which remains the most authoritative decision in English law, bears a striking resemblance to the German approach in privacy disputes. German law employs doctrinal tests that help promote clarity and transparency, while at the same time giving expression to clear ideals of justice and core

---

[4] *Ibid.*

[5] Fenwick & Phillipson, *Media Freedom under the Human Rights Act* (2006) p 700.

[6] Rawls, *Political Liberalism* (1993) p 57.

[7] Alder, 'Dissents in Courts of Last Resort' (2000) at 224.

[8] Berlin *The Crooked Timber of Humanity*,(2003) p 13.

constitutional and private law principles. The upshot, as noted earlier, is a clearer sense of purpose. This is important because as Lord Woolf emphasises in *Kent* v *Griffiths*,[9] tort law doctrine is a collection 'of tools not rules.' We can see this in German law when the doctrines on privacy and image are used to advance certain informing purposes. The doctrine on privacy finds its origins in constitutional provisions on *dignity* and *self-determination*; however other ideals of justice and principles can be extrapolated from the case law. In publicity claims, for example, recognition of 'incomplete commodification' of personality in Radin's sense is implicit in German law. Interests in personal autonomy and the commercial complexities of the media and digital age mean that we cannot (even if we were so inclined) prohibit the commodification of personality. However, complete commodification of personality is anathema to us. Understood in these terms, we require a legal framework that does not simply posit complete commodification against non-commodification but allows for a reasonable degree of commodification of personality, while emphasising its 'special non-market significance'. In German law, the general personality right acts as a *Monistischer Ansatz*, allowing for the co-existence of dignitarian and commercial interests. While the English Court of Appeal thinks that a publicity claim has 'nothing to do' with privacy, in German law we find an appreciation for the complexity of the relationship between these interests—the *ideelle* and *materielle* interests are inseparable.

Alongside these features of German doctrine, we should note that the German approach does not call for the sole application of (supposedly) rigid tests in order to determine the outcome of individual cases. We must remember that the approach remains context-specific and if an individual claims an invasion of privacy, the court will normally proceed to a multi-factorial balancing exercise, but one which is based on a clearer set of guidelines than found in English law. Clear principles are enumerated so that the law's addressees know how to 'go on' (in Wittgenstein's sense).[10] This point is important because the liability of others does not begin with the silence of the law. We need 'basic rules' if we are to act on the 'law's reasonably ascertainable implications'.[11] Vague pronouncements on the need to respect 'physical and psychological integrity' do not adhere to the 'fundamental premise of equality before the law'; in other words, 'the content of the law must be accessible to all'.[12]

[9] *Kent* v *Griffiths* [2001] QB 36.

[10] See Wittgenstein, *Philosophical Investigations* (1953).

[11] Mullender, 'Negligence Law and the Concept of Community' (2008) at 88.

[12] Beever, 'Particularism and Prejudice in the Law of Tort' (2003) at 167. Kay criticises the ECtHR on similar grounds arguing that the 'court that departs from [its] role [as a court of *law*] to pursue a deeply felt, but only vaguely defined, idea of justice, puts [its] fragile legitimacy to the test'. See Kay, 'The European Convention on Human Rights and the Control of Private Law' (2005) at 479.

5.2 Privacy and Rank

But perhaps the severest criticism we can make of the English approach to civil liability for invasion of privacy is that it does not conform to the regulative ideal of equality before the law. At the very foundation of our understanding of justice and the rule of law is equality. It is for this reason that Dworkin argues that '[n]o government is legitimate unless... it [shows] equal concern for the fate of every person over whom it claims dominion.'[13] Yet, in developing a tort of invasion of informational privacy, English courts have responded to the privacy concerns of a very small class of potential claimants: public figures. In doing so, they have (surely unintentionally) ensured that every other privacy concern is pushed to the margins of judicial and academic debate. This means that there are relatively few cases in English tort law in which counsel advise a non-public claimant to take an action for invasion of privacy (and there are even fewer successful claims).[14]

Of course journalists will be more interested in the personal information of public figures, increasing the likelihood that such information will be misused. But given our shared experience of privacy and its importance for normative agency, it cannot be the case that only public figures suffer invasions of privacy that are serious enough to merit the law's attention. Perhaps, then, courts are simply hesitant to expand the privacy action in private law? In a *vertical relationship* between the injured party and the state (or public body), we might suppose that courts would be willing to entertain direct actions on the basis of Article 8 for intrusion into a person's seclusion. But even here, developments have been disappointing. Mullender points to recent cases in which 'some obvious violations of privacy have passed lawyers by.'[15] These include *Hussain* v *Lancaster City Council*,[16] *Mitchell* v *Glasgow City Council*[17] and *X* v *Hounslow London Borough Council*.[18] Each of these cases concerned claimants living in social housing, all of whom had suffered abuse that was 'highly intrusive and impacted detrimentally on their home life.'[19] While in *Hussain* the claimant attempted to invoke Article 8, counsel for the claimants in *Mitchell* and in *X* failed to highlight the interests under Article 8 despite the defendant in both cases being a 'public authority' within the meaning of section 6 of the Human Rights Act. Mullender argues that there is 'a lack of grip on the relationship between lower-order private law and higher-order public law' on the part of counsel in such cases. On his account, they exhibit a lack of 'legal imagination.'[20]

---

[13] Dworkin, *Justice for Hedgehogs* (2011) p 2.

[14] I am aware of only one successful action though it was a dual libel and privacy action. See *Applause Store Productions* v *Raphael* [2008] All ER (D) 321.

[15] Mullender, 'Privacy, Imbalance and the Legal Imagination' (2011) at 112.

[16] *Hussain* v *Lancaster City Council* [2000] QB 1.

[17] *Mitchell* v *Glasgow City Council* [2009] 1 AC 874.

[18] *X* v *Hounslow London Borough Council* [2009] EWCA Civ 286.

[19] Mullender, 'Privacy, Imbalance and the Legal Imagination' (2011) at 112.

[20] *Ibid* p 112.

One way of explaining this 'lack of grip' on the relationship between the ECHR and private law is by revisiting the general privacy narrative that has emerged from case law and academic comment. Consider, for example the recent parliamentary report on privacy and injunctions.[21] The report begins by emphasising that privacy is 'rooted in a belief in the dignity of the human being' but then proceeds to focus only on misuse of private information claims. The privacy narrative, then, understands invasion of privacy as misuse of private information and associates these claims with celebrities and public figures.[22] Understood in this way, it is perhaps no surprise that other forms of invasion of privacy do not feature in the arguments of counsel.[23]

This narrative is now ingrained in tort law. Despite the excitement about a new 'privacy tort' in English law, there are at least three reasons why the tort cannot function as a general privacy action. First, when developing the tort of misuse of private information, the English courts stressed that this was an incremental development of the law as a result of the indirect horizontal effect of Article 8 ECHR. The doctrinal vehicle chosen for this purpose was breach of confidence, the primary function of which (pre-HRA) was to afford equitable protection to trade secrets in the form of an injunction. So, from the very outset, the courts made it abundantly clear that the new action covered misuse of *information* only. Second, the decision procedure of the new tort stresses 'limiting principles' such as the public interest and the need to engage in a balancing of Articles 8 and 10. Understood in this way, the decision procedure presupposes that freedom of expression is at stake in such cases. While it is easy to see how courts might reach this conclusion in misuse of private information cases, it is less apparent why interests in freedom of expression should necessarily be a factor in cases involving intrusion into a person's seclusion. In light of this point, we can conclude that the new tort is not designed to cater for privacy claims other than misuse of private information (or else it suffers from a very significant design flaw).[24] Third, despite the various references on the part of

[21] House of Lords and House of Commons Joint Report on Privacy and Injunctions (2012).

[22] This narrative has been further reinforced by recent high profile cases involving celebrities and the media coverage of 'super-injunctions' (also known as anonymised injunctions). See, for example, *Terry* v *Persons Unknown* [2010] EWHC 119 (QB); *Rio Ferdinand* v *MGN Ltd* [2011] EWHC 2454 (QB).

[23] Mullender attributes the development of a tort of invasion of informational privacy partly to the fact that celebrities are normally in a position to pay for the advice of expert counsel. See Mullender, 'Privacy, Imbalance and the Legal Imagination' (2011) at 113.

[24] Moreham argues that the 'preferable' approach to protecting the 'physical privacy interest' is to extend the misuse of privacy information action to cover privacy intrusions generally. She argues that '[n]o change in the formulation of the action would be required' as long as courts recognise that autonomy and dignity are at the base of these interests and that the intrusion has 'upset a claimant's reasonable desire for or expectation of privacy.' Although she mentions a potential Art 10 defence for some intrusion cases, she does not seem to think it problematic that the basic decision procedure for the current tort presupposes that interests in free expression are at stake. See Moreham, 'Privacy in the Common Law' (2005) at 655.

the English courts to the importance of dignity and autonomy,[25] so far as I am aware, there is absolutely nothing in recent case law to suggest that the new tort could potentially encompass other forms of invasion of privacy. Instead, courts have generally sidestepped the issue simply by saying that it is a point that does not need to be considered at present.[26]

Assuming that this analysis is broadly correct, we reach the unhappy conclusion that the principle in *Wainwright* v *Home Office* remains valid: there is no general right of privacy in the English common law. Understood in these terms, if *Kaye* v *Robertson* were to come before the English courts today, it is difficult to see how the courts would be able to award an adequate remedy in common law. What emerges from this analysis is that Article 8 ECHR has had minimal impact in *private law* and English lawyers are left with a skewed understanding of privacy as a preserve of the rich and famous.[27]

I suspect that a critic of this argument would say:

> But are the courts not simply responding to the cases that come before them? Surely they are not to blame if these claims happen to be brought by public figures (who are more likely to suffer an invasion of privacy in the first place)? And, anyway, if we are committed to corrective justice, surely these individuals are entitled to a remedy when they suffer a legal wrong?

I would respond to observations of this sort by drawing on the work of Gregory Vlastos. In what Waldron labels a 'neglected' essay,[28] Vlastos sets out to imagine what a social order based on 'acquired merit' would look like—he calls this social order an 'M-system'.[29] Vlastos understands 'merit' as consisting of 'all the kinds of valuable qualities or performances in respect of which persons may be graded.'[30] He contrasts this system with our social order (or at least the platonic ideal of it),

[25] See for example, Lord Hoffman's remarks in *Campbell.* According to him, the new action focuses on 'the protection of human autonomy and dignity – the right to control the dissemination of information about one's private life and the right to the esteem and respect of other people.' See *Campbell* v *MGN* [2004] 2 AC 457 at 473 (per Lord Hoffmann).

[26] Lord Nicholls has come closest to engaging this question. In Campbell he remarks that '[i]n the case of individuals this tort, however labelled, affords respect for one aspect of an individual's privacy. That is the value underlying this cause of action. An individual's privacy can be invaded in ways not involving publication of information. Strip-searches are an example. The extent to which the common law as developed thus far in this country protects other forms of invasion of privacy is not a matter arising in the present case. It does not arise because, although pleaded more widely, Miss Campbell's common law claim was throughout presented in court exclusively on the basis of breach of confidence, that is, the wrongful *publication* by the 'Mirror' of private *information.*' See *Campbell* v *MGN* [2004] 2 AC 457 at 465 (per Lord Nicholls).

[27] As Lord Smith of Finsbury has argued, '[o]ne of the big issues [in] privacy law. . .is that this is justice only for the wealthy'. See Mullender, 'Privacy, Imbalance and the Legal Imagination' (2011) at 113.

[28] Waldron, 'Dignity and Rank' (2007) at 221.

[29] Vlastos, 'Justice and Equality' (1984) p 54.

[30] *Ibid* p 51.

which he describes an 'equalitarian community'.[31] In our community, we attach value to 'a person's individual existence, over and above his merit'; Vlastos calls this 'individual worth'.[32] We find examples of a commitment to equalitarianism throughout our legal system—consider, for instance, the principle of 'equal protection of the laws' or the right to vote; everyone enjoys these rights; they are clearly not based on merit.[33]

In contrasting the 'M-system' with our equalitarian community, Vlastos comes to the conclusion that:

> in one fundamental respect our society is much more like a caste society (with a *unique* caste) than like the M-system. The latter has no place for a rank of dignity which descends on an individual by the purely existential circumstance (the "accident") of birth and remained unalterably for life. ... We do not [elevate] in rank for rare merit or [degrade] for extreme demerit. In our legal system no such thing can happen: even a criminal may not be sentenced to second-class citizenship. ... It is the simple truth... to speak of it... as a "rank of dignity" in some ways comparable to that enjoyed by hereditary nobles of the past.[34]

Our equalitarian legal order is one in which each individual enjoys the same high rank by virtue of his or her humanity (or the 'capacity for moral personality', as Rawls puts it).[35] In Chap. 3 of this book, we found similar sentiments expressed by prominent historical figures. Consider again Pufendorf's *De jure natuerae et gentium*. In it, he refers to the 'first foundations in the very constitution of human nature'. On his account, our response to someone who insults us should be: 'I am not a Beast, a Dog, but I am a Man as well as yourself.' This is because:

> ...human nature agrees equally to all persons, and since no one can live a sociable life with another, who does not own and respect him as a man; it follows as a command of the law of nature, *that every man should esteem and treat another as one who is naturally his equal, or who is a man as well as he.*

The philosophers and scholars of the Enlightenment described a process of socio-genetic change. But whatever we call this process—'levelling-up', 'universalization of rank' or 'rank reversal'[36]—it was very real and took root. Hence, the idea, for instance, that a 'great man of the realm' could have recourse to the *scandalum magnatum* became increasingly untenable as the seventeenth and eighteenth centuries progressed. So, when John Locke writes of men being of the 'same species and rank', the notion of rank is used here, as Waldron explains, 'to articulate an aggressively egalitarian position. Humans are basically one another's equals,

[31] *Ibid* p 50.
[32] *Ibid* p 52.
[33] *Ibid* p 53.
[34] *Ibid* p 54.
[35] Rawls, *A Theory of Justice* (1999) p 505.
[36] Waldron, 'Dignity and Rank' (2007) at 226.

because denial of equality in this fundamental sense would relegate some to the status of animals or elevate some to the status of gods.'[37]

This conception of equality underlies our understanding of justice and the rule of law. But we can come to a better understanding of the fundamental importance of equality by paying close attention to Rawls' idea of 'justice as fairness'. Rawls draws a distinction between 'two conceptions of equality'. He explains that:

> [s]ome writers have distinguished between equality as it is invoked in connection with the distribution of certain goods, some of which will almost certainly give higher status or prestige to those who are more favoured, and equality as it applies to the respect which is owed to persons irrespective of their social position. Equality of the first kind is defined by the second principle of justice which regulates the structure of organizations and distributive shares so that social cooperation is both efficient and fair. But equality of the second kind is fundamental. It is defined by the first principle of justice and by such natural duties as that of mutual respect; it is owed to human beings as moral persons.[38]

The process of socio-genetic change, described in Chap. 3, has led to an understanding of equality as the 'respect ... owed to persons irrespective of their social position'. According to Rawls, this is 'fundamental', so much so, as Dworkin in his reading of Rawls explains, that 'the right to equal respect is not... a product of the contract, but a condition of admission to the original position.'[39] Equality, then, is fundamental in more ways than one. In the Rawlsian scheme it pre-exists all other rights, goods and interests.

But equalitarian justice does not simply mean that the equality of each individual should be formally recognised by the legal system. It demands much more. Vlastos explains that equalitarian justice:

> implies that the fundamental and distinctive idea in its notion of just distribution is (i) not equal distribution of benefits, but (ii) their equal distribution at the highest obtainable level.[40]

In other words, equalitarian justice 'has a direct stake not only in equalizing the distribution of those goods whose enjoyment constitutes well-being but also in promoting their creation.'[41] Following Vlastos, then, I can respond to my critic in the following way:

> It may well be the case that courts are simply responding to the privacy claims coming before them and it so happens that the majority of these claims are brought by public figures (whose private lives are the subject of much media interest). But should the courts not be mindful of the language they use? If they are to remain faithful to the regulative ideals of justice and the rule of law, should they not avoid creating the *impression* of inequality at all costs? After all, on their own account, courts (as public bodies) must act compatibly with ECHR rights when applying the common law. In some cases, this may mean developing an

[37] *Ibid* p 218.

[38] Rawls, *A Theory of Justice* (1999) p 511.

[39] Dworkin, *Taking Rights Seriously* (1997) p 181.

[40] Vlastos, 'Justice and Equality' (1984) p 65.

[41] *Ibid*.

> existing cause of action by means of indirect horizontal effect (as was the case with informational privacy). But in other cases this may mean *creating* a new cause of action through a bold judicial stroke where there are obvious gaps in the law. Where basic interests in dignity, autonomy and equalitarian justice are at stake, surely courts must explore the bounds of legal possibility in the same way Lord Atkin did some eighty years ago?[42]

On the question of the remedies available to celebrity claimants and my commitment to corrective justice, I would add:

> Most certainly, if an individual has being wronged, she is entitled to seek redress. The worst thing we could do at this juncture is revert to a situation in which there are no privacy actions of any sort available in English private law.

This is because 'equalizing the restriction' of privacy (though it may *seem* like equal treatment) does not help matters. As Vlastos emphasises, this sort of equalization:

> would be to aggravate, not to alleviate, its injustice. Would any of us feel that no injustice was suffered by Soviet citizens by the suppression of Doctor Zhivago if we were reliably informed that no one, not even Khrushchev, was exempted...?[43]

In a system of justice as fairness, as Rawls indicates, '[t]he social order can be justified to everyone and in particular to those who are least favoured; and in this sense it is egalitarian.'[44] The principal problem with the current English law on liability for invasion of privacy, however well-intentioned, is that it leads to an appearance of inequality. This is particularly troubling given the egalitarian justifications for the introduction of the Human Rights Act. The levelling-up of rank is an important aspect of our shared experience of privacy. Actions on the part of public bodies that appear to emphasise rank (of the sort we have encountered throughout this book) are a deep insult to human dignity, to our commitment to treat each individual as a full member of the human community by virtue of his or her moral capacity. This is, surely, the gravest injustice of them all.

---

[42] *Donoghue* v *Stevenson* [1932] AC 562.

[43] Vlastos, 'Justice and Equality' (1984) p 67.

[44] Rawls, *A Theory of Justice* (1999) p 103.

Bibliography

Alder, J, 'Dissents in Courts of Last Resort: Tragic Choices?' (2000) 20 (2) *Oxford Journal of Legal Studies* 221

Aplin, T, 'The Development of the Action for Breach of Confidence in the Post-HRA Era' [2007] *Intellectual Property Law Quarterly* 19

Arendt, H, *The Human Condition* (2nd edn, Chicago: University of Chicago Press: 1999)

Ariès, P, 'Introduction' in Chartier, R (ed), *A History of Private Life Volume III: Passions of the Renaissance* (Cambridge: Harvard University Press, 1989)

Bajohr, F, 'The "Folk Community" and the Persecution of the Jews: German Society under National Socialist Dictatorship, 1933–1945' (2006) 20 (2) *Holocaust Genocide Studies* 183

Bakhtin, M, *Problems of Dostoevsky's Poetics* (edited and translated by Emerson, C) (Minneapolis: University of Minnesota Press, 1984)

Bamforth, N, 'Parliamentary Sovereignty and the Human Rights Act 1998' [1998] *Public Law* 572

Baston-Vogt, M, *Der sachliche Schutzbereich des zivilrechtlichen allgemeinen Persönlichkeitsrechts* (Tübingen: Mohr Siebeck, 1997)

Baynes, K, 'Freedom and Recognition in Hegel and Habermas' (2002) 28 (1) *Philosophy & Social Criticism* 1

Beckmann, P, Colombi Ciacchi, A, Ferreira, N, Moulin-Doos, C, O'Callaghan, P, Russo T, & Turney, J, 'Germany' in Brüggemeier, G, Colombi Ciacchi, A, & Comandé, G (eds), *Fundamental Rights and Private Law in the European Union: Volume 1* (Cambridge: Cambridge University Press, 2010)

Beever, A, 'Particularism and Prejudice in the Law of Tort' (2003) 11 *Tort Law Review* 146

Bennett, T, 'Corrective Justice and Horizontal Privacy: A Leaf Out of Wright J's Book' (2010) 7 *The Journal Jurisprudence* 545

Berlin, I, *The Crooked Timber of Humanity: Chapters in the History of Ideas* (edited by Hardy, H) (London: Pimlico 2003)

Berlin, I, *The Roots of Romanticism* (edited by Hardy, H) (London: Pimlico, 2000)

Beverley-Smith, H, *The Commercial Appropriation of Personality* (Cambridge: Cambridge University Press, 2002)

Black, G, *Publicity Rights and Image: Exploitation and Legal Control* (Oxford: Hart Publishing, 2011)

Blackstone, W, *Commentaries on the Laws of England, Book the Second* (1770)

Blackstone, W, *Commentaries on the Laws of England, Book the Third* (1768)

Bloustein, E, 'Privacy as an Aspect of Human Dignity: An Answer to Dean Prosser,' (1964) 39 *New York University Law Review* 962

Braunstein, P, 'Toward Intimacy: The Fourteenth and Fifteenth Centuries' in Duby, G (ed), *A History of Private Life Volume II: Revelations of the Medieval World* (Cambridge: Harvard University Press, 1988)

DOI 10.1007/978-3-642-31884-9,

Brown, P, 'Late Antiquity' in Ariès, P, & Duby, G (eds), *A History of Private Life Volume I: From Pagan Rome to Byzantium* (Cambridge: Harvard University Press, 1987)
Brüggemeier, G, 'Constitutionalisation of Private Law – The German Perspective' in Barkhuysen, T, & Lindenburgh, SD (eds), *Constitutionalisation of Private Law* (Leiden: Martinus Nijhoff, 2006)
Brüggemeier, G, *Haftungsrecht: Struktur, Prinzipien, Schutzbereich – Ein Beitrag zur Europäisierung des Privatrechts* (Berlin/Heidelberg/New York: Springer, 2006)
Brüggemeier, G, Colombi Ciacchi, A, & O'Callaghan, P, *Personality Rights in European Tort Law* (Cambridge: Cambridge University Press, 2010)
Cairns, D, 'Honour and Shame: Modern Controversies and Ancient Values' (2011) 53 (1) *Critical Quarterly* 23
Caney, S, 'Liberalism and Communitarianism: A Misconceived Debate' (1992) 40 (2) *Political Studies* 273
Carolan, E, & Delany, H, *The Right to Privacy: A Doctrinal and Comparative Analysis* (Dublin: Thomson Round Hall, 2008)
Clapham, A, *Human Rights Obligations of Non-State Actors* (Oxford: Oxford University Press, 2006)
Chartier, R, 'The Practical Impact of Writing' in Chartier, R (ed), *A History of Private Life Volume III: Passions of the Renaissance* (Cambridge: Harvard University Press, 1989)
Cole, SW, Kemeny, ME, Taylor, SE, & Visscher, BR, 'Elevated physical health risk among gay men who conceal their homosexual identity' (1996) 15 (4) *Health Psychology* 243
Coors, C, 'Headwind from Europe: The New Position of the German Courts on Personality Rights after the Judgment of the European Court of Human Rights' (2010) 11 (6) *German Law Journal* 527
Corbin, A, 'The Secret of the Individual' in Perrot, M (ed), *A History of Private Life Volume IV: From the Fires of Revolution to the Great War* (Cambridge: Harvard University Press, 1990)
Dannemann, G, 'Of Princesses and Politicians: Current Developments in the German Law of Personality Rights and the Media', in Beater, A, & Habermeier, S (eds), *Verletzungen von Persönlichkeitsrechten durch die Medien* (Tübingen: Mohr Siebeck, 2005)
Dworkin, R, 'Hard Cases' (1975) 88(6) *Harvard Law Review* 1057
Dworkin, R, *Justice for Hedgehogs* (Cambridge: Harvard University Press, 2011)
Dworkin, R, *Life's Dominion: An Argument about Abortion, Euthanasia, and Individual Freedom* (New York: Alfred A Knopf, 1993)
Dworkin, R, *Taking Rights Seriously* (London: Duckworth, 1977)
Duby, G, 'Introduction' in Duby, G (ed), *A History of Private Life Volume II: Revelations of the Medieval World* (Cambridge: Harvard University Press, 1988)
Duby, G, 'Solitude: Eleventh to Thirteenth Century' in Duby, G (ed), *A History of Private Life Volume II: Revelations of the Medieval World* (Cambridge: Harvard University Press, 1988)
Eberle, EJ, 'Human Dignity, Privacy, and Personality in German and American Constitutional Law' (1997) 4 *Utah Law Review* 963
Edison Research Study, *The Social Habit* (May 2011), www.edisonresearch.com/home/archives/2011/05/the_social_habit_2011.php
Elias, N, *The Civilizing Process* (rev edn, Oxford: Blackwell, 2000)
Emerson, T, *The System of Freedom of Expression* (New York: Random House, 1970)
Emerson, T, 'Toward a General Theory of the First Amendment' (1963) 72 *Yale Law Journal* 877
Farge, A, 'The Honor and Secrecy of Families' in Chartier, R (ed), *A History of Private Life Volume III: Passions of the Renaissance* (Cambridge: Harvard University Press, 1989)
Fenwick, H, & Phillipson, G, *Media Freedom under the Human Rights Act* (Oxford: Oxford University Press, 2006)
Fish, S, *There's No Such Thing as Free Speech and It's a Good Thing, Too* (New York/Oxford: Oxford University Press, 1994)
Forkel, H, 'Das "Caroline-Urteil" aus Straßburg – richtungsweisend für den Schutz auch der seelischen Unversehrtheit' (2005) 49 (3) *Zeitschrift für Urheber- und Medienrecht* 192

Forster, MN, *Hegel's Idea of a Phenomenology of Spirit* (Chicago: University of Chicago Press, 1998)
Freud, S, *Drei Abhandlungen Zur Sexualtheorie* (Leipzig and Vienna: Deuticke, 1905)
Frevert, U, *Ehrenmänner. Das Duell in der bürgerlichen Gesellschaft* (Munich: CH Beck, 1991)
Funkenstein, A, *Perceptions of Jewish History* (Berkeley: University of California Press, 1993)
Gadamer, HG, *Truth and Method* (London: Sheed and Ward, 1975)
Gavison, R, 'Privacy and the Limits of Law' (1980) 89 (3) *Yale Law Journal* 421
Gibbons, T, 'Defamation Reconsidered' (1996) 16 (4) *Oxford Journal of Legal Studies* 587
Giddens, A, *Modernity and Self-Identity: Self and Society in the Late Modern Age* (Stanford: Stanford University Press, 1991)
Götting, HP, 'Allgemeine Fragen' in Götting, HP, Schertz C, & Seitz W (eds), *Handbuch des Persönlichkeitsrechts* (München: CH Beck, 2008)
Götting, HP, 'Geschichte des Persönlichkeitsrechts' in Götting, HP, Schertz C, & Seitz W (eds), *Handbuch des Persönlichkeitsrechts* (München: CH Beck, 2008)
Götting, HP, 'Ideeller und kommerzieller Persönlichkeitsschutz' in Götting, HP, Schertz C, & Seitz W (eds), *Handbuch des Persönlichkeitsrechts* (München: CH Beck, 2008)
Götting, HP, 'Inhalt, Zweck und Rechtsnatur des Persönlichkeitsrecht' in Götting, HP, Schertz C, & Seitz W (eds), *Handbuch des Persönlichkeitsrechts* (München: CH Beck, 2008)
Gordley, J, *Foundations of Private Law: Property, Tort, Contract, Unjust Enrichment* (Oxford: Oxford University Press, 2006)
Goulemot, JM, 'Literary Practices: Publicizing the Private' in Chartier, R (ed), *A History of Private Life Volume III: Passions of the Renaissance* (Cambridge: Harvard University Press, 1989)
Griffin, J, *On Human Rights* (Oxford: Oxford University Press, 2008)
Habermas, J, 'The Concept of Human Dignity and the Realistic Utopia of Human Rights' (2010) 41 (4) *Metaphilosophy* 464
Hagemann, M, *Iniuria: von den XII-Tafeln bis zur Justinianischen Kodifikation* (Köln: Böhlau Verlag, 1998)
Halfmeier, A, *Die Veröffentlichung privater Tatsachen als unerlaubte Handlung. Eine rechtsvergleichende Untersuchung* (Frankfurt am Main: Lang, 2000)
Hanafin, P, *Constituting Identity: Political Identity Formation and the Constitution in Post-Independence Ireland* (Aldershot: Ashgate, 2001)
Hall, JB, 'Taking "Rechts" Seriously: Ronald Dworkin and the Federal Constitutional Court of Germany' (2008) 9 (6) *German Law Journal* 771
Hart, HLA, *The Concept of Law* (2nd edn, Oxford/New York: Oxford University Press, 1997)
Hartmann, G, 'Der Civilgesetzentwurf, das Aequitätaprincip und die Richterstelung' (1888) *Archiv für die civilistische Praxis* 309
Hegel, GWF, *Phenomenology of Spirit* (translated by Miller, AV) (Oxford: Oxford University Press, 1977)
Heidegger, M, *The Concept of Time* (translated by McNeill, W) (Oxford: Blackwell, 2002)
Helmholz, RH, *The Oxford History of the Laws of England, Volume I: The Canon Law and Ecclesiastical Jurisdiction from 597 to the 1640s* (Oxford: Oxford University Press, 2004)
Hendrickson, GL, 'Verbal Injury, Magic, or Erotic Comus?' (1925) 20 (4) *Classical Philology* 289
Hendrickson, GL, 'Convicium' (1926) 21 (2) *Classical Philology* 114
Herrmann, G 'Anmerkung zum Urteil des EGMR vom 24.6.2004' (2004) *Zeitschrift für Urheber- und Medienrecht* 665
Herrmann, M, *Der Schutz der Persönlichkeit in der Rechtslehre des 16.-18. Jahrhunderts* (Stuttgart: Kohlhammer, 1968)
Hesse, K, *Grundzüge des Verfassungsrechts der Bundesrepublik Deutschland* (19th edn, Heidelberg: Müller, 1993)
Heuchemer, M, 'Die Verletzung des persönlichen Lebens- und Geheimbereichs' in Götting, HP, Schertz C, & Seitz W (eds), *Handbuch des Persönlichkeitsrechts* (Munich: CH Beck, 2008)
Hoffmann, The Rt Hon Lord, 'Causation' (2005) 121 *Law Quarterly Review* 592

Honderich, T (ed), *The Oxford Companion to Philosophy* (Oxford/New York: Oxford University Press, 1995)
Hong Kong Law Reform Commission, *Consultation Paper on Civil Liability for Invasion of Privacy* (1999)
House of Lords and House of Commons Joint Committee on Privacy and Injunctions Report, Session 2010-2012, HL Paper 273, HC 1443, published on 27 March 2012.
Hubmann, H, *Das Persönlichkeitsrecht* (2nd edn, Wien/Köln/Graz: Böhlau, 1967)
Hunt, L, 'The Unstable Boundaries of the French Revolution' in Perrot, M (ed), *A History of Private Life Volume IV: From the Fires of Revolution to the Great War* (Cambridge: Harvard University Press, 1990)
Inness, JC, *Privacy, Intimacy and Isolation* (New York/Oxford: Oxford University Press, 1992)
Jaspers, K, *Allgemeine Psychopathologie* (Berlin: Springer, 1913)
Kalven Jr, H, 'Privacy in Tort Law – Were Warren and Brandeis Wrong?' (1966) 31 *Law & Contemporary Problems* 326
Kant, I, *Critique of Pure Reason* (edited and translated by Weigelt, M) (London: Penguin, 2007)
Kant, I, *Groundwork of the Metaphysics of Morals* (edited by Gregor, M) (Cambridge University Press, 2011)
Kant, I, *Lectures on Logic* (edited and translated by Young, JM) (Cambridge: Cambridge University Press, 1992)
Kateb, G, *Human Dignity* (Cambridge: Harvard University Press, 2011)
Kaufmann, M, 'Rational Egoism, Morality and Human Rights' in Kühnelt, J (ed), *Political Legitimization without Morality?* (Berlin: Springer, 2008)
Kay, RS, 'The European Convention on Human Rights and the Control of Private Law' (2005) 5 *European Human Rights Law Review* 466
Kelly, JM, *A Short History of Western Legal Theory* (Oxford: Clarendon, 1992)
Kiralfy, A (ed), *Potter's Historical Introduction to English Law and its Institutions* (4th edn, London: Sweet & Maxwell, 1962)
Kiralfy, A, *The Action on the Case* (London: Sweet & Maxwell, 1970)
Kumm, M, 'Who's Afraid of the Total Constitution? Constitutional Rights as Principles and the Constitutionalization of Private Law' (2006) 7(4) *German Law Journal* 341
Larenz, K (ed), *Grundfragen der neuen Rechtswissenschaft* (Berlin: Junker & Dünnhaupt, 1935)
Larson, DG, & Chastain, RL, 'Self-concealment: Conceptualization, measurement, and health implications' (1990) 9 (4) *Journal of Social and Clinical Psychology* 439
Lassiter, JC, 'Defamation of Peers: The Rise and Decline of the Action for *Scandalum Magnatum*, 1497-1773' (1978) 22 *American Journal of Legal History* 216
Leage, RW, *Roman Private Law* (2nd edn by Ziegler. CH) (London: Macmillan, 1954)
Leuze, D, *Die Entwicklung des Persönlichkeitsrechts im 19. Jahrhundert* (Bielefeld: Gieseking Verlag, 1962)
Lindsay, R, 'Defamation and the Law under Sulla' (1949) 44 (4) *Classical Philology* 240
Markesinis, BS, *Always on the Same Path: Essays on Foreign Law and Comparative Methodology Volume II* (Oxford: Hart Publishing, 2001)
Markesinis, BS, 'The Calcutt Report must not be forgotten' (1992) 55 *Modern Law Review* 118
Markesinis, BS, Auby, JB, Coester-Waltjen, D, & Deakin SF, *Tortious Liability of Statutory Bodies* (Oxford: Hart Publishing, 1999)
McCarthy, JT, *The Rights of Publicity and Privacy: Volumes I & II* (2nd edn, St Paul: Thomson/West, 2008)
McNamara, L, *Reputation and Defamation* (Oxford: Oxford University Press, 2007)
Mead, GH, *Mind, Self, & Society* (Chicago: Chicago University Press, 1934)
Mill, JS, *On Liberty* (Boston: Ticknor & Fields, 1863)
Mommsen, T, *Römisches Strafrecht* (Leipzig: Duncker &. Humblot, 1899)
Moosheimer, T, *Die actio injuriarum aestimatoria im 18. und 19. Jahrhundert: eine Untersuchung zu den Gründen ihrer Abschaffung* (Tübingen: Mohr Siebeck, 1997)
More, T, *Utopia* (edited by Logan, GM, & Adams, RM) (Cambridge: Cambridge University Press, 2002)

Moreham, N, 'Privacy in the Common Law: A Doctrinal and Theoretical Analysis' (2005) 121 *Law Quarterly Review* 628
Morgan, J, 'Privacy, Confidence and Horizontal Effect: "Hello" Trouble' (2003) 62 (2) *Cambridge Law Journal* 444
Morgan, J, 'Hello! Again: Privacy and Breach of Confidence' (2005) 64 (3) *Cambridge Law Journal* 549
Mulheron R, 'A Potential Framework for Privacy? A Reply to Hello!' (2006) 69 *Modern Law Review* 679
Mullender, R, 'Negligence Law and the Concept of Community' (2008) 16 *Tort Law Review* 85
Mullender, R, 'Privacy, Imbalance and the Legal Imagination' (2011) 19 (2) *Tort Law Review* 109
Nagel, T, 'Concealment and Exposure' (1998) 27 (1) *Philosophy and Public Affairs* 3
Nagel, T, *The View From Nowhere* (New York/Oxford: Oxford University Press, 1986)
Negley, G, 'Philosophical Views on the Value of Privacy' (1966) 31 *Law & Contemporary Problems* 319
Nicholas, B, *Introduction to Roman Law* (Oxford: Clarendon Press, 1962)
Nussbaum, M, 'Kant and Stoic Cosmopolitanism' (1997) 5 (1) *The Journal of Political Philosophy* 1
O'Callaghan, P, 'Monologism and Dialogism in Private Law' (2010) 7 *The Journal Jurisprudence* 405
Office of Communications (Ofcom), *Research Report on Social Networking: A quantitative and qualitative research report into attitudes, behaviours and use* (2 April 2008)
Peifer, KN, *Individualität im Zivilrecht: der Schutz persönlicher, gegenständlicher und wettbewerblicher Individualität im Persönlichkeitsrecht, Immaterialgüterrecht und Recht der Unternehmen* (Tübingen: Mohr Siebeck, 2001)
Peikoff, AL, 'The Right To Privacy: Contemporary Reductionists and Their Critics' (2006) 13 (3) *The Virginia Journal of Social Policy & the Law* 474
Perrot, M, 'Introduction' in Perrot, M (ed), *A History of Private Life Volume IV: From the Fires of Revolution to the Great War* (Cambridge: Harvard University Press, 1990)
Perrot, M, 'The Family Triumphant' in Perrot, M (ed), *A History of Private Life Volume IV: From the Fires of Revolution to the Great War* (Cambridge: Harvard University Press, 1990)
Perrot, M, 'At Home' in Perrot, M (ed), *A History of Private Life Volume IV: From the Fires of Revolution to the Great War* (Cambridge: Harvard University Press, 1990)
Phillipson, G, 'Transforming Breach of Confidence? Towards a Common Law Right of Privacy under the Human Rights Act' (2003) 66 (5) *Modern Law Review* 726
Plucknett, TFT, *A Concise History of the Common Law* (5th edn, London: Butterworths, 1956)
Popper, K, *Conjectures and Refutations* (London: Routledge Classics, 2002)
Popper, K, 'Two Kinds of Definitions' in Miller, D (ed), *A Pocket Popper* (Glasgow: Fontana Press, 1987)
Posner, RA, 'The Right of Privacy' (1978) 12 (3) *Georgia Law Review* 393
Posner, RA, 'Savigny, Holmes and the Law and Economics of Possession' (2000) 86 (3) *Virginia Law Review* 535
Post, RC, 'The Social Foundations of Defamation Law: Reputation and the Constitution' (1986) 74 *California Law Review* 691
Postema, GJ, *Bentham and the Common Law Tradition* (Oxford: Clarendon Press, 1986)
Pound, R, 'Interests of Personality' (1915) 28 *Harvard Law Review* 343 (Part 1) /445 (Part 2)
Prosser, WL, 'Privacy' (1960) 48 (3) *California Law Review* 383
Raber, F, *Grundlagen klassischer Injurienansprüche* (Wien: Böhlau Verlag, 1969)
Rachels, J, 'Why Privacy is Important' (1975) 4 (4) *Philosophy and Public Affairs* 323
Radin, MJ, *Contested Commodities: The Trouble with Trade in Sex, Children, Body Parts and Other Things* (Cambridge: Harvard University Press, 2001)
Räikkä, J, 'Is Privacy Relative?' (2008) 39 (4) *Journal of Social Philosophy* 534
Rawls, J, *A Theory of Justice* (revised edn, Cambridge: Belknap Press of Harvard University Press, 1999)
Rawls, J, *The Law of Peoples* (Cambridge: Harvard University Press, 1999)
Rawls, J, *Political Liberalism* (New York: Columbia University Press, 1993)
Raz, J, 'The Problem About the Nature of Law' (1983) 21 (2) *University of Western Ontario Law Review* 203

Reiter, EH, 'Personality and Patrimony: Comparative Perspectives on the Right to One's Image' (2002) 76 *Tulane Law Review* 673

Revel, J, 'The Uses of Civility' in Chartier, R (ed), *A History of Private Life Volume III: Passions of the Renaissance* (Cambridge: Harvard University Press, 1989)

Robertson, G, & Nicol, A, *Media Law* (5th edn, London: Sweet and Maxwell, 2007)

Rousseau, JJ, *The Social Contract and Other Later Political Writings* (edited by Gourevitch, V) (Cambridge: Cambridge University Press, 1997)

Rouche, M, 'The Early Middle Ages in the West' in Ariès, P, & Duby, G (eds), *A History of Private Life Volume I: From Pagan Rome to Byzantium* (Cambridge: Harvard University Press, 1987)

Schertz, C, 'Das Recht am eigenen Bild' in Götting, HP, Schertz C, & Seitz W (eds), *Handbuch des Persönlichkeitsrechts* (Munich: CH Beck, 2008)

Schilpp, PA (ed), *The Philosophy of Karl Jaspers* (New York: Tudor Publishing Company, 1957)

Scott, A, 'Introduction: Privacy and Publication' in Doley, C, & Mullis, A (eds), *Carter Ruck on Libel and Privacy* (6th edn, London: LexisNexis, 2010)

Scott, A, 'Harassment' in in Doley, C, & Mullis, A (eds), Carter Ruck on Libel and Privacy (6th edn, London: LexisNexis, 2010)

Scott, A, 'Misuse of Private Information: The Reasonable Expectation of Privacy' in in Doley, C, & Mullis, A (eds), Carter Ruck on Libel and Privacy (6th edn, London: LexisNexis, 2010)

Seipp, DJ, 'English Judicial Recognition of a Right to Privacy' (1983) 3 (3) *Oxford Journal of Legal Studies* 325

Sims, A, 'A Shift in the Centre of Gravity: The Dangers of Protecting Privacy through Breach of Confidence' [2005] *Intellectual Property Law Quarterly* 27

Singer, P, 'Hegel' in Honderich, T (ed), *The Oxford Companion to Philosophy* (Oxford/New York: Oxford University Press, 1995)

Smith, RE, 'The Law of Libel at Rome' (1951) 1 (3/4) *The Classical Quarterly* 169

Sohm, R, *The Institutes: A Textbook of the History and System of Roman Private Law* (Oxford: Clarendon Press, 1901)

Solove, DH, *Understanding Privacy* (Cambridge: Harvard University Press, 2008)

Strauss, A (ed), *George Herbert Mead on Social Psychology* (Chicago: Chicago University Press, 1964)

Sunstein, CR, *Radicals in Robes: Why Extreme Right-Wing Courts are Bad for America* (New York: Basic Books, 2005)

Susman, WI, 'History and the American Intellectual: Uses of a Usable Past' (1964) 16 (2) *American Quarterly* 243

Teichmann, C, 'Abschied von der absoluten Person der Zeitgeschichte', [2007] *Neue Juristische Wochenschrift* 1917

Thomson, JJ, 'The Right to Privacy' (1975) 4 (4) *Philosophy and Public Affairs* 295

Toulson, RG, & Phipps, CM, *Confidentiality* (2nd edn, London: Sweet & Maxwell, 2006)

Tugendhat, M, & Christie, I, *The Law of Privacy and the Media* (Oxford: Oxford University Press, 2002)

Unger, RM, 'The Critical Legal Studies Movement' (1983) 96 *Harvard Law Review* 561

Veeder, VV, 'The History and Theory of the Law of Defamation I' (1903) 3 *Columbia Law Review* 546

von Jhering, R, 'Rechtsschutz gegen injuriöse Rechtsverletzungen', in *Gesammelte Aufsätze, Volume III* (Jena: Fischer, 1886)

von Pufendorf, S, *Of the Law of Nature and Nations* (translated by Kennett, B) (London, Printed for Walthoe, J, Wilkin, R [*et al*], 1729)

Vesting, T, 'Einführung' in Götting, HP, Schertz C, & Seitz W (eds), *Handbuch des Persönlichkeitsrechts* (Munich: CH Beck, 2008)

Veyne, P, 'The Roman Empire' in Ariès, P, & Duby, G (eds), *A History of Private Life Volume I: From Pagan Rome to Byzantium* (Cambridge: Harvard University Press, 1987)

Vignale, G, *The Beautiful Invisible: Creativity, Imagination, and Theoretical Physics* (New York/Oxford: Oxford University Press, 2011)

Vincent, G, 'The Secrets of History and the Riddle of Identity' in Prost, A, & Vincent, G, *A History of Private Life Volume V: Riddles of Identity in Modern Times* (Cambridge: Harvard University Press, 1991)

Vlastos, G, 'Justice and Equality' in Waldron, J (ed), *Theories of Rights* (Oxford: Oxford University Press, 1984)

Wacks, R, *Law, Morality and the Private Domain* (Hong Kong: Hong Kong University Press, 2000)

Wacks, R, *Personal Information, Privacy and the Law* (Oxford: Clarendon Press, 1993)

Wadham, J, Mountfield, H, & Edmundson, A, *Blackstone's Guide to Human Rights Act 1998* (3rd edn, Oxford: Oxford University Press, 2003)

Wagner, G, 'The Protection of Personality Rights Against Invasions By Mass Media in Germany', in Koziol, H, & Warzilek, A (eds), *The Protection of Personality Rights against Invasions by Mass Media* (Wien: Springer, 2005)

Waldron, J (ed), 'Dignity and Rank' (2007) XLVIII *Archive Europe´ene de Sociologie* 201

Wanckel, E, 'Der Schutz vor Indiskretion' in Götting, HP, Schertz C, & Seitz W (eds), *Handbuch des Persönlichkeitsrechts* (Munich: CH Beck, 2008)

Warren, S, & Brandeis, R, 'The Right to Privacy' (1890) 4 *Harvard Law Review* 193

Wenzel, KE, *Das Recht der Wort- und Bildberichterstattung* (4th edn, Köln: Verlag Dr Otto Schmidt, 1994)

Westin, AF, *Privacy and Freedom* (New York: Atheneum, 1967)

Whitman, JQ, *The Legacy of Roman Law in the German Romantic Era* (Princeton: Princeton University Press, 1990)

Whitman, JQ, 'On Nazi "Honour" and the New European "Dignity"' in Joerges, C, & Ghaleigh, NS (eds) *The Darker Legacies of Law in Europe* (Portland/Oxford: Hart Publishing, 2003)

Whitman, JQ, 'The Two Western Cultures of Privacy: Dignity versus Liberty' (2004) 113 *Yale Law Journal* 1151

Wieacker, F, *A History of Private Law in Europe* (translated by Weir, T) (Oxford: Clarendon Press, 1995)

Wittgenstein, L, *Philosophical Investigations* (Blackwell, Oxford, 1953)

Wittmann, R, 'Entwicklungslinien der klassischen Injurienklage' (1974) 91 *Zeitschrift der Savigny-Stiftung fur Rechtsgeschichte, Romanistische Abteilung* 285

Witzleb, N, 'Monetary Remedies for Breach of Confidence in Privacy cases' (2007) 27 (3) *Legal Studies* 430

Wolff, HJ, 'The Historical and Constitutional Background of Roman Law' in Wolff, HJ, *Roman Law: An Historical Introduction* (Norman: University of Oklahoma Press, 1951)

Wright Mills, C, *The Sociological Imagination* (New York/Oxford: Oxford University Press, 2000)

Zimmerman, DL, 'The "New" Privacy and the "Old": Is Applying the Tort Law of Privacy Like Putting High-Button Shoes on the Internet?' (2012) 17 (2) *Communication Law and Policy* 107

Zimmermann, R, *The Law of Obligations: Roman Foundations of the Civilian Tradition* (Munich: CH Beck, 1992)

Zogby International, *Polling/Market Research - Results from June 4-7 Nationwide Poll* (7 June 2010), www.precursorblog.com/files/pdf/topline-report-key-findings.pdf

Zweigert, K, & Kötz, H, *An Introduction to Comparative Law* (translated by Weir, T) (3rd edn, Oxford: Clarendon Press, 1998)

Index

P. O'Callaghan, *Refining Privacy in Tort Law*,
DOI 10.1007/978-3-642-31884-9, © Springer-Verlag Berlin Heidelberg 2013

MIX
Papier aus verantwortungsvollen Quellen
Paper from responsible sources
FSC® C105338

If you have any concerns about our products,
you can contact us on
ProductSafety@springernature.com

In case Publisher is established outside the EU,
the EU authorized representative is:
Springer Nature Customer Service Center GmbH
Europaplatz 3, 69115 Heidelberg, Germany

Printed by Libri Plureos GmbH
in Hamburg, Germany